DOING BUSINESS IN ARIZONA

Doing Business in Arizona

A Legal Guide

SECOND EDITION

BY

SNELL & WILMER L.L.P.

PUBLISHED FOR
SNELL & WILMER L.L.P.
BY
THE UNIVERSITY OF ARIZONA PRESS
TUCSON

The University of Arizona Press, Tucson, Arizona
© 1992, 1998 Snell & Wilmer L.L.P.
First University of Arizona Press paperbound edition 1998

This book was written, edited, designed, and typeset by
Snell & Wilmer L.L.P., Phoenix, Arizona

This book is printed on acid-free, archival-quality paper.
Manufactured in the United States of America

03   02   01   00   99   98   6   5   4   3   2   1

Cover photograph by William Lesch, "Old Saguaro and
Catback Mountain, Gates Pass, 1990," Courtesy of Etherton
Gallery, Tucson, Arizona

Library of Congress Cataloging-in-Publication Data
Doing business in Arizona: a legal guide / by Snell & Wilmer L.L.P.
–2nd ed.
p. cm.
ISBN 0-8165-1888-2 (cloth). –ISBN 0-8165-1889-0 (pbk.)
1. Business law–Arizona. 2. Business enterprises–Law and
legislation–Arizona. 3. Arizona–Economic conditions. I. Snell &
Wilmer.
KFA2481.D65 1997
346.79107–dc21   97.45267

British Library Cataloguing-in-Publication Data
A catalogue record for this book is available from the
British Library.

*Dedicated to the continued growth of
good business in Arizona.*

Snell & Wilmer is a law firm that is focused on delivering exceptional, cost-effective, and efficient quality legal services to our clients. We are committed to continuous improvement through the use of advanced technology and open communication and feedback with our clients and staff. Our attorneys provide quality legal representation to meet our clients' evolving needs by frequently expanding practice areas, sponsoring client seminars, and publishing newsletters devoted to specific practice areas. We rely on teamwork, hard work, creativity, innovation, and dedication to provide the best possible service to our clients.

Founded in 1938, Snell & Wilmer is a full-service law firm that has grown to be one of the largest in the western United States, with more than 260 attorneys in Phoenix and Tucson, Arizona, Irvine, California, and Salt Lake City, Utah. The firm represents more than 10,000 clients, ranging from publicly-traded national and multinational corporations to emerging enterprises and individuals in all areas of general civil practice.

CONTENTS

PART III: SELECTED LEGAL SUBJECTS*

> *Note: Each chapter in Part III is preceded by a separate
> outline and summary.

DOING BUSINESS IN ARIZONA
A LEGAL GUIDE
SECOND EDITION

INTRODUCTION

This book brings together in one place, the essential legal information needed when planning to start a business, locate a facility, or invest in Arizona. Snell & Wilmer published the first edition, in 1992, primarily for foreign investors, and quickly learned that domestic business persons also found it useful. Therefore, we have prepared this second edition with both the domestic and the international readerships in mind. We have attempted to strike a fair balance, including both basic information for the reader who knows little of Arizona or the U.S. legal system and information of more depth and complexity.

In a work of this scope, many subjects must be only briefly mentioned or entirely omitted. For example, there are no extended discussions of family law, community property, banking, bankruptcy, uniform laws such as the Uniform Commercial Code, nor of Indian law.

We have chosen topics that experience has shown are among the first about which many foreign investors wish more information, information that often is not readily available elsewhere.

Because of the many complex issues discussed and the evolving nature of the law, this guide is neither legal advice nor intended to be a substitute for the services of an attorney. Users should remember that laws, regulations, and procedures change and, although the information in this guide was current as of its publication date, a lawyer should be consulted before proceeding with any matter.

The book is presented in three main parts. Part I is a brief look at Arizona, with factual information of special interest to foreign investors. Part II contains a general overview of the U.S. legal system. Selected legal subjects are discussed in Part III.

We hope this work will be of help to you.

Snell & Wilmer L.L.P.

PART I

A BRIEF FACTUAL LOOK
AT
ARIZONA

A BRIEF FACTUAL
LOOK AT ARIZONA

POPULATION

Growth is a feature of the entire Southwest. From 1970 to
1986, the region grew from 40 million people to almost 60 million, and is expected to reach 80 million by 2010 *(Illustration
One)*. For decades, Arizona has been one of the leading growth
states in not only the Southwest, but also the nation, in both
employment and population. Beyond its employment and population increases, Arizona has also achieved unprecedented
growth in business and become one of the more powerful economic magnets in the country.

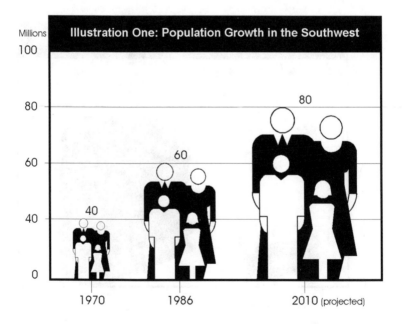

Illustration One: Population Growth in the Southwest

Ranked fourth in population growth in the United States in the '50s, third in the '60s, '70s, and '80s, and second for the first six years of this decade, Arizona has grown more than 20 percent. From 1980 to 1990, Arizona's population grew 34.9 percent, almost four times the growth rate of the United States *(Illustration Two)*, and greatly exceeded the growth rates of Canada, France, Germany, Italy, Japan, and the United Kingdom. The U.S. Census Bureau projects Arizona's population growth rate in the 1990s will exceed that of not only every other state again, but also the United States, by more than 250 percent *(Illustration Three)*. In 1995, Arizona's population was 4,307,150, and is expected to reach 7,363,625 by the year 2020 *(Illustration Four)*.

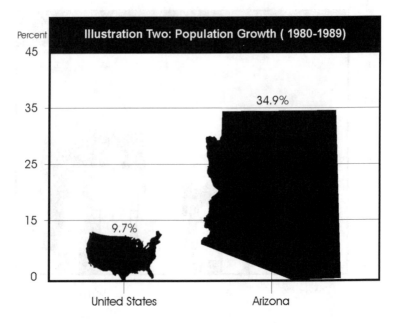

Illustration Two: Population Growth (1980-1989)

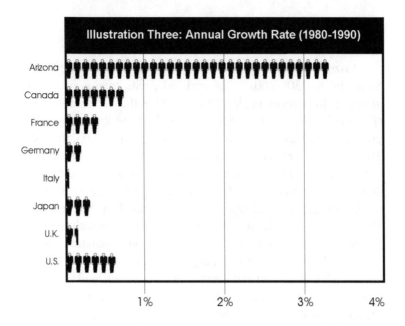

Illustration Three: Annual Growth Rate (1980-1990)

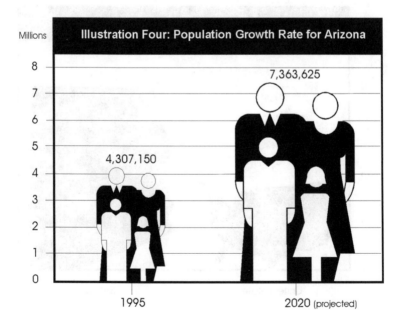

Illustration Four: Population Growth Rate for Arizona

EMPLOYMENT

Arizona was ranked third in employment growth in the United States in the '50s, '60s, '70s, and '80s, with total employment growing 40 percent in the '80s, to twice the national average *(Illustration Five)*. In 1995, Arizona had the third fastest job growth rate in the nation at 4.2 percent, creating 103,500 jobs. That number increased 5.6 percent (almost three times the national average) in 1996 *(Illustration Six)*, creating an estimated 100,000 jobs and ranking Arizona fourth best in the country. In total, an estimated 322,000 jobs were created in Arizona from 1993 to 1996, and the state was ranked first in the nation for the number of new jobs created per one million population for the years 1993-1995. As of February 1997, Arizona had the second highest job growth rate in the nation at 4.92 percent, and the state's labor force is expected to increase a total of 5 percent in 1997, creating 95,000 additional jobs.

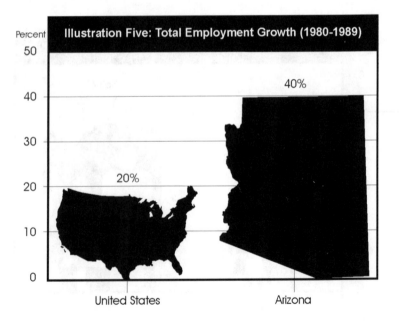

Illustration Five: Total Employment Growth (1980-1989)

DOING BUSINESS IN ARIZONA

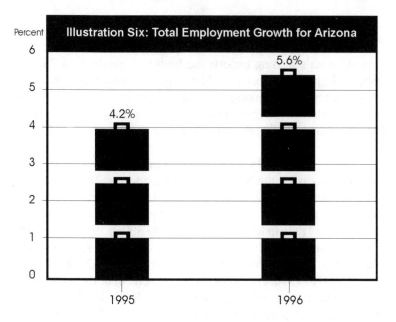

Percent

Illustration Six: Total Employment Growth for Arizona

6

5.6%

5

4.2%

4

3

2

1

0

1995   1996

INCREASING INCOME AND COMPETITIVE WAGE RATES

The state's population and employment increases have been accompanied by corresponding increases in personal income. For the 10 years ending 1988, the personal income of Arizonans rose 178 percent, ranking Arizona third in the United States. Over the next 10 years, the total annual personal income of Arizonans is projected to increase to almost $60 billion. In 1995, Arizona's personal income increased 9.4 percent and was tied for the highest growth rate in the nation, while the state's per capita income rose 5.7 percent. In 1996, Arizona's personal income increased another 4.5 percent, and currently, the state is tied for 20th in per capita income growth.

LEADING INDUSTRIES

Arizona's leading exports are high-tech products at 75 percent. High-tech industries add nearly $10 billion a year to the Arizona economy, ranking Arizona eighth in the country in high-tech exports. Employment (direct and indirect) by high-tech companies totals 180,000 jobs within the state, ranking Arizona 17th in high-tech jobs.

From 1987 to 1996, the two largest industries in Arizona have consistently been the Services industry and the Trade industry. The Services industry grew from 345,300 in 1987 to 561,400 in 1996, and accounts for 25 percent of the state's total workforce today. The Trade industry grew from 340,300 in 1987 to 466,200 in 1996, and is 21 percent of the total workforce in Arizona. Not far behind, is the Government, which grew from 232,000 in 1987 to 320,600 in 1996, and accounts for 14 percent of the workforce, and Manufacturing, which grew from 187,400 in 1987 to 199,500 in 1996, and is 9 percent of the state's workforce. The Construction industry has grown to 126,500 and 6 percent, the Finance, Insurance, and Real Estate industry to 115,100 and 5 percent, the Transportation and Utilities industry to 92,100 and 4 percent, and the Mining industry to 14,400 and 1 percent *(Illustration Seven)*.

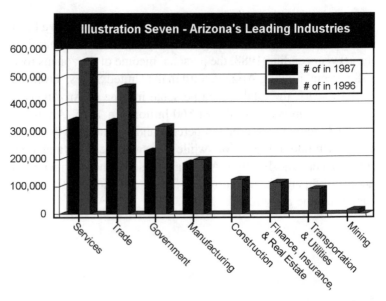

DOING BUSINESS IN ARIZONA

EXPORTS

At nearly $10 billion, exports from Arizona-based companies are significant. Mexico accounts for $1.6 billion of the outgoing shipments from the state, Japan $1.356 billion, Canada $970.1 million, Taiwan $895.4 million, and the United Kingdom $827.1 million.

Arizona has an exporters loan program that guarantees short-term, pre-shipment finance for Arizona-based small business exporters, and the state also has offices in Mexico City; Hermosillo; Sonora; Tokyo; and Taipei, to assist Arizona businesses with sales leads, local buyers, and joint venture partners located in those areas *(Illustration Eight)*.

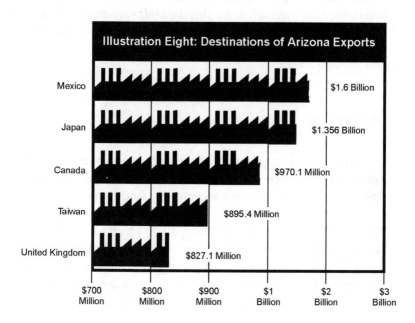

Illustration Eight: Destinations of Arizona Exports

Mexico	$1.6 Billion
Japan	$1.356 Billion
Canada	$970.1 Million
Taiwan	$895.4 Million
United Kingdom	$827.1 Million

$700 Million $800 Million $900 Million $1 Billion $2 Billion $3 Billion

Foreign Investment in Arizona

As one of the most visited places in the nation, Arizona's phenomenal growth is well known in the United States, but to many foreign visitors, it is still considered part of the American West. The state's attractive climate, natural and man-made wonders, and many tourist attractions, however, are quickly developing a reputation throughout the world. In 1996, the Arizona Department of Commerce helped 73 businesses to either locate new, or expand existing, operations in the state.

Among the state's many special features that make it particularly attractive to foreign investors are its location; land availability; low operating costs; proximity to Mexico; skilled labor force; business-friendly government; competitive taxes; affordable housing; convenient transportation; abundant infrastructure, including communications, energy, utilities, and water services; agreeable climate; diverse geography, and enjoyable lifestyle.

Location

Arizona consistently rates as one of the best states in which to establish a business. Centrally located in the southwestern United States, Arizona provides easy access to the world's most dynamic and fastest growing markets, including California, Nevada, New Mexico, Utah, Colorado, and Texas, all of which are within two hours via air transportation and two days via ground transportation *(Illustration Nine)*. Traveling to the countries of Latin America and the Pacific Rim from Arizona is also quite effortless from any of the state's six international airports.

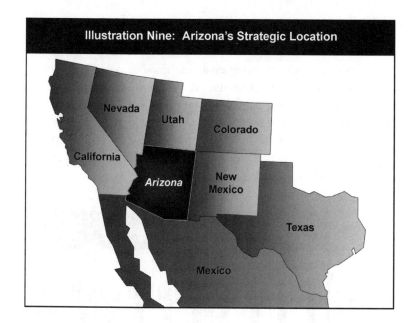

Illustration Nine: Arizona's Strategic Location

Nevada

Utah

Colorado

California

Arizona

New Mexico

Texas

Mexico

LAND AVAILABILITY

Since the frontier days, Arizona has been associated with wide open spaces. Many companies have recently expanded into Arizona because of the abundance of land available for growth that still exists today. Sizable tracts of land for office space, industrial sites, and residential use are available at competitive prices throughout the state. The cost of leasing office space in the Phoenix area was $18.12 per square foot in the fourth quarter of 1996, compared to $29.46 in San Francisco, $24.53 in San Jose-Silicon Valley, $22.50 in Las Vegas, $22.12 in Dallas-Fort Worth, $22.04 in Los Angeles, $21.98 in Denver, and $19.86 in San Diego.

LOW OPERATING COSTS

Lower overall operating costs are another positive factor in locating a business in Arizona. A recent study found that the annual cost, including wages, of operating a 200,000 square foot manufacturing facility in Maricopa County, which includes metropolitan Phoenix, was 10 to 20 percent less than the cost of operating a similar facility in California in either Orange County or Los Angeles County. *(Illustration Ten)*

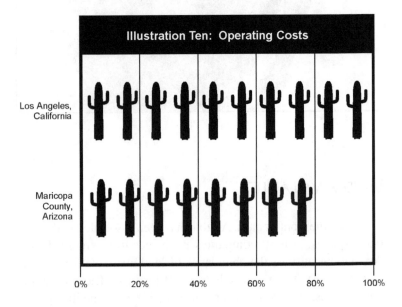

Illustration Ten: Operating Costs

PROXIMITY TO MEXICO

Arizona's link to Mexico is an ever-increasing asset as Mexico develops economic importance and trade ties strengthen. The opportunity to participate in the maquiladora program with Mexico is a valuable advantage of doing business in Arizona. Maquiladoras are border plants in Mexico that manufacture, process, assemble, and repair materials and components imported into Mexico duty-free on a temporary basis. The finished or semi-finished products are then shipped back to Arizona for distribution, where the goods are exempt from additional taxation. The Maquiladora program is scheduled to end in 2001, but maquila companies can still take advantage of the accomplishments of the North American Free Trade Agreement (NAFTA) and the relatively low labor costs in Mexico.

NAFTA is the agreement between the United States, Canada, and Mexico, that became effective January 1, 1994, and has further enhanced the region's economy. The advantages provided by NAFTA include such direct benefits as tariff reductions and the promise of bringing an improved and stable economy to Mexico, as well as indirect benefits such as the heightened awareness and increased number of projects focusing on Arizona's border region.

The Arizona/Sonora Regional Economic Development Vision is a unique bi-state, bi-national effort to develop an integrated regional plan for the area. The Arizona International Development Authority (AIDA), created in 1994, issues tax-exempt bonds for border projects. The Border Environment Cooperation Commission (BECC) addresses concerns about environmental degradation along the border. The Border Infrastructure Finance Office (BIFO), established in 1995, helps border communities access funding for constructing much-needed infrastructures.

LABOR FORCE

An average 10,100 more jobs are created annually in right-to-work states than in states that allow forced payment of union dues. In 1996, Arizona was ranked third in job growth among right-to-work states. Arizona's membership in labor unions is small when compared with other states - fewer than 4 percent of the state's manufacturing employees are affiliated with unions.

Arizona's labor force is competitively priced, which also contributes to the state's favorable business climate. The United States as a whole had a 14 percent increase in manufacturing wage rates from 1984 through 1989, and Arizona's rates increased less than 10 percent, ninth lowest of the 50 states. In the Phoenix metropolitan area, residents ages 25-34 make up the largest section of the population with more than 2.29 million people, a major reason that the state has such a young labor force; at an average age of 32. Arizona's labor force, while young, is extremely skilled, motivated, and productive, and among the nation's leaders in productivity because of the state's commitment to education, research, and vocational training programs. Arizona's universities excel in producing engineers, scientists, and other leading technology professionals.

EDUCATION

Arizona has a strong commitment to education. Three state universities, 19 community colleges, 20 accredited degree-granting private colleges and universities, and 180 trade and technical schools make up the state's education system and serve to produce a highly-trained workforce. Seventy-nine percent of Arizonans age 25 or older have a high school diploma, which is higher than the national average of 75 percent. The Phoenix metropolitan area ranks eighth in the nation with 81 percent of its entire population having graduated from high school. Approximately 65 percent of state education funding is spent at the primary and secondary school levels, where the state has several innovative teaching programs, including pay-for-performance and outstanding continuing education training. Of particular interest to industry, the schools have programs that allow faculty members to divide time between the classroom and technology-based firms.

The post-secondary education enrollment rate in Arizona exceeds the enrollment rate in the United States and most other countries (Illustration Eleven). The state's community college system trains 150,000 students annually through 250 vocational education programs. Arizona ranks sixth nationally in the percentage of population enrolled in vocational education programs. Maricopa Community College District is the second largest community college district in the United States. The district's innovative programs such as its special turnkey employment service for companies moving into the county in which the district designs a training program for the company, recruits employees, and trains them prior to the facility's opening, and retraining sessions for employees to upgrade or modify their manufacturing skills have brought national recognition. The Greater Phoenix area ranks tenth in the nation with 20 percent of its population having earned a college degree or higher.

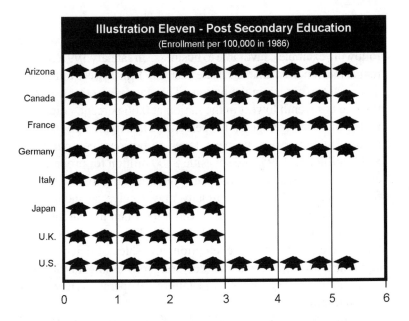

GOVERNMENT

Arizona is known for sound, fiscally responsible government that is accessible to all types and sizes of businesses, responsive to their needs, and committed to providing a favorable environment in which to conduct business throughout their development. *Financial World* magazine ranks Arizona as the ninth best-managed state in the nation. The state's unemployment benefits and workers' compensation premiums are substantially lower than in most other states in the nation, and Arizona's Constitution also requires the state and its political subdivisions to have balanced budgets that prohibit deficit financing and unlimited spending. The state has a budget surplus of approximately $780 million. Arizona has been relatively free of anti-business government regulations and "slow-growth" measures, unlike several other states in which initiative measures have significantly restricted development.

TAXES

Arizona's tax structure is highly competitive and given the following examples, favorable to business. In January 1997, *Money* magazine reported that the state has the 14th lowest total state and local tax burden in the nation. The state's effective property tax rate is seventh lowest in the nation at 0.66 percent, compared with a national average of 1.5 percent. The Arizona Legislature reduced state personal property taxes on business equipment by $31.7 million in 1995, and set aside $200 million for property tax cuts in 1996. Businesses may carry net operating losses forward for five years. A parent company may receive an income tax exemption on dividends from subsidiaries when the parent company owns at least 50 percent of the subsidiary. Business inventories have a property tax exemption, and sales of machinery or equipment used directly in manufacturing, processing, fabricating, job printing, refining, and other metallurgical operations have sales tax exemptions.

Lawmakers approved a $431.7 million tax relief that included an average income tax reduction of 13 percent in 1995, and during the past four years, personal income taxes have been cut by approximately 28 percent.

HOUSING

Affordable housing is still another reason for Arizona's business growth. At an average $80,100 per home, housing is both readily available and affordable in Arizona. The state had an estimated 25,100 new home sales and 43,775 home resales in 1996. According to a 1990 study by *The Wall Street Journal*, home prices in Phoenix averaged less than one-third of home prices in the California cities of Los Angeles and San Francisco and less than one-half of home prices in New York and Seattle. In the final quarter of 1996, the cost of living in the Phoenix area was less expensive than most other western urban areas - 16.9% less than San Diego, 14.6% less than Los Angeles, and 1.9% less than Denver *(Illustration Twelve)*.

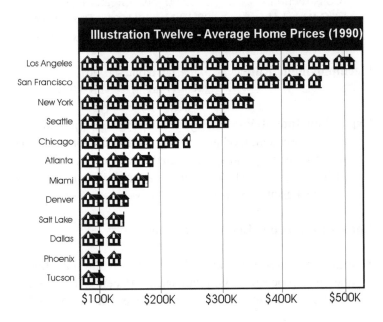

Arizona at a Glance

Capitol: Phoenix

Population: 3.77 million (Arizona - 1991)
2.33 million (Greater Phoenix
area - 1995)

Labor Force: 2,249,328 (1996)

Major Industries:

Services -	561,400 jobs (Greater Phx - 1996)
Trade -	466,200 jobs (Greater Phx - 1996)
Government -	320,600 jobs (Greater Phx - 1996)
Manufacturing -	199,500 jobs (Greater Phx - 1996)
Finance, Insurance, and Real Estate	
Construction -	126,500 jobs (Greater Phx - 1996)
T.C.P. and U. -	92,100 jobs (Greater Phx - 1996)
Mining -	14,400 jobs (Greater Phx - 1996)

Unemployment Rate: 5.5 % (Arizona - 1996)
2.8 % (Phoenix - May 1997)

Expanding Industries: High technology, electric and electronic equipment, food processing, semiconductors, information processing, printing, fabricated metals, communications, business services, wholesale and retail trade, financing, insurance, real estate, tourism.

Corporate Income Tax: 9.3 percent

Transaction Privilege (Sales) Tax: 5 percent state tax on the gross proceeds from retail sales. Phoenix, Tucson, and other communities add an additional sales tax of up to 1.7%.

FINANCIAL ADVANTAGES AND INCENTIVES

- Enterprise Zones
- Foreign Trade Zones
- Maquiladoras
- Arizona Enterprise Development Corp. (subordinated mortgages, SBA loans, and guarantees)
- Bridge loans (short-term, interim financing)
- Industrial Development Bonds
- Commerce and Economic Development Commission (direct loans, loan guarantees, grants, interest-rate subsidies, shared or subordinated liens)
- Revolving Energy Loans for Arizona (direct loans)

TRANSPORTATION

The state's integrated network of federal interstate highways which includes I-8, I-10, I-17, I-19, I-40, and U.S. 60, enables trucking companies to provide overnight service to Los Angeles, San Diego, Las Vegas, El Paso, Albuquerque, and many points in northern Mexico. In addition, Arizona is home to six international airports located in Phoenix, Tucson, Nogales, Yuma, Douglas, and Bullhead City, more than 200 public and private airports, and several air parks. The state's transportation system also includes an extensive rail service, consisting of two transcontinental railroads and 10 intrastate railroads, which links most of Arizona's metropolitan and industrial areas.

COMMUNICATIONS, ENERGY, UTILITIES, AND WATER

Arizona offers a modern, extensive, and highly advanced fiber optic communication network with virtually unlimited expansion capabilities. Electricity, natural gas, and solar energy are abundant and competitively priced. The state has several sources of electricity including the nation's largest nuclear generating plant - the Palo Verde Nuclear Generating Plant. Arizona Public Service Company provides electric power to 700,000 customers, the Salt River Project serves an additional 625,000 customers, and coal-fired, oil-fired, and hydroelectric generating plants throughout Arizona, such as those at Glen Canyon and Hoover dams, also supply the state's electricity.

Despite being partially desert, Arizona's water supply is so abundant that it more than meets the state's needs through a water allocation system that is an example to the world and is widely recognized for its fair and effective management of water resources. Major irrigation projects such as the Central Arizona Project and the Salt River Project deliver Colorado River water throughout the state, and irrigation dams create the miles-long lakes of Mead and Powell on the Colorado River that provide Arizona with unrivaled recreational waters.

CLIMATE AND GEOGRAPHY

Contrary to the familiar image of Arizona, the state is less than one-third desert. The northern third of the state is high plateau and includes spectacular scenic wonders such as Monument Valley, Meteor Crater, the Petrified Forest, the Painted Desert, Canyon de Chelly, Native American country, and the Grand Canyon. The middle third is central mountains and is home to the world's largest Ponderosa pine forest, the new-age city of Sedona, Oak Creek Canyon, and the Mogollon Rim that is the site of Zane Grey's western novels. While the lower third of the state is Sonoran Desert, it is more alive with plants and animals than most other deserts in the world and is home to the historic cities of Old Tucson and Tombstone.

Enjoyable Lifestyle

Arizona offers a complete range of intellectual and cultural activities, both those common elsewhere, and those that feature the state's unique Native American, Hispanic, and western heritages. The state has symphony orchestras, opera companies, chamber music, theater groups, and ballet troupes. Its many museums and galleries house some of the world's finest western collections. The Heard Museum in Phoenix is nationally known for its outstanding collection of southwestern Native American art and artifacts.

Popular attractions across the state include 67 natural and man-made lakes, 22 national parks, monuments and preserves, 16 state historical and recreational parks, ancient Native American ruins, ghost towns, rodeos, and pioneer day celebrations. Well-known places of interest include, the Mission San Xavier del Bac, the Phoenix Zoo, the Botanical Garden, the Arizona Science Center, and the Kitt Peak Observatory at the University of Arizona.

Arizona's recreational opportunities include snow skiing at any of the nine cross-country ski areas or four alpine ski areas, waterskiing, hiking, camping, mountain climbing, hot air ballooning, hang gliding, boating, fishing, and tubing. As host to five professional golf tournaments each year and home to 240 golf courses, Arizona is a golfer's paradise. The same can also be said of tennis, which is played year-round in the state. Arizona has more than 2,000 tennis facilities.

Sports enthusiasts enjoy major league baseball with the Arizona Diamondbacks, NHL hockey with the Phoenix Coyotes, NFL football with the Phoenix Cardinals, AFL football with the Arizona Rattlers, NBA basketball with the Phoenix Suns, WNBA basketball with the Phoenix Mercury, CISL soccer with the Arizona Sandsharks, and RHI roller hockey with the Phoenix Cobras.

Additionally, Arizona is the spring training site for six major league baseball teams, including the Chicago Cubs, Colorado Rockies, Milwaukee Brewers, San Diego Padres, San Francisco Giants, and Seattle Mariners. The state is an avid supporter of college football, hosting two bowl games - the Fiesta Bowl and the Copper Bowl. Two professional rodeos are held in Arizona each year, and racing fans have their choice of automobiles, horses, and greyhounds.

Part II

THE UNITED STATES LEGAL SYSTEM

THE UNITED STATES LEGAL SYSTEM

The reader already familiar with the legal system of the United States can pass quickly through this "overview." It is intended for those with little knowledge of the system who would appreciate a brief basic introduction.

THE UNITED STATES SYSTEM OF LAWS

The laws of the United States are found in its federal Constitution, in the constitutions of the 50 states, in federal laws passed by Congress, in state laws passed by state legislatures, in ordinances passed by governing bodies of counties, cities, and towns, in rules and regulations adopted by federal and state agencies, in tribal laws that apply on Indian reservations, and in the "common law," a body of law, originally unwritten that originated in England and arose out of customs. Judges also make significant law in two ways: by interpreting existing laws to determine how the legislative body intended a particular law to apply to a given situation, a process that has the effect of expanding or contracting the scope of statute law, and by ruling in cases where no written law precisely applies, which has the effect of further developing the common law. Judicial rulings, and the opinions that support them, become "precedent" and influence the outcome of subsequent similar cases.

The two main bodies of law are criminal law and civil law. Criminal cases are prosecuted by the state or federal government. Convictions lead to fines or imprisonment. Enforcement of civil laws is through suits brought by private parties. Criminal and civil law often overlap, and some behavior may subject a person both to criminal penalties and to civil liability. Violation of antitrust laws is a good example, but not the only one. Within the broad civil law field there are many separate areas of the law, such as contracts, product liability, and torts, the last of which deals with civil remedies for intended or negligent injuries to persons or property.

THE UNITED STATES COURT SYSTEM

The United States has two major court systems – a single federal system that administers federal law, principally the statutes enacted by the U.S. Congress, and separate state court systems in each of the 50 states. State courts, in general, interpret and enforce the laws passed by state legislatures. Indian tribes, which are independent but subordinate sovereignties within the United States, have their own laws that apply within tribal reservations and are administered by tribal courts. In addition, there are also courts that apply within tribal reservations. Each state has both federal and state courts, but most cases are processed through courts that have broad subject-matter jurisdiction.

Each court system has several levels. At the lowest level is the "trial court" or "court of first impression." In the federal system, the court of first impression is the district court. In Arizona, it is the Superior Court or, for smaller claims, the Justice courts and small claims courts. Most courts hear and try both criminal prosecutions and civil suits. Criminal suits are brought in the name of the United States or of the particular state and are prosecuted by U.S. attorneys, state attorneys-general, county attorneys, and city attorneys. Civil suits, each commenced by filing a written "complaint" with the clerk of the court, are brought by private litigants. Individuals are permitted to represent themselves in court actions, and sometimes do, but more often they are represented by attorneys. Cities and towns have municipal courts that administer local ordinances. Justice and small claims courts handle relatively minor civil matters, such as lawsuits where the total amount claimed is small – $5,000 or less in Arizona Justice courts. Justice courts also have a role in the initial stages of criminal prosecutions.

Disputed questions of fact are tried and decided at the trial court, which can be a municipal court, a justice court, a superior court, or a district court, depending on which has "jurisdiction" (a concept discussed below). Legal principles are applied to the facts as so decided, and a judgment is rendered. In a criminal case, the verdict is either "guilty" or "not guilty." In a civil case, the judgment will be to award or deny relief to the plaintiff, the party who brought the suit against the other side, the defendant. In a civil suit, a judgment is usually for monetary relief, but in appropriate cases, an injunction may issue directing the defendant to do, or to refrain from doing, something. In a civil suit, the winning side also recovers its allowable court costs from the other side, and in many cases, recovers its own attorneys' fees. The amount of damages recovered includes actual dollar loss and sometimes, recovery for pain and suffering, or a multiple of actual damages or, for particularly outrageous conduct, punitive damages. In the trial court, a jury of laymen, usually 12, but sometimes as few as eight or six, decides which version of contested facts is the true version. The judge decides and applies the law and renders judgment. Not all cases involve a jury; some are decided entirely by the judge based on the facts and law. In criminal cases, the defendant has a right to a trial by jury. In civil cases, the defendant or plaintiff cannot always insist upon a jury, because the nature of the particular case determines whether a jury is required.

The appellate courts are above the trial courts. In the state court system, the decision of the trial court may be appealed to the state Court of Appeals, from there to the Arizona Supreme Court and, if a question of federal constitutional law is involved, ultimately to the U.S. Court of Appeals, and from there to the U.S. Supreme Court. Both the U.S. Supreme Court and state supreme courts have broad discretionary powers to decide whether to review decisions of lower courts. Each year the U.S. Supreme Court accepts only a handful of cases for review, out of thousands of "petitions for certiorari" filed.

Courts of appeal do not hold trials, hear witnesses, or receive new evidence. Instead, they review written "briefs" and hear oral arguments presented by attorneys in almost all instances. Appellate courts decide whether the proceedings of the lower courts were procedurally correct and whether the proceedings and the result were in accord with applicable law. An appellate court may let the lower court decision stand by affirming the lower court's decision, reverse the lower court and direct an opposite result, dismiss the case entirely, or return the case to the trial court for a new trial, sometimes with express instructions as to how to correct errors made in the first trial.

At the heart of the justice system is the "adversary" concept of opponents who fight a battle of words in court before unbiased neutrals, the judge, and a jury, if there is one. The judge requires the parties to follow the rules and decides questions of law. The jury, or if there is no jury, the judge, decides the facts and determines a winner. The underlying rationale is that each side will present its best possible case, so that the impartial judge and jury will be able to discern the truth, apply correct law, and fairly decide the outcome.

Court proceedings are often slow and expensive. A case may take a year or more to come to trial. If appealed, it may take five years or more to come to final conclusion. In civil matters, speedier and less expensive ways of resolving disputes are available through private agreement. There are a number of alternate dispute methods and public and private organizations who administer them, such as the American Arbitration Association and the Federal Mediation and Conciliation Service.

In mediation, a neutral third party goes between the parties conveying offers and counteroffers of settlement. Conciliation is like mediation, except the conciliator takes a more active role in proposing compromise solutions. Arbitration is the alternate method of longest standing and the one most often used. In arbitration, the parties select a neutral arbitrator or panel of arbitrators who perform the roles of both judge and jury and decide the matter after a hearing, usually far shorter, always less formal and more flexible, and often less expensive, than court proceedings. Arbitration awards can be enforced through court proceedings and can be appealed only on very limited grounds, such as arbitrator bias, or that the arbitration award went beyond the scope of the matter the parties agreed to arbitrate. Arbitration is mandatory in civil cases in Arizona in which the plaintiff seeks to recover $50,000 or less.

INTERRELATIONSHIP AND PRIORITIES AMONG FEDERAL, STATE, AND LOCAL LAWS

For a court to be able to issue a binding judgment, it must have "jurisdiction" of two kinds. The first is jurisdiction over the litigants (*in personam*) or, in some cases, over a physical thing such as over certain goods or a piece of land (*in rem*). A court acquires *in personam* or *in rem* jurisdiction by having the persons or things within the boundaries of the physical area within which the court is authorized to act, and by having given formal notice in the manner required by law, such as by service upon a defendant of a "summons" issued by the court. In some cases, persons physically outside the area of jurisdiction of a court can be brought within its jurisdiction for legal purposes, by mailing copies of the summons and other pleadings to them or, when their whereabouts are unknown, by publishing the summons in a newspaper. This alternate means of service is available when the absent defendant has caused a significant event to take place within the area of the court's jurisdiction.

Second, the court must also have "subject matter" jurisdiction. This means that the court must be authorized to apply the particular laws being invoked by the parties. The starting point here is the general rule that each court administers the laws enacted by the legislative body of the system to which it belongs. Municipal courts enforce city ordinances, state courts enforce state laws, federal courts enforce federal laws, Indian courts enforce tribal laws, but it is not that simple. Certain acts may violate both state and federal laws. Some actions may take place in more than one state or violate the laws of more than one state. Some laws take precedence over others. Physical areas overlap. Tribal reservations are within counties, counties within states, and states within the United States. With two major court systems – federal and state, two major bodies of law – federal and state, some courts having broad general jurisdiction and others only limited subject-matter jurisdiction, and with three and sometimes four levels of appeal, one would expect to find (and does) a complex set of rules governing which court has jurisdiction over a particular matter and which law applies. In a given matter, a single court may have exclusive jurisdiction, but in other situations, more than one court may have concurrent jurisdiction. Sometimes a case begun in state court can be removed to a federal court, or vice versa. Depending on the facts, a given court, state or federal, may apply federal law, state law, constitutional law, or more than one set of laws to various aspects of the case.

Whatever the court, there is a clear order of priority to resolve conflicts of law. The U.S. Constitution has the highest priority, and the U.S. Supreme Court is the final authority on the reach and meaning of the U.S. Constitution. The Supreme Court has the power to invalidate laws passed by Congress or by state legislatures as being "unconstitutional." Next in order of priority, are the laws passed by the U.S. Congress, which take priority over (preempt), state and tribal laws, but only if the federal law is enacted on a subject on which the U.S. Constitution gives Congress authority to act. Congressional legislative authority is very broad. Congress, for example, can pass laws which preempt state laws having anything to do with "interstate commerce." But Congress' legislative authority is not total. Matters of purely state concern are reserved to state legislatures; in those areas state laws prevail. County and municipal ordinances are subordinate to state laws, because counties and municipalities are subordinate state instrumentalities. On reservations, tribal laws take precedence, except when Congress has preempted tribal laws or has given authority to the states to enact laws that reach into tribal reservations.

ADMINISTRATIVE AGENCIES AND REGULATIONS

The influence of the many administrative agencies – state, federal, and local – is extensive and pervasive. Agencies have the authority to adopt rules and regulations, many with the "force of law." Agencies are the creatures of the legislatures that created them, and their authority and scope is determined by the legislatures. Agencies always deal with a single subject matter, although the subject may be broad and far-reaching. Agencies

DOING BUSINESS IN ARIZONA

adopt rules and regulations through a formal procedure that usually provides for notice to the public and for public hearings before adoption. Enforcement of agency rules and regulations is most often through a "citation" for alleged violations, followed by a hearing. The final agency determination is much like a court judgment. Many agency proceedings are so similar to court proceedings that they are referred to as "quasi-judicial."

To name but a few of the federal agencies: the National Labor Relations Board (NLRB) administers federal labor law, the Occupational Safety and Health Administration (OSHA) administers federal safety and health measures, the Equal Employment Opportunity Commission (EEOC) administers federal civil rights laws, the Federal Communication Commission (FCC) regulates the communication industry, and the Securities and Exchange Commission (SEC) regulates the issuance and sale of securities. In Arizona, in addition to agencies that administer state laws that parallel federal laws, such as state civil rights laws and security regulations, the Arizona Corporation Commission regulates public utilities and, among others, agencies that license and regulate professions such as law, medicine, and engineering. For the foreign investor in real property, zoning is a very important concern, governed by county and municipal ordinances and administered by local zoning boards and commissions.

A basic principle of matters with agency jurisdiction is that the parties must first "exhaust their administrative remedies" before going to court. Agency determinations are often given great weight; it is difficult to overturn an agency ruling in a court action. Nevertheless, recourse to the courts is always available, both as to the adoption of agency rules and regulations that can be challenged in court proceedings, and as to the agency rulings and decisions that can be appealed to the courts. The requisite exhaustion of administrative remedies prior to court action is always time consuming, and often expensive. This is particularly true in tax matters, because to appeal an adverse tax ruling, generally the full amount of the contested tax must be paid as a precondition of bringing a suit. However, a winning taxpayer will get not only the return of taxes paid under protest, but also interest.

PART III

SELECTED LEGAL SUBJECTS

FORMS OF BUSINESS OWNERSHIP

CHAPTER OUTLINE

SUMMARY
ENTITY CONSIDERATIONS CHART
SOLE PROPRIETORSHIPS
GENERAL PARTNERSHIPS
LIMITED PARTNERSHIPS
LIMITED LIABILITY COMPANIES
CORPORATIONS

SUMMARY

An individual may choose among several alternate forms of ownership to make an investment or to conduct business in Arizona. The choice of form of ownership is important, because it affects not only the manner in which the investment or business will be operated, but also the extent to which federal and state laws will apply. The choice will determine who will make management decisions, whether owners will be liable for investment or business related obligations, whether interests in the investment or business can be easily transferred, and how the owner's income tax liability will be determined.

The five most common forms of ownership in Arizona are sole proprietorships, general partnerships, limited partnerships, registered limited liability partnerships, limited liability companies, and corporations. Each form of ownership offers specific advantages.

The following should be considered:

- Required formalities

- Suitability of the form of ownership as a vehicle for raising capital and borrowing funds

- Method by which the owners manage and control the business

- Manner of dividing profits and losses

- Extent to which owners may be personally liable for business obligations

- Ability of owners to transfer their interests

- Effect of an owner's death, bankruptcy, or withdrawal upon the continuing existence of the business

- Recordkeeping requirements

The objectives of the owners can sometimes be accomplished through a combination of forms of ownership when a single form would not suffice. The following chart summarizes these criteria.

Foreign persons also may use forms of ownership initiated or created outside of Arizona or the United States to take action or conduct business in Arizona. Arizona law permits foreign corporations and other types of business entities or associations to qualify to do business in Arizona. However, foreign persons may encounter reluctance on the part of local lenders or merchants to do business with businesses organized outside of the United States. For this reason, it may be advisable for foreign persons to use one or more entities organized in Arizona or in another state of the United States to make investments or to conduct business. A business organized under Arizona law can be a subsidiary or affiliate of a foreign business organization.

CHART: ENTITY CONSIDERATIONS

	Organizational Formalities	Capitalization and Debt Financing
Sole Proprietorship	Generally none	Capital limited to amount committed by proprietor; ability to obtain financing generally limited to financial condition of proprietor
General Partnership	Oral partnership agreement is permitted; advisable to adopt written partnership agreement	Partners free to structure their respective capital obligations as they may agree; ability to obtain financing generally limited to financial condition of the partners
Limited Partnership	Certificate of limited partnership must be filed; advisable to adopt written limited partnership agreement	Partners free to structure their respective capital obligations as they may agree; absent limited partner guarantees, ability to obtain financing generally limited to financial condition of the general partners
Corporation	Articles of incorporation must be filed; directors' meeting must be held; bylaws must be adopted	Capital raised through issuance of shares; significant freedom to develop share structure best suited for corporate needs; debt financing may require shareholder guarantees
Limited Liability Company	Articles of organization must be filed	Members free to structure their respective capital obligations as they may agree; debt financing may require member guarantees

	Control	Profits and Losses
Sole Proprietorship	Exclusively vested in proprietor	Exclusively allocable to proprietor
General Partnership	Partners have equal voice in all management decisions unless the partnership agreement establishes different management rights	Significant freedom to allocate among partners in partnership agreement
Limited Partnership	Typically exercised by general partners with rights of limited partners to ratify certain decisions, including sale of assets and liquidation	Significant freedom to allocate among partners by partnership agreement
Corporation	Vested in board of directors; members are subject to election and removal by shareholders	Dividends generally allocated among shareholders in accordance with stock ownership; exception for holders of preferred stock, who may be given dividend rights superior to common shareholders
Limited Liability Company	Vested in managers or members, depending on management structure	Significant freedom to allocate among members by operating agreement

	Personal Liabilities	Transferability of Interest
Sole Proprietorship	Generally unlimited personal liability	Assets of proprietorship generally freely transferable
General Partnership	Generally, unlimited personal liability except in the case of a limited liability partnership	Generally requires agreement of all partners
Limited Partnership	General partners generally have unlimited personal liability except in the case of a limited liability limited partnership; liability of limited partners generally limited to contributions made or agreed to be made	Transfer of general partners' interest typically requires consent of all partners; limited partner may substitute another party if permitted under partnership agreement
Corporation	Liability of shareholders generally limited to investment in shares	Shares freely transferable unless restricted by articles, bylaws, agreement, or securities laws
Limited Liability Company	Liability of members generally limited to investment in membership interests	Generally, consent of members needed for transfer of membership interest

Continuity of Existence

Sole Proprietorship	No continuity; death terminates proprietorship
General Partnership	Withdrawal, bankruptcy, death, or expulsion causes dissolution of partnership unless remaining partners elect to continue business in accordance with partnership agreement
Limited Partnership	Withdrawal, bankruptcy, death, or expulsion of general partner causes dissolution of partnership unless remaining general partners elect to continue business in accordance with partnership agreement or, if no remaining general partners, all limited partners appoint one or more new general partners to continue partnership
Corporation	A corporation has perpetual existence unless other wise specified in the articles; continuity not disrupted by events affecting shareholders
Limited Liability Company	Generally, withdrawal, bankruptcy, death, or expulsion of a member causes dissolution unless remaining members elect to continue business in accordance with operating agreement or unless provided to the contrary in an operating agreement

	Taxability	Reports
Sole Proprietorship	Not a separate taxable entity; income or loss exclusively allocable to proprietor	Preparation of tax return
General Partnership	Not a separate taxable entity; income or loss generally allocable to partners in accordance with partnership agreement	Preparation of tax return; maintenance of books and records
Limited Partnership	Not a separate taxable entity; income or loss generally allocable to partners in accordance with partnership agreement	Preparation of tax return; maintenance of books and records
Corporation	Generally, a separate taxable entity that pays tax on entity profits; additional tax results to shareholders upon distribution of dividends	Annual reports must be filed with Arizona Corporation Commission; corporation must provide annual financial reports to shareholders; preparation of annual tax returns; certain corporate transactions involving foreign parties subject to special federal tax recordkeeping requirements
Limited Liability Company	Not a separate taxable entity; income or loss generally allocable to members in accordance with operating agreement	Preparation of annual tax returns except in the case of certain single member companies; maintenance of books and records

Sole Proprietorships

Chapter Outline

Summary

"Sole proprietorship" describes the direct ownership of a business enterprise by a single individual or single marital community of husband and wife. The characteristics are summarized in the preceding chart and detailed in the following paragraphs.

Organizational Formalities

No formalities are involved nor documents required to organize a sole proprietorship. However, if the owner conducts business operations under a name other than the owner's own, a certificate of "fictitious name" must be recorded with the county recorder of each county in which the business is conducted.

Capitalization and Debt Financing

In a sole proprietorship the owner's ability to obtain capital and financing is likely to be limited by the owner's net worth or financial strength, which tends to limit proprietorships to smaller businesses.

Management and Control

The operation of a sole proprietorship is within the owner's sole control. The owner is not required to keep a written record of management decisions. Because there is a single owner, there can be no management conflicts, except as between husband and wife in a marital community proprietorship. Under Arizona's community property laws husband wife have equal rights in, and equal control over, community property, unless they otherwise agree.

Profits and Losses

A sole proprietor retains all profits of the business and bears all losses. If the owner should enter into any agreement with another for the sharing of income or expenses relating to a business or investment, the agreement may create a general partnership, with unintended consequences.

Extent of Owner's Liability

Because a sole proprietorship is not a separate legal entity, a sole proprietorship does not protect its owner from personal liability for business obligations. A sole proprietor has unlimited personal liability for the debts and obligations of the business, even after the business is sold or terminated. Insurance can be purchased to protect the sole proprietor's personal assets from some liability risks.

Transferability of Interest

The sale of a proprietorship can be accomplished through a sale of the assets used in the business. Assets, as a general rule, are freely transferable, but restrictions may apply to some. For example, the sale of a franchise might be restricted by the terms of the franchise agreement.

A sale of all assets of a business, including an inventory of merchandise, requires compliance with the "bulk transfer" law, intended to protect the claims of business creditors by requiring advance notice of any pending sale of business assets. If the required notice is not given to creditors, the creditors may pursue their claims against the assets in the hands of the buyer.

Continuity of Existence

A sole proprietorship has no continuity of existence independent of its owner and ends upon the owner's death.

Tax Considerations

Because a sole proprietorship is not a separable taxable entity, the income or loss from operation of a sole proprietorship is included with the owner's other income or loss in calculating the owner's taxable income. Taxes are further discussed in the chapter "Taxation."

RECORDKEEPING REQUIREMENTS

A sole proprietorship is not subject to any special reporting requirements. The owner is required to file federal and state income tax returns, payroll tax returns for employees, license applications, and other regulatory reports applicable to the business being conducted. In license applications for certain businesses, the owner may be required to disclose more information regarding the owner's personal affairs than if the business were a partnership or corporation.

CONCLUSION

The principal advantage of a sole proprietorship is that the owner has exclusive control. The owner does not need to obtain the consent of partners, directors, or shareholders. Another advantage is simplicity. No formalities are required to organize or maintain a proprietorship. The chief shortcomings of a sole proprietorship are the exposure of all the owner's personal assets to liabilities of the business and the difficulties that may be encountered in obtaining sufficient funds to finance the business.

General Partnerships

Chapter Outline

SUMMARY
ORGANIZATIONAL FORMALITIES
CAPITALIZATION AND DEBT FINANCING
MANAGEMENT AND CONTROL
PROFITS AND LOSSES
EXTENT OF OWNERS' LIABILITY
TRANSFERABILITY OF INTERESTS
CONTINUITY OF EXISTENCE
TAX CONSIDERATIONS
RECORDKEEPING REQUIREMENTS
CONCLUSION

Summary

Partnerships are a common forms of business ownership used by two or more persons to acquire investment property or to operate a business. The two kinds of partnerships under Arizona law are general partnerships and limited partnerships. The principal differences between a general partnership and a limited partnership are that each of the partners of a general partnership can incur liabilities on behalf of the partnership, and that generally each is personally liable for the payment of all partnership liabilities. The partners of a general partnership enjoy significant freedom under Arizona law to fix their rights and obligations by agreement as to most partnership matters.

ORGANIZATIONAL FORMALITIES

A general partnership can be created with little formality. Under Arizona law a general partnership is formed among two or more persons whenever they associate together to carry on a common business enterprise as co-owners for profit. Generally there is no requirement to file any certificate or other organizational documents with any governmental agency. However, if the partners conduct the partnership business under a "fictitious" name, one which does not consist of the individual names of all partners, a certificate showing the name and address of each partner must be filed in the county recorder's office of each Arizona county in which the partnership transacts business.

A partnership can be created without a written partnership agreement if the co-owners orally agree to form a partnership, or if they conduct their enterprise in a manner that demonstrates their intention to share profits and losses as partners. For this reason, a general partnership sometimes arises inadvertently when two or more persons jointly acquire property and share income and expenses. Because a partnership relationship creates significant rights and obligations among co-owners, any arrangement involving the sharing of income and expenses should be carefully considered to determine whether it creates a partnership. If so, a *written* partnership agreement should be prepared to clearly define the partners' respective rights and obligations, including such items as the sharing of profits and losses, the obligations to fund the ongoing business of the partnership, management decisions, and transfer rights. In the absence of a written agreement, Arizona law will dictate the partners' rights and obligations in a manner that may or may not conform to the partners' expectations or desires.

CAPITALIZATION AND DEBT FINANCING

Partners may contribute cash, property, or services to the capital of a general partnership. Arizona law permits the partners broad discretion to arrange their capital contribution in any way they choose. In most cases the partners will describe in their partnership agreement, the specific capital contributions required of each partner when the partnership is formed. The partnership agreement should also set forth the respective obligations of the partners to contribute additional capital if the business of the partnership requires. The partners may agree to make capital contributions in proportions different from their share of profits and losses or may agree to make additional contributions in proportions different from their initial contributions.

Arizona law permits a general partnership to borrow money or obtain credit from lenders in the name of the partnership. A general partnership may also borrow money from one or more of its partners. Each partner in a general partnership is personally liable to partnership creditors to repay partnership debts if the partnership's assets are insufficient. Consequently, a partnership's ability to borrow money or obtain credit will be influenced by each partner's individual financial condition and credit history, as well as by the partnership's financial condition. Because of each partner's financial responsibility for partnership debts, generally, the partners usually include a provision in their partnership agreement limiting the partnership's ability to borrow money without the consent of all, or a majority, of the partners.

As an alternative to obtaining its cash requirements from its existing partners or third party lenders, the partnership may create and issue additional interests in the partnership to new partners who agree to contribute additional capital. Arizona law requires the consent of each existing partner before a new partner is admitted as a member of a general partnership, because the admission of an additional partner may alter the management control of the existing partners and dilute the value of their interests in the partnership's assets and profits.

MANAGEMENT AND CONTROL

The partners of a general partnership are free to divide management authority and responsibilities among themselves in whatever manner they agree. If the partners fail to describe any specific management arrangement in their partnership agreement, Arizona law provides that each partner will have an equal voice in all management decisions and that a majority vote of the partners is controlling as to ordinary partnership matters.

In many general partnerships, the partners modify the general rule that all partners have equal management rights. It is quite common, for instance, to give partners voting rights according to their respective contributions to the partnership or their percentage of shares of partnership profits. Partners may appoint a management committee for the purpose of approving all, or a specified list of, management decisions. The partners may also agree that one specific partner will be the "managing partner" with responsibility for conducting routine transactions within described limitations. One of the most important advantages of the partnership form is the wide range of freedom the partners have to devise internal management rules that reflect the needs of the enterprise and the individual partners.

Arizona law provides certain rules that cannot be modified by the partners in their partnership agreement. For example, no matter how the partners may agree to divide management responsibilities among themselves, third parties who are unaware of the partnership agreement are entitled to rely on the presumed authority of each partner to represent the partnership. Therefore, even if the partnership agreement deprives some of the partners of the right to participate in management, each of the partners is treated as an *agent* of the partnership for the purpose of carrying on ordinary partnership business. This means that each of the partners has the power to incur partnership debts and liabilities to third parties in the ordinary course of the partnership's business that will obligate both the partnership and all individual partners. Obviously, it is advisable to carefully evaluate the trustworthiness and reliability of all other partners before entering into a general partnership.

PROFITS AND LOSSES

Partners are free to allocate partnership profits and losses by agreement. If the partners do not specify in their partnership agreement how profits and losses are to be shared, Arizona provides that profits and losses are shared equally among the partners. Partnership agreements often provide for unequal sharing of profits and losses to reflect differences in amounts or types of contributions made by the partners and, if one of the partners has contributed management or other services to the partnership rather than cash or property, the "service" partner may be given a percentage share of profits greater than the proportion of any cash or property he or she contributed.

In cases in which one partner contributes services and another partner contributes cash, the partners often agree upon complex profit and loss sharing arrangements. One common arrangement is to allocate all or most of the profits to those partners who contribute cash until they receive a "targeted" return on their investment equal to an agreed-upon percentage per year. After the target is achieved, additional profits are then divided between the "service" partner and the other partners in equal shares or in some other agreed upon proportion. The variety of possible arrangements is limitless.

The partnership agreement should describe when and how the partnership will make distributions of cash or other property to the partners. Frequently the partners will desire to distribute cash flow from ordinary business operations in the same proportions that they share profits, but following a sale by the partnership of a capital asset, the partners will usually require that the partnership distribute the sale proceeds in proportion to the partners' net capital contributions until capital is returned and that excess proceeds be distributed in proportion to the partners' profit shares. A related issue is the need to decide whether proceeds must be distributed immediately or retained in the partnership to satisfy future requirements.

EXTENT OF OWNERS' LIABILITY

One of the principal disadvantages of a general partnership is that each of the partners is generally fully liable for the payment of all the partnership's debts and liabilities. The partners' liability is "joint and several". Each partner alone can be sued by a partnership creditor for the full amount of an unpaid partnership liability, even though the partners may have agreed among themselves to share responsibility for the payment of partnership debts in specified portions.

Several steps can be taken to minimize the risk of unlimited liability of the individual partners. Under agreements with a third party, such as leases or loan agreements, the partners may be able to negotiate an agreed-upon limit to the liability of individual partners. A lender also may agree to limit the partners' individual liability for all, or a portion, of a loan, to the assets given as collateral by the partnership to secure the loan. Non-contractual partnership liabilities, such as for a personal injury caused by the negligence of a partner, the partners may be able to protect themselves by obtaining liability insurance.

Further, Arizona law authorizes a general partnership to elect classification as a registered limited liability partnership. If a general partnership elects classification as a registered limited liability partnership, each partner is shielded from "vicarious" liability associated with the debts and obligations of the partnership, whether arising in contract, negligence, or otherwise. The liability shield of a registered limited liability partnership does not, however, protect a partner from direct liability on account of a partner's own actions, including wrongful acts, negligence, or misconduct of the partner, or the wrongful actions of others under the partner's direct supervision and control.

Transferability of Interests

Under Arizona law, a partnership is viewed as a personal relationship of trust and confidence among the partners. Therefore, absent special agreement, no partner alone can transfer the partner's rights and duties as a partner to another person. If a partner desires the ability to transfer his or her interest in a partnership to a new partner, the partner should insist that the partnership agreement provide this right.

Arizona law does permit a partner to transfer the partner's *economic* rights to receive future partnership distributions of the partner's share of profits and return of contributions. No agreement of any other partners is necessary to transfer such economic rights unless the partnership agreement specifically restricts such transfers. However, because a person who acquires all, or a part, of a partner's economic rights generally cannot participate in the management of the partnership's business and cannot review the partnership's financial or business records, it is usually difficult or impossible for a partner, without the agreement of the other partners, to sell economic rights for the full value of the partner's interest in the partnership.

Continuity of Existence

One of the important characteristics of a general partnership is that any partner has the ability at any time, to cause the dissolution of the partnership, by withdrawing from the partnership. In addition, the death, bankruptcy, or expulsion of any partner will also cause the dissolution of the partnership.

Arizona law requires the partnership to wind up its business and liquidate its assets, upon any dissolution of the partnership, absent agreement otherwise. The partners often agree in advance to remain in the partnership for a fixed period or until a specific project is completed to avoid an undesirable and unplanned liquidation. If one of the partners should then withdraw, die, become bankrupt, or be expelled prior to this time, Arizona law permits the other partners to continue the partnership business if their partnership agreement so provides. The partnership agreement usually provides a formula for valuing such partner's interest, and requires one or more of the continuing partners to pay that value to the former partner to protect the interest of the withdrawn, bankrupt, deceased, or expelled partner. This payment can be required immediately in cash, or the partnership agreement may specify deferred payment terms.

If the partnership business is wound up and liquidated after dissolution, Arizona law provides that liquidation proceeds must first be used to pay partnership debts and liabilities owing to persons who are not partners and the remainder distributed among the partners as the partners may agree or, if there is no agreement first to pay partnership debts owing to partners, next to return to the partners, their previous contributions, and, finally, to pay the partners in proportion to their profit shares.

TAX CONSIDERATIONS

Typically, a general partnership is not treated as a separate entity taxable for purposes of either the U.S. or Arizona income tax codes. A general partnership is only required to file an annual information return reflecting the partnership's income or loss for the year and each partner's share of the partnership's taxable income or loss. Each individual partner then includes his or her share of the partnership's taxable income or loss in computing taxable income on that partner's individual tax return. In effect, the partnership is treated for income tax purposes as a mere conduit that passes its income and expenses through to the partners. No income tax is imposed upon the partnership itself.

Each partner's share of partnership income or loss for income tax reporting purposes must conform to that partner's share of the economic profits or losses under the partnership agreement. In other words, if partners have agreed to share partnership profits and losses equally, they cannot report partnership income or expenses for tax purposes in different proportions. Furthermore, each partner must include his or her share of partnership taxable income in that partner's annual individual taxable income, even if the partnership does not distribute the income to the partners. For this reason, it is common for the partners to include in their partnership agreement a provision that requires that, in any year in which the partnership has taxable income, there will be a cash distribution sufficient to ensure that the individual partners will have enough funds to pay their tax liability arising out of the partnership.

In the case of a foreign partner who is considered a nonresident alien for federal income tax purposes, the partnership is required to pay a withholding tax on the partnership income associated with a U.S. trade or business that is allocable to the nonresident alien. A discussion of the classification of foreign persons as resident and nonresident aliens is included in the "Taxation" chapter. When the foreign partner files his or her income tax return, the amount withheld by the partnership is treated as a credit against the tax due by the foreign partner. Under the terms of most partnership agreements, the amounts withheld by the partnership and paid to the federal taxing authorities on behalf of the foreign partner are treated as distributions to the partner that reduce the amount of subsequent partnership distributions to which the foreign partner would otherwise be entitled. Alternatively, the withholding payments may be treated as loans by the partnership to the foreign partner, to be recovered by the partnership, with interest, out of subsequent partnership distributions to which the partner would otherwise be entitled. Under a third option, the partnership agreement may require the foreign partner to contribute the funds necessary for the partnership to make the withholding payments.

Although a partnership is typically not treated as a separate entity for U.S. or Arizona tax purposes, there are circumstances in which a partnership may elect to be taxed as a corporation. In such case, the partnership and the "partners" are taxed in the same manner as corporations and corporate shareholders.

RECORDKEEPING REQUIREMENTS

An Arizona general partnership must file annual federal and state informational tax returns that reflect the partnership's income or loss for the year and each partner's share of the partnership's taxable income or loss. Additionally, a general partnership must maintain correct and complete books or records, which may be inspected by any partner. However, no reports of partnership activity are required to be filed with any state agency.

CONCLUSION

The primary benefit associated with use of a general partnership is the significant freedom afforded the partners to determine by agreement their respective rights and obligations relating to partnership matters such as capital requirements, sharing of profits and losses, and business management. Another benefit is the single level of income taxation resulting from the status of the partnership as a mere non-taxed conduit for tax purposes. The chief disadvantage is that each partner is subject to unlimited personal liability for partnership obligations unless the partnership elects classification as a registered limited liability partnership or takes other steps to insulate the partners from partnership liabilities. Another disadvantage is the considerable practical difficulty in the ability of partners to transfer their interests in the partnership.

LIMITED PARTNERSHIPS

CHAPTER OUTLINE

SUMMARY
ORGANIZATIONAL FORMALITIES
CAPITALIZATION AND DEBT FINANCING
MANAGEMENT AND CONTROL
PROFITS AND LOSSES
EXTENT OF OWNERS' LIABILITY
TRANSFERABILITY OF INTERESTS
CONTINUITY OF INTEREST
TAX CONSIDERATIONS
RECORDKEEPING REQUIREMENTS
CONCLUSION

SUMMARY

A limited partnership may be used by two or more persons or other forms of ownership to acquire investment property or to operate a business. The principal distinction between a *limited* partnership and a *general* partnership is that a limited partnership is permitted to have one or more "limited partners" who are not personally liable for the partnership's obligations unless they actively participate in management. As in a general partnership, Arizona law provides significant freedom to partners to fix by agreement, their respective rights and obligations regarding most partnership matters.

ORGANIZATIONAL FORMALITIES

A limited partnership is not created under Arizona law until partners have filed a "certificate of limited partnership" with the Arizona Secretary of State and have paid the requisite filing fee. If the partners conduct business prior to filing the required certificate of limited partnership, they run a substantial risk of having the entity treated as a general partnership with liability of *all* partners for all partnership obligations incurred prior to filing the certificate.

The certificate of limited partnership must disclose basic information about the limited partnership for public inspection, including, among other items:

- The name of the limited partnership, which may not be the same as, nor deceptively similar to, the name of any existing Arizona limited partnership, nor any Arizona corporation, nor any foreign limited partnership or corporation authorized to transact business in the state. The name must include the words "limited partnership" and must not include the name of any limited partner.

- The address of the partnership's office where the partners may inspect copies of the partnership agreement, financial statements, and other partnership records.

- The name and address of an agent for service of legal process on the partnership, who may be an individual, an Arizona corporation, or a foreign corporation authorized to do business in Arizona.

- The name and address of each general partner.

- The latest date on which the partnership is to dissolve.

If the information in the certificate of limited partnership changes, the general partners are required to file an appropriate amendment with the Arizona Secretary of State.

The partners in a limited partnership customarily enter into a written partnership agreement at the time the certificate of limited partnership is filed. The purpose of the partnership agreement is to describe the partners' financial responsibilities and economic rights in greater detail than in the certificate and to describe other responsibilities and rights (such as management rights) not covered in the certificate. As with general partnerships, if the partners do not define their rights and obligations in a written partnership agreement, Arizona law will supply any missing rights or obligations in a manner that may or may not be consistent with the partners' expectations.

The limited partners' interests in a limited partnership are generally considered securities under both U.S. and Arizona laws. Care must be taken to ensure that the issuance of the limited partnership interests complies with the securities laws discussed in the "Securities Law" chapter.

CAPITALIZATION AND DEBT FINANCING

As in general partnerships, Arizona law permits the partners of a limited partnership, broad discretion to determine among themselves how cash, other property, or services will be contributed to the partnership by each partner at the time of formation or at any time thereafter.

A limited partnership is permitted under Arizona law to borrow money from its partners or from third parties. A limited partnership's ability to obtain debt financing may be based upon the financial condition of its *general* partners, who are individually liable under Arizona law for all partnership debts. The financial condition of a *limited* partner is not normally taken into account by a partnership lender, except to the extent that the lender is relying upon the limited partner's initial or future capital contribution commitment as a source of repayment of the debt. Limited partnership, to sign promissory notes payable to the partnership in the amounts of their future contributions. The promissory notes are then assigned as collateral to the lender to secure the loan to the partnership.

A limited partnership may also raise additional capital by creating and issuing additional partnership interests to new partners. If the new partner desires to become a general partner, existing partners must consent. If the new partner desires to become a limited partner, the consent of all the existing partners is *not* required if the partnership agreement gives the partners authority to issue additional limited partnership interests. Because the issuance of additional interests to new partners almost always will dilute the profit shares of the existing partners, partnership agreements that give the general partners this authority, usually impose conditions such as requiring a minimum capital contribution for any new limited partner or that any additional limited partner interests be offered first to the existing limited partners.

MANAGEMENT AND CONTROL

Arizona law permits the partners of a limited partnership to divide management rights and responsibilities in any manner that they may agree, but a limited partner may become personally liable for partnership debts as a general partner if the limited partner participates in the control of the partnership's business. Arizona law permits limited partners to vote on certain specific management matters (for example, the sale of all of the partnership's assets) without risking personal liability as a general partner. Most partnership agreements restrict the management rights of limited partners to these specific matters.

If there are two or more general partners in a limited partnership, the partners may delegate management rights and responsibilities among the general partners as they choose. In the absence of a division of management rights in the partnership agreement, management decisions relating to the partnership's business are made by the general partners, each of whom has an equal voice in the management and conduct of the partnership business.

Because limited partners may not be involved in the day-to-day management of the partnership's business, a limited partner, concerned that the general partners may not have taken the necessary steps to enforce a claim of the partnership against a third party, has a special right to bring a legal action (derivative action) against a third party if the general partners refuse to sue the third party. If the limited partner is successful in obtaining a judgment or a settlement of the claim, the court may award the limited partner reimbursement for expenses and legal fees. The remainder of the recovery will belong to the partnership.

PROFITS AND LOSSES

The partners in a limited partnership have significant freedom to divide partnership profits and losses and partnership distributions in any manner. If the partners do not allocate profits and losses in their partnership agreement, Arizona law provides that they share profits and losses or distributions of cash or other property in the same proportions as their actual unreturned contributions to the partnership as stated in the partnership records required to be kept by the partnership.

Freedom to allocate profits, losses, and distributions by agreement is one of the important advantages of limited (and general) partnerships under Arizona law. The different profit and loss sharing arrangements available to general partnerships are also available to limited partnerships. However, there are considerations that do not arise in general partnerships. The limited partnership agreement generally will, and should, provide that losses in excess of profits be allocated to the limited partners only up to their contributions to the partnership and that all other losses be allocated to the general partners. Also, if any distribution by the partnership causes the net worth of the partnership (the amount by which the value of the partnership's total assets exceeds its total liabilities) to be less than the total contribution of the partners as set forth in the partnership records, the partners who receive the distributions may be required to return the amount distributed if needed to pay partnership debts.

EXTENT OF OWNERS' LIABILITY

The general partners of a limited partnership generally have the same "joint and several" liability for partnership debts as do general partners in a general partnership. However, the principal advantage of a limited partnership is that each *limited* partner's liability for partnership debts is limited, with exceptions, to the contribution that the limited partner has made or agreed to make to the partnership.

There are several exceptions to the limitation on the personal liability of a limited partner. The most important applies when a limited partner participates in the control of the partnership's business. If a limited partner's management participation is substantially the same as a general partner, the limited partner will have joint and several liability for all partnership debts. If a limited partner participates in management but does not exercise substantially the same powers as a general partner, he or she will be liable only to partnership creditors who actually know of his or her management participation.

Several activities in which a limited partner may engage will *not* be considered participation in control under Arizona law. A limited partner may consult with and advise a general partner concerning management decisions. A limited partner may be an employee or agent of a general partner or the limited partnership. A limited partner is also permitted to act as a surety or guarantor for the limited partnership, may have a right of approval regarding any amendment to the partnership agreement, and may request or attend a meeting of partners. A limited partner will not be treated as participating in partnership control by reason of a right to vote on any of the following basic decisions:

- The sale, exchange, lease, mortgage, pledge, or other transfer of substantially all of the partnership's assets other than in the ordinary course of the partnership's business,

- The partnership's incurrence of indebtedness other than in the ordinary course of its business,

- The dissolution and winding up of the partnership,

- A change in the nature of the partnership's business,

- The admission or removal of a general partner,

- The admission or removal of a limited partner,

- A transaction involving an actual or potential conflict of interest between a general partner and the limited partnership or the limited partners,

- An amendment to the partnership agreement or certificate of limited partnership,

- Other matters specifically provided for in the partnership agreement.

Another important exception to the general rule of limited liability of a limited partner is that a limited partner must repay excessive partnership distributions. Arizona law prohibits partnership distributions to partners if the value of the partnership's remaining assets is less than the aggregate partnership liabilities owing to third parties. If a limited partner receives a distribution in violation of this prohibition, for six years thereafter the limited partner may be required to repay the distribution to the partnership. Additionally, if a limited partner receives the return of his or her contribution from the partnership, the limited partner may be required during the following year to return the distribution if necessary to pay partnership debts incurred prior to the distribution.

Arizona law authorizes a limited partnership to elect classification as a registered limited liability partnership. If a general partnership elects classification as a registered limited liability partnership, each partner is shielded from "vicarious" liability associated with the debts and obligations of the partnership, whether arising in contract, negligence, or otherwise. The liability shield of a registered limited liability partnership does not, however, protect a partner from direct liability on account of the partner's own actions, including wrongful acts, negligence, or misconduct of the partner, or the wrongful actions of others under a partner's direct supervision and control.

To elect classification as a registered limited liability partnership, the partnership must file an application with the Arizona Secretary of State. Further, the name of the partnership must reflect the status of the partnership as a registered limited liability partnership. The partnership must file an annual report to retain status as a registered limited partnership.

TRANSFERABILITY OF INTERESTS

A *general* partner of a limited partnership may sell or assign his or her interest in the partnership to another person and make that person a general partner only as provided in writing in the partnership agreement or, if not provided in the partnership agreement, then only with the consent of all other partners. A *limited* partner may substitute a buyer or assignee of his or her partnership interest as a new limited partner, if done in accordance with the provisions of the partnership agreement or, if not provided in the partnership agreement, then upon the consent of all other partners. Compliance with state and federal securities laws may be required in connection with any such transfer of rights.

If a general partner or limited partner desires merely to sell or assign the partner's *economic* rights to receive partnership distributions, without providing the buyer or assignee any management or voting rights as a partner, Arizona law permits the transfer of these economic rights, unless the transfer is prohibited by the partnership agreement. In many cases the limited partners will desire to restrict the assignment of a general partner's economic rights in order to maintain the general partner's incentive to manage the partnership's business. Also, the general partners may desire to restrict a limited partner's assignment of economic rights until the limited partner has made all of his or her agreed-upon capital contributions.

CONTINUITY OF INTEREST

A limited partnership is dissolved at the time of a *general* partner's withdrawal, removal, bankruptcy, death or, if the general partner is a corporation or other legal entity, upon termination of a general partner's legal existence. However, any such event affecting a *limited* partner will not cause a dissolution of a limited partnership, unless the partnership agreement provides otherwise. Absent other agreement, if a limited partnership is dissolved, the partnership's business must be wound up and liquidated.

In order to prevent an unwanted liquidation of a limited partnership following its dissolution, the remaining general partners, if any, may continue the business of the partnership without liquidation if the partnership agreement so permits. If there are no remaining general partners, the partnership business may be continued without liquidation if, within 90 days of dissolution, all of the limited partners (or a lesser number or percentage as specified in the partnership agreement) agree to appoint one or more new general partners.

If the partnership's business is not continued following a dissolution, the proceeds of liquidation must first be used to pay existing partnership liabilities other than liabilities for distributions to existing or former partners. If the proceeds of liquidation exceed the partnership's liabilities, the remaining proceeds are distributed in whatever manner the partnership agreement provides. In the absence of a provision in the partnership agreement for distribution of liquidation proceeds, the remaining proceeds must be distributed first to satisfy unpaid obligations to partners who withdrew from the partnership prior to dissolution, second to the existing partners until they have received the return of their contributions, and third to the existing partners in the same proportions as their prior contributions to the partnership.

TAX CONSIDERATIONS

The income tax treatment of a limited partnership and its partners is generally the same under the U.S. and Arizona tax codes as the treatment of general partnerships. A limited partnership typically is not required to pay income tax on its net income but simply reports each partner's share of partnership income or loss to be included in the partner's individual income tax return. Like a general partnership, a limited partnership is required to pay a withholding tax on behalf of a foreign partner characterized as a nonresident alien for federal income tax purposes. Like a general partnership, a limited partnership may elect to be taxed as a corporation. In such case, the partnership and the partner, are treated in the same manner as a corporation and corporate shareholders.

RECORDKEEPING REQUIREMENTS

An Arizona limited partnership must file annual federal and state informational tax returns that reflect the partnership's income or loss for the year and each partner's share of the partnership's taxable income or loss. A limited partnership must maintain correct and complete financial records that may be inspected by any limited partner. No annual activity reports need to be filed with any state agency.

CONCLUSION

The principal benefit available with use of a limited partnership is the protection against the personal liability of the *limited* partners. A limited partner's risk associated with the partnership is generally confined to the amount contributed or required to be contributed to the limited partnership. Other benefits arising from use of a limited partnership include the significant freedom of the partners to allocate the sharing of profits and losses and the single level of taxation resulting from the status of the partnership as a mere non-taxed conduit for tax purposes. The primary shortcoming of a limited partnership is that, in contrast to a corporation, one or more of the owners (the general partners) will be subject to unlimited personal liability for the obligations of the partnership unless the partnership elects classification as a registered limited liability partnership.

LIMITED LIABILITY COMPANIES

CHAPTER OUTLINE

SUMMARY
ORGANIZATIONAL FORMALITIES
CAPITALIZATION AND DEBT FINANCING
MANAGEMENT AND CONTROL
PROFITS AND LOSSES
EXTENT OF OWNERS' LIABILITY
TRANSFERABILITY OF INTERESTS
CONTINUITY OF EXISTENCE
TAX CONSIDERATIONS
RECORDKEEPING REQUIREMENTS
CONCLUSION

SUMMARY

Limited liability companies are a relatively new forms of business organization in Arizona. The limited liability company is intended to give flexibility to businesses in meeting their tax and business objectives.

A limited liability company combines some of the best characteristics of partnerships and corporations while eliminating some of their less desirable characteristics. The owners (called "members") of a limited liability company, like shareholders of a corporation, are not generally liable for the debts of the business. Yet, like a partnership, double taxation is avoided because the profits of a limited liability company are not subject to income tax liability imposed upon the company. Furthermore, unlike limited partners in a limited partnership, members of a limited liability company may actively participate in management without becoming subject to unlimited personal liability. The members of a limited liability company enjoy significant freedom under Arizona law to fix their rights and obligations by agreement as to most matters.

ORGANIZATIONAL FORMALITIES

One or more persons may form a limited liability company by signing and filing with the Arizona Corporation Commission articles of organization. The person or persons need not be members of the limited liability company at the time of or after formation. If the members conduct business prior to filing the articles of organization, they run a substantial risk of having the limited liability company treated as a general partnership with liability of *all* members for all obligations incurred prior to filing the articles.

The articles of organization must disclose basic information about the limited liability company for public inspection, including, among other items:

- The name of the limited liability company. The name must include the words "limited liability company" or "limited company" or the abbreviation "L.L.C." or "L.C." and must not include the words "association," "corporation," or "incorporated" nor an abbreviation of these words.

- The name and address of an agent for service of legal process on the limited liability company. This agent may be an individual, an Arizona limited liability company or corporation, or a foreign limited liability company or corporation authorized to do business in Arizona.

- Either of the following statements:

  - Management of the limited liability company is vested in a manager or managers, or

  - Management of the limited liability company is reserved to the members.

- If management is vested in a manager or managers, each person who is a manager of the limited liability company, and each person who owns a 20% or greater interest in the company.

- If management is reserved to the members, each person who is a member of the limited liability company.

- The latest date, if any, on which the limited liability company must dissolve.

- The articles of organization may include any other legal provisions.

A limited liability company's articles of organization are amended by filing an amendment with the Arizona Corporation Commission. A limited liability company must amend its articles of organization if there is a statement in the articles that is false when it was made, or if facts described in the articles have changed, making the articles inaccurate in any respect. For example, an amendment is required if the membership changes and management has been reserved to the members. If management has not been reserved to the members, an amendment is required after any change in managers or in the members holding 20% or greater interest in the limited liability company.

The members in a limited liability company customarily enter into an operating agreement at the time the articles of organization are filed. The purpose of the operating agreement is to describe the members' financial responsibilities, management rights, and profit and distribution shares. As with general partnerships and limited partnerships, if the members do not define their rights and obligations in an operating agreement, Arizona law will supply any missing rights or obligations in a manner which may or may not be consistent with the members' expectations.

The members' interests in a limited liability company may be securities under both U.S. and Arizona laws. Care must be taken to ensure that the issuance of members' interests complies with the securities laws discussed in the "Securities Law" chapter to the extent that the members' interests are securities.

CAPITALIZATION AND DEBT FINANCING

As in general partnerships and limited partnerships, Arizona law permits the members of a limited liability company broad discretion to determine among themselves how cash, other property, or services will be contributed to the limited liability company by each member at the time of formation or at any time thereafter.

A limited liability company is permitted under Arizona law to borrow money from its members or from third parties. The financial condition of a member is not normally taken into account by a lender, except to the extent that the lender is relying upon the member's initial or future capital contribution commitment as a source of repayment of the debt. Members will sometimes be asked by a lender to the limited liability company to sign promissory notes payable to the limited liability company in the amounts of their future contributions. The promissory notes are then assigned as collateral to the lender to secure the loan to the limited liability company.

A limited liability company may also raise additional capital by creating and issuing additional interests in the limited liability company to new members. Unless the operating agreement provides otherwise, the consent of all members is required to issue new interests in the limited liability company. Because the issuance of additional interests to new members almost always will dilute the profit shares of the existing members, operating agreements that give the limited liability company the authority to issue additional interest usually impose conditions, such as requiring a minimum capital contribution for any new member or that any additional interests be offered first to the existing members.

Management and Control

Arizona law permits the members of a limited liability company to divide management rights and responsibilities among the members or to grant management rights and responsibilities to "managers" designated or elected by the members. Unlike a limited partner in a limited partnership, a member does not become personally liable for limited liability company debts if the member participates in the control of the limited liability company's business. In the absence of an operating agreement to the contrary, Arizona law permits members to vote on certain specific management matters, such as the approval of a plan of merger or consolidation or the issuance of a new interest in the limited liability company.

If the members delegate management responsibilities to managers, the members will not be involved in the day-to-day management of the limited liability company's business. If a member becomes concerned that the managers may not have taken the necessary steps to enforce a claim of the limited liability company against a third party, each member has a special right to bring a legal action (called a "derivative action") to obtain a judgment in the name of the limited liability company against the third party, if the managers refuse to sue the third party. If the member is successful in obtaining a judgment or a settlement of the claim, the court may award the member reimbursement for expenses and legal fees. The remainder of the recovery will belong to the limited liability company.

Profits and Losses

The members in a limited liability company have significant freedom to divide limited liability company profits and losses and limited liability company distributions in any manner they choose. If the members do not allocate distributions in their operating agreement, Arizona law provides that distributions will be shared by the members in proportion to their actual contributions to the limited liability company and, after all contributions have been returned, distributions will be shared equally by the members.

EXTENT OF OWNERS' LIABILITY

Any member, manager, employee, officer, or agent of a limited liability company is not liable, solely by reason of being a member, manager, employee, officer, or agent, for the debts of the limited liability company. This is different than the liability of general partners in a general partnership or of the general partners in a limited partnership, who have "joint and several" liability for partnership obligations. It is also different from the liability of limited partners in a limited partnership. In a limited partnership, each limited partner's liability for partnership debts is generally limited to the contribution that the limited partner has made or agreed to make to the partnership. However, if a limited partner participates in the control of the partnership's business, the limited partner will also become liable for all partnership debts.

TRANSFERABILITY OF INTERESTS

A member cannot sell or assign his or her interest in a limited liability company to another person and make that person a member without the consent of all other members, unless all of the members have previously agreed in their operating agreement that such consent is not necessary. As noted above, compliance with state and federal securities laws may be required in connection with any such transfer of rights.

If a member desires merely to sell or assign the member's *economic* rights to receive limited liability company distributions, without giving the buyer or assignee any management or voting rights as a member, Arizona law permits the transfer of these economic rights, unless the transfer is prohibited by the members' operating agreement.

CONTINUITY OF EXISTENCE

A limited liability company is dissolved by the consent of all the members unless all of the members have previously agreed in their operating agreement that such consent is not necessary, at the time of a member's withdrawal, removal, bankruptcy, death, or, if the member is a corporation or other legal entity, upon termination of the member's legal existence unless otherwise provided in the operating agreement. Absent other agreements among the members, if a limited liability company is dissolved, the limited liability company's business must be wound up and liquidated.

In order to prevent an unwanted liquidation of a limited liability company following its dissolution, the members may continue the business of the limited liability company pursuant to a right in the operating agreement or, if the operating agreement does not provide such a right, by agreement or consent of all of the remaining members. The Arizona Corporation Commission may involuntarily dissolve a limited liability company if the company fails to amend its articles as required by law or if the company has failed to make a required publication.

If the limited liability company's business is not continued following a dissolution, the proceeds of liquidation must first be used to pay existing limited liability company obligations other than liabilities for distributions to existing or former members. If the proceeds of liquidation exceed the limited liability company's obligations, the remaining proceeds are distributed in whatever manner the members' operating agreement provides. In the absence of a provision in the operating agreement for distribution of liquidation proceeds, the remaining proceeds must be distributed, first, to satisfy unpaid obligations to members who withdrew from the limited liability company prior to dissolution; second, to existing members until they have received a return of their contributions; and, third, to the members in equal shares.

TAX CONSIDERATIONS

The income tax treatment of a limited liability company and its members is generally the same under U.S. and Arizona tax codes as the treatment of limited partnerships. A limited liability company is not required to pay income tax on its net income, but simply reports each member's share of limited liability income or loss to be included in the member's individual income tax return. Like a limited partnership, a limited liability company is required to pay a withholding tax on behalf of a foreign member characterized as a nonresident alien for federal income tax purposes.

Similar to limited partnerships, a limited liability company may elect to be taxed as a corporation. In such case, the limited liability company and its members are treated in the same manner as a corporation and corporate shareholders.

RECORDKEEPING REQUIREMENTS

An Arizona limited liability company must file annual federal and state informational tax returns that reflect the limited liability company's income or loss for the year and each member's share of the limited liability company's taxable income or loss. The company must maintain copies of a current list of the names and addresses of its members, the original articles of organization, and all written operating agreements and amendments. A limited liability company must also maintain correct and complete financial records, which may be inspected by any member. No annual activity reports need to be filed with any state agency.

Conclusion

The principal benefit available with use of a limited liability company is the protection against the personal liability of the members. A member's risk associated with the limited liability company is generally confined to the amount contributed or required to be contributed to the limited liability partnership. Other benefits arising from use of a limited liability company include the significant freedom of the members to allocate the sharing of profits, losses, and distributions and the single level of taxation resulting from the treatment of the limited liability company as a nontaxable partnership for income tax purposes.

CORPORATIONS

CHAPTER OUTLINE

SUMMARY
ORGANIZATION FORMALITIES
CAPITALIZATION AND DEBT FINANCING
MANAGEMENT AND CONTROL
PROFITS AND LOSSES
EXTENT OF OWNERS' LIABILITY
TRANSFERABILITY OF INTERESTS
CONTINUITY OF EXISTENCE
TAX CONSIDERATIONS
RECORDKEEPING REQUIREMENTS
CONCLUSION

SUMMARY

Corporations, popular vehicles for making investments or conducting business, can accommodate wide variations in the number of owners ("shareholders"), ranging from the corporation in which all the outstanding shares are owned by one person, through the "closely-held" corporation, in which the shares are held by a limited number of persons, to "publicly-held" corporations, in which share ownership is held by hundreds or thousands of shareholders. Arizona laws governing corporations are designed to permit corporate operations with minimum red tape.

Organizational Formalities

Several formalities must be observed in forming a corporation. Articles of incorporation must be filed with the Arizona Corporation Commission and a filing fee paid. A corporation's articles of incorporation must include the following information:

The name of the corporation, which must include one of the following words (or an abbreviation), "association," "bank," "corporation," "company," "incorporated," or "limited." The name selected for a corporation must be distinguishable from, among other names, the name of any existing Arizona corporation, limited partnership, or limited liability company, any foreign corporation, limited partnership, or limited liability company authorized to do business in Arizona, and certain fictitious and trade names of other entities.

- A statement of the character of the business that the corporation initially intends to conduct. The business that the corporation may conduct is not limited to that stated.

- The aggregate number of authorized shares. A corporation's articles of incorporation usually authorize a greater number of shares than the corporation intends to issue in its initial capitalization. This provides flexibility to issue additional shares in the future without amending the articles of incorporation.

- The names, addresses, and signatures of each incorporator who performs the mechanical function of filing the articles of incorporation. Incorporators need not be shareholders of the corporation, nor Arizona residents.

- The name and street address of the corporation's initial statutory agent and the street address of the corporation's known place of business if different from that of its statutory agent. Every corporation doing business in Arizona must appoint a statutory agent to receive formal notices and to accept service of process in lawsuits filed against the corporation. A statutory agent must be either a corporation authorized to do business in Arizona or an individual who is a resident of Arizona. A statutory agent, although merely ministerial, is important, because service of process gives a court jurisdiction and starts the running of the time within which the corporation must respond in order to avoid entry of judgment by default against it.

■ The name and address of each of the initial directors of the corporation.

The articles may also include other provisions not in conflict with law, including provisions eliminating or limiting liability of directors to the corporation or its shareholders for monetary damages for actions taken or any failure to take action as a director, with certain specified exceptions.

After filing the articles of incorporation, the directors named in the articles of incorporation must hold an organizational meeting to elect officers and transact other appropriate business. The adoption of corporate bylaws is among the first items of business. The bylaws of a corporation set out the details of corporate governance and normally contain provisions relating to the conduct of business and to the rights and powers of shareholders, directors, and officers. Bylaws must be consistent with Arizona law and with the articles of incorporation.

CAPITALIZATION AND DEBT FINANCING

The proceeds from the sale of its shares normally provide the principal source of capital for a corporation. An Arizona corporation may issue any number of shares, up to the maximum specified in its articles of incorporation. The board of directors establishes the price for each share to be issued. Payment for shares may be made to the corporation in cash, other property, or in past services actually performed for the corporation. Promissory notes and promises of future services cannot be used for the payment of shares.

Corporate shares are "securities" under both federal and state securities law. Care must be taken to assure that all applicable securities law requirements have been satisfied. See the chapter "Securities Laws."

An Arizona corporation has great flexibility to issue various classes of shares, each with different rights, to develop a share structure suited to its needs. For example, as a means of attracting additional investors and selling additional shares, the corporation may issue shares that provide preferred rights, such as to dividends or to the first proceeds of corporate assets in the event of dissolution. The corporation also may issue shares that lack voting rights or that provide either limited or preferential voting rights.

In general, subject to the securities laws, shares can be sold by the corporation to any party at any time. However, the articles of incorporation may grant "preemptive" rights to existing shareholders, giving them the first opportunity to purchase additional shares in proportion to the number of shares already held. Preemptive rights are often useful in closely-held corporations to preserve the relative proportion of share ownership among the existing shareholders.

Funds needed for corporate operations can also be obtained through the sale of debt securities, such as bonds or debentures. Bonds and debentures are repaid over a period of time with interest. They do not grant the holder any ownership interest in the corporation, but they rank ahead of stock in payment priority. Additionally, corporations can borrow money from financial institutions. Corporations which are new, closely-held, or thinly capitalized, often encounter difficulties in borrowing funds, unless shareholders personally guarantee the debt.

MANAGEMENT AND CONTROL

Management of a corporation is vested in its board of directors, which must consist of individuals, from one to any number.

Directors are required to manage the business of the corporation with the ordinary care that a prudent person would exercise under similar circumstances. Directors need not be shareholders of the corporation nor Arizona residents unless the articles of incorporation or bylaws so provide. Meetings of the board of directors may be held within or outside Arizona and may be held by conference telephone or other communications equipment. The directors also may take action by unanimous written consent without holding a meeting. Unless a different number is specified in the bylaws or articles of incorporation, a majority of directors constitutes a sufficient number of directors, or "quorum," necessary for the transaction of business at a meeting.

Directors are elected annually by the holders of the corporation's voting shares. At the annual election of directors, each shareholder has the right to vote the number of shares owned by the shareholder, multiplied by the number of directors to be elected. A shareholder may cast all of his or her votes for one candidate or allocate votes in any manner among the candidates. Under this system of "cumulative" voting, shareholders can elect directors in rough proportion to the percentage of shares they own.

If the articles of incorporation provide, a corporation's board of directors may be divided to any extent that does not infringe upon the shareholders' cumulative voting rights. Such a "staggered board" usually consists of two or three groups. With a staggered board, only the directors in a particular group stand for election at each annual meeting, so that only a half or third of the board is elected that year. Staggered boards promote continuity of management by preventing a shareholder or group of shareholders from replacing all of the directors at a single annual shareholder meeting.

Subject to certain exceptions, one or more of a corporation's directors may be removed from office for any reason by the shareholders at a shareholders' meeting called expressly for that purpose. If less than the entire board is to be removed, no director may be removed if the votes cast against removal would be sufficient to elect the director to the board under the cumulative voting system. Subject to certain exceptions, any vacancy on the board of directors may be filled by either the remaining directors or the shareholders. The replacement director holds office until the next election of directors.

Shareholders enjoy rights in addition to the rights associated with the election and removal of members of the board of directors. If the directors desire to sell, exchange, or otherwise dispose of all or substantially all of the corporation's property, other than in the usual and regular course of the corporation's business, a majority of the outstanding voting shares of the corporation usually must approve the transaction. If the directors desire to merge the corporation with another corporation, approval by a majority of the outstanding voting shares of each corporation is required in most instances.

If a shareholder dissents from, among other things, any disposition of all or substantially all of the corporation's assets, or any merger, subject to certain limitations, the shareholder, by complying with statutory notice and other requirements, may require the corporation to purchase his or her shares. If the corporation and the dissenting shareholder cannot agree on a value for the shares, the corporation must request a court to determine their value. These "dissenters' rights" do not extend to holders of shares of an Arizona corporation registered on a national securities exchange or listed on the NASDAQ National Market System, nor to a class or series of shares that are held by 2,000 or more shareholders of record, unless the corporation's articles of incorporation otherwise provide.

In certain cases, Arizona law provides rights to existing management to avoid the effects of hostile takeovers. For example, the voting rights of shares of "issuing public corporations" that are acquired in a "control share acquisition" may be limited. An "issuing public corporation" would include certain publicly-held companies and companies that elect to be subject to such rules in their articles of incorporation if certain additional conditions are satisfied. Arizona law also permits a corporation to specify in its articles of incorporation that certain matters must be approved by a greater voting requirement than would otherwise be required by law.

The day-to-day operations of a corporation are conducted by its officers, whose authority is determined by the board of directors or described in the bylaws. The corporation may have such officers as the shareholders or directors deem appropriate. The officers are elected by the board of directors, and may then appoint one or more assistant officers if authorized by the bylaws or the board of directors. The same individual may hold any two or more offices. Any officer may be removed at any time by the directors, but, by contract, an officer may be entitled to severance compensation or to continued employment in some other capacity.

PROFITS AND LOSSES

Profits are shared by the shareholders in the form of dividends. Generally, dividends are distributed to shareholders proportionately in accordance with share ownership. Holders of preferred shares enjoy preferential rights to dividend distributions.

Subject to any restriction contained in the articles of incorporation, a corporation may pay dividends in cash, in property, or in its own shares. A distribution of dividends may not be made if the corporation would not be able to pay its debts in the normal course of business. Also, payment of dividends would not be permitted when the corporation's total assets would be less than the sum of its total liabilities plus, unless the articles permit otherwise, the amount needed to satisfy the rights of preferential shareholders on dissolution.

Losses incurred by a corporation may reduce the payment of dividends to shareholders and the price obtainable by shareholders upon a sale of shares. Except in the case of a "Subchapter S" corporation, the losses incurred by a corporation are not shared by the shareholders on a current basis. See "Tax Considerations" below in this chapter.

EXTENT OF OWNERS' LIABILITY

As a general rule, each shareholder's liability for corporate obligations is limited to the shareholder's investment in the shares of the corporation, insulating unrelated assets of the shareholder from corporate debts. In some situations, however, a court may "pierce the corporate veil" and disregard the corporation as a legal entity, with the effect of making shareholders personally liable for the corporation's obligations as if it were a proprietorship or partnership.

The corporate veil may be pierced by a court if the corporation is not sufficiently capitalized to meet the obligations reasonably foreseeable for a business of its size and character. Other factors that may lead a court to pierce the veil and disregard the corporation as a distinct legal entity include whether the corporation was used to defraud creditors, whether the corporation failed to maintain adequate records, and whether the corporation disregarded corporate legal formalities. Arizona courts seldom grant relief to corporate creditors under the theory of piercing the corporate veil except in extreme factual circumstances. By providing adequate capital, by honest business practices, and by paying attention to simple formalities, the protection of shareholders' separate assets from claims of corporate creditors afforded by use of the corporate structure can easily be maintained.

TRANSFERABILITY OF INTERESTS

The ownership interest of shareholders in a corporation are usually represented by share certificates, which, in most cases, are freely transferable, although the corporation need not recognize a purchaser as a shareholder until the transfer is recorded on the corporation's books. Reasonable restrictions on share transfers may be imposed by the corporation's articles of incorporation or bylaws or by the provisions of an agreement among the shareholders if the existence of such restriction is noted conspicuously on the share certificate. The board of directors of an Arizona corporation may authorize issuance of shares without certificates as long as the shareholder receives relevant information regarding his or her rights. Federal and state securities laws may also impose restrictions on the transferability of shares.

CONTINUITY OF EXISTENCE

An Arizona corporation will have perpetual existence unless its articles of incorporation provide otherwise. A corporation with perpetual existence will not terminate until formal steps are taken to dissolve the corporation. The death, bankruptcy, or transfer of shares of any shareholder will not interrupt the continuing existence of a corporation.

TAX CONSIDERATIONS

Generally, a corporation is treated for both federal and state tax purposes as a taxable entity, separate and apart from its shareholders. A corporation computes its taxable income or loss each year and pays tax at the corporate level on its taxable income. After payment of income taxes, if the corporation distributes dividends to its shareholders, the shareholders usually must include the dividend distributions in their own individual taxable income. Consequently, corporate profits are taxed twice, once when earned by the corporation and a second time when distributed to the shareholders.

Certain corporations may avoid the liability for corporate-level income taxes by filing a special election under Subchapter S of the federal tax code. A corporation can make this special election only if, among other requirements, it has permissible shareholders, including individuals (other than nonresident aliens), estates, certain trusts, and commencing in 1997, certain tax exempt entities. Corporations owned in whole or in part by other corporations, by partnerships, or by nonresident aliens are not eligible to make the special election and cannot avoid liability for corporate-level income taxes. Classification of foreign persons as resident or nonresident aliens is discussed in the chapter "Immigration." Tax considerations are further considered in the chapters "Taxation" and "Real Property."

RECORDKEEPING REQUIREMENTS

Every Arizona corporation is required to file an annual report with the Arizona Corporation Commission that includes, among other things, the following information:

- The name of the corporation and the state or country under whose law it is incorporated

- The corporation's address and the name and address of its statutory agent

- The address of its principal office

- A statement of the character of the corporation's business

- The names and addresses of the directors and principal officers of the corporation

- The number of authorized and issued shares for each class of shares

- The name of each shareholder who holds more than 20 percent of any class of shares

- A statement of the corporation's financial condition

An Arizona corporation must file annual federal and state income tax returns. Certain corporations are subject to special recordkeeping requirements in connection with transactions involving "related" foreign persons.

In addition to the reports that must be filed with state and federal authorities, a corporation must annually provide shareholders with a financial report. Every corporation, regardless of size or numbers of shareholders, is required to maintain appropriate accounting records, as well as minutes of meetings of its shareholders and board of directors. A corporation must also keep a

DOING BUSINESS IN ARIZONA

record of its shareholders, with the names and addresses of all shareholders and the number and class of shares held by each. Under certain circumstances, shareholders have the right to inspect the corporation's books and records.

CONCLUSION

The primary benefit of forming a corporation is protection against the personal liability of the owners. A shareholder's risk is limited to the amount of capital invested in the corporation, unless there is abuse of the corporate form that justifies "piercing the corporate veil." The disadvantages of the use of a corporation include the greater formalities that must be observed and, except when a Subchapter S election is used, the double taxation of business profits, once by taxing the corporation and a second time by taxing shareholders' income.

REAL PROPERTY

CHAPTER OUTLINE

DEVELOPMENT OF ARIZONA REAL ESTATE
    PUBLIC REGULATION
        ZONING AND LAND USE REGULATIONS
        SITE PLANS AND SPECIAL USE PERMITS
        ANNEXATION
        MUNICIPAL SUBDIVISION REGULATIONS
        DEVELOPMENT FEES
        OTHER REGULATIONS
    PRIVATE REGULATION
        DEED RESTRICTIONS
        RECIPROCAL EASEMENT AGREEMENTS
        DECLARATIONS (CC&Rs)
    MANAGEMENT AND MARKETING
        PROPERTY MANAGEMENT
        BROKERS
        SALE OR LEASE OF SUBDIVIDED LAND
CONSTRUCTION OF BUILDINGS
    PUBLIC REGULATION OF CONSTRUCTION
    SELECTION OF CONSTRUCTION
        PROFESSIONALS
    CONSTRUCTION CONTRACTS
    PAYMENT OF CONTRACTORS
    CONSTRUCTION DISPUTES

SUMMARY

A common investment in Arizona is ownership and development of real estate. Business operations in Arizona are often accompanied by the purchase or lease of local real estate. Foreign persons who contemplate investment or business activities that involve real estate will find Arizona attractive from a legal standpoint. Arizona has no "alien land laws" that restrict the acquisition or lease of real estate by foreign persons. Foreign persons have the same rights and opportunities as U.S. citizens to acquire or lease Arizona real estate.

Acquisition of Arizona Real Property

In acquiring Arizona real estate an investor usually acquires either outright ownership of the property ("fee simple" ownership) or a leasehold interest.

Purchases

Purchase Agreements

The purchase of fee simple ownership of Arizona real estate is best accomplished through a written purchase agreement. An oral agreement to purchase or sell Arizona real estate generally is not enforceable. Arizona laws leave wide latitude to the parties to structure their transactions. As a result, a written purchase agreement in Arizona is often lengthy and detailed.

A purchase agreement will cover basic matters such as the purchase price of the property, the identity of the property, the timing of the transaction, and the allocation between the potential buyer and seller of ongoing income and expense such as rents or utilities. Most real estate purchases also require investigation of the property by the potential buyer, a process that can involve substantial expenditures of time and money. Therefore, most written purchase agreements provide for a period of time during which the buyer may investigate the property for defects or problems.

Such matters as title, the physical condition and state of repair of any improvements to the property, soil and subsurface conditions, zoning and land use regulations, environmental matters, the availability of financing, the availability of water and other utilities, the financial history of the property, and the economic feasibility of the particular investment are of concern to the buyer. The buyer's satisfaction as to such matters may be made an explicit condition of the buyer's obligation to purchase the property. The importance of such investigations and of the prospective buyer making a thorough analysis of all aspects of the transaction are particularly important if the seller is unwilling to make representations and warranties with respect to the property, because without them the buyer may be left without legal recourse against the seller for problems discovered after the property is purchased.

In Arizona it is customary for a purchase agreement to provide for an "escrow," an arrangement in which an independent third party (such as a title insurance company) holds documents and money until the parties are prepared to complete the transaction. When the transfer of title and payment of purchase price finally take place (called the "closing"), the escrow agent disburses the purchase money deposited by the buyer to the seller and records the deed to the property in the public records, completing the purchase.

Often the prospective buyer will be required to place money into escrow when the purchase agreement is signed. This "earnest money deposit" shows the seller that the prospective buyer is seriously interested in the property and intends to proceed in good faith. By agreement the earnest money deposit either may or may not be refundable if the prospective buyer does not consummate the transaction.

LETTERS OF INTENT

Early in the course of negotiating a real estate transaction, a prospective buyer and seller may wish to memorialize the basic transaction terms in order to have a common framework for further negotiations that may lead to a binding agreement. A letter of intent or letter of understanding may be used for this purpose. A prospective buyer or seller should take care that such a letter does not constitute a binding agreement. The letter should clearly state that it is not intended to be binding but only a basic outline of terms and conditions that the parties will discuss and negotiate further, and that the parties will have no liability to each other if they fail to enter into a final contract.

TITLE INSURANCE

The condition of title to property is a key consideration for prospective buyers. A purchase agreement will often require the seller to provide the buyer with a status report on the condition of title to the property, a preliminary title report or commitment for title insurance (known as a "title report") issued by a company in the business of investigating and insuring title to real property. The title report will describe the current ownership of the property, will list any matters that may affect title to the property such as delinquent property taxes and assessments, covenants, conditions, restrictions, easements, liens, and any other encumbrances, and will identify the requirements that must be satisfied before the title company will insure title.

Both the title report and the copies of the "title exceptions" must be reviewed carefully by the prospective buyer during the investigation period to confirm marketable title and that the title exceptions will not interfere with the proposed use or development of the property. Often it is necessary to obtain a survey of the property, so that the property boundaries can be determined, easements, improvements, and encroachments can be located, and other physical characteristics of the property examined. The purchase agreement also may obligate the seller to remove title matters unacceptable to the buyer or to provide protective title insurance. The prospective buyer's obligation to purchase the property should be conditioned upon review of a title report and upon receipt of a written commitment by a title insurance company to issue a title insurance policy at closing, insuring the title to be in satisfactory condition approved by the buyer.

At the closing, or very shortly thereafter, the title insurance policy will be issued to the owner. There are two forms of title insurance policies available to owners in Arizona, standard coverage and extended coverage. A number of policy modifications, called endorsements, also are available. Legal counsel should be consulted to determine appropriate policies and endorsements for specific transactions.

The premium for a title insurance policy is determined by the title company that issues the title policy, subject to state regulated schedules. In Arizona it is common for the seller to pay the premium cost of a standard owner's policy of title insurance. Payment of the additional premium for any "extended coverage" policy (which provides additional protections such as insuring the accuracy of boundary line locations) is as negotiated between buyer and seller.

DEEDS

Ownership of Arizona real estate is conveyed by delivery to the buyer of a deed. To be valid a deed must be in writing, must adequately describe the property, must be signed by the seller, and must be acknowledged before a notary public. There are additional requirements that apply to deeds to or from trustees or to or from two or more individuals who give or take title in some form of co-ownership, discussed in more detail below.

A deed may or may not contain warranties concerning the condition of title. A buyer would prefer to receive a "general warranty deed" in which the seller warrants that the seller owns the property and that no one, including the seller, has done anything to cause the title to be less than as described in the deed. The seller would prefer to provide only a "special warranty deed" in which the seller warrants merely that the seller owns the property and that the seller has not done anything to diminish the title from that described in the deed. An alternative to a general warranty deed or to a special warranty deed is a "quit claim deed." In a quit claim deed the seller makes no promise or warranty whatsoever concerning ownership or condition of title, but merely transfers to the buyer all rights, if any, that the seller has in the property. A buyer should carefully consider the consequences in a given situation before accepting a quit claim deed.

A deed to Arizona real estate should be recorded promptly with the county recorder of the county in which the property is located. Failure to record a deed promptly may permit third parties, such as innocent purchasers or lien holders, to acquire rights superior to the rights of the buyer.

Arizona law generally requires that an "affidavit of property value" be completed and signed by the parties. The affidavit, which includes a number of details concerning the real estate transaction, must be filed with the county recorder at the same time as the deed is recorded. All of the information disclosed on the affidavit of property value is a matter of public record.

There is a small recording fee for both deeds and affidavits of property value. Arizona does not impose a documentary stamp tax or real estate transfer tax on real estate transactions.

METHODS OF HOLDING TITLE

In acquiring Arizona real estate, attention must be given to the manner in which title to the real estate will be held. Arizona real estate may be owned by any natural person or legal entity or by combinations of persons and legal entities.

▪ Individual Ownership

Any natural person, regardless of age, nationality, religion, or race, may own any Arizona real estate interest. Individual ownership may not be the most advisable method by which to acquire property, particularly if the individual is a foreign person. For example, on the death of an individual who owns real estate in Arizona, Arizona law may require an Arizona probate proceeding to confirm the passage of title to an heir or legatee. Substantial time and expense may be incurred by the heirs of a foreign person in Arizona probate court proceedings.

■ Corporate Ownership

Any foreign or domestic corporation may hold title to Arizona real estate. A foreign corporation should determine whether or not the corporation must qualify to do business in Arizona prior to the acquisition. If a foreign corporation merely purchases, holds, and later sells, an interest in undeveloped Arizona real estate in an isolated transaction, this alone would not require the foreign corporation to qualify to do business in the state. However, if the corporation's ownership of an interest in Arizona real property will involve substantial and continuous business activities, such as leasing of property or sales of lots, it is advisable that the foreign corporation qualify to do business in Arizona.

■ Partnership Ownership

Foreign or domestic partnerships may also own Arizona real estate. Foreign general partnerships are required to file a certificate of "fictitious name" with the county recorder of each Arizona county in which the partnership will conduct business. This document sets forth the names of the partners as a matter of public record. Every foreign limited partnership must file an "application for registration" as a foreign limited partnership with the Arizona Secretary of State.

■ Trust and Estate Ownership

Any legally existing trust or estate, whether foreign or domestic, may hold title to Arizona real estate.

■ Multiple Ownership

Any interest in Arizona real estate may be owned by more than one person or entity. There are four forms of multiple ownership in Arizona real estate: "community property," "community property with right of survivorship," "tenancy in common," and "joint tenancy with right of survivorship."

Unless the deed conveying title specifies to the contrary, all interests in Arizona real estate acquired by a husband or wife during their marriage are presumed to constitute "community property" of the husband and wife, regardless of where they reside, although spouses may own property individually ("separate property") as well. In community property ownership each spouse owns an undivided one-half interest. Both spouses must sign a deed in order to convey any interest in their community property to another person or entity. Generally, when property is acquired by gift or inheritance or with the separate funds of a spouse, the acquired property is the separate property of the acquiring spouse, and the signature of that spouse alone on the deed is sufficient to transfer the property.

Husband and wife may also acquire title to real property as "community property with right of survivorship." This form of ownership retains all the essential characteristics of "community property" ownership, in that each spouse owns an undivided one-half interest and both spouses must sign a deed in order to convey any interest in their community property to another person or entity. Community property with right of survivorship eliminates some of the potential disadvantages associated with other forms of ownership. Unlike community property, which requires a probate proceeding upon the death of either spouse, with community property with right of survivorship the deceased spouse's interest is automatically transferred to the surviving spouse without probate, regardless of any provision to the contrary in the deceased spouse's will. Community property with right of survivorship can also provide a tax advantage upon the death of the first spouse if the sale of the home will result in significant gain because both the deceased and surviving spouses' interest in the property receive a step-up in basis.

Any combination of natural persons or entities may acquire title to real property as "tenants in common." When title to real property is acquired by tenants in common, each tenant in common has a separate and distinct, proportionate, undivided, interest in the property, which separate interest is freely transferable. The proportionate interest in the property of the different tenants in common may be equal or unequal. Unless fractional interests are specifically fixed in the instrument of conveyance, each tenant is presumed to own an equal share. Each tenant in common is entitled to the full use and enjoyment of the property, subject to the equal rights of use of the other co-tenants. Except in the cases of conveyances to executors or trustees, or to husbands and wives, any conveyance of an interest in Arizona real estate to two or more persons or entities that fails to specify the form of ownership is presumed to create a tenancy in common.

Any combination of natural persons may acquire title to Arizona real estate as "joint tenants with right of survivorship." A joint tenancy with right of survivorship differs from a tenancy in common in one significant aspect. In the event of the death of an individual joint tenant, the deceased co-owner interest goes automatically to the survivor, joint tenant, or if more than one, is divided equally among the surviving joint tenants, without probate, regardless of any provision to the contrary in the deceased owner's will. In contrast, the interest of a co-owner under a tenancy in common can be transferred by a tenant in common while alive to any other person. On an individual tenant in common's death, the interest passes by will, if there is one, to the deceased's legatees. If there are none, it passes by intestate succession to the deceased's heirs.

■ **Disclosure of Acquisition**

Although foreign persons have the same rights and opportunities as U.S. persons to acquire Arizona real estate, U.S. law requires that certain investments in real estate by   foreign persons be disclosed to the federal government. Generally, all information disclosed is confidential and access to the disclosed information is limited to officials and employees of U.S. governmental agencies. However, certain disclosure information required in connection with the ownership of agricultural land is available to the public. There is further discussion of the disclosure requirements associated with ownership of real estate by foreign persons in the chapter "Disclosure of Foreign Investments."

Leases

In General

A foreign investor may prefer to lease, rather than own, real estate. A lease of real estate is the exclusive right to possess and use real estate for a specified period of time in consideration for the payment of money as rent. The property owner under a lease is the "landlord" or "lessor." The party acquiring the "leasehold" interest in the property is the "tenant" or "lessee." The time period when the lease is in effect is the "term." Although the lessor transfers the use and possession of the leased property to the lessee for the term of the lease, the lessor retains ownership of the property. Upon expiration of the term of the lease, the right to use and possess the property reverts back to the lessor. Leases with a term over one year must be in writing to be enforceable.

A lease allocates the economic risks and expenses of property ownership, possession, and operation between the lessor and lessee. For example, a lease generally specifies which of the parties will be responsible for the payment of taxes, assessments, utility charges, building maintenance charges and other costs, what type of insurance coverage each party must maintain, which of the parties is to bear the risk of loss if buildings, structures, improvements or personal property on the leased property are damaged or destroyed, and which of the parties is responsible for maintaining and repairing the property.

Various factors, including the proposed use of a particular property, determine the appropriate contents of a specific lease. Most leases of non-residential property fall within one of the following categories: "ground leases," "agricultural leases," or "commercial leases."

Ground Leases

A ground lease is often made by a landowner who wants to retain ownership of real property but to avoid an active role in its development. A ground lease entitles the lessee to use, develop, and operate the leased property without actually owning the property. In turn, a ground lease generally obligates the lessee to assume most of the burdens and responsibilities associated with ownership of the property, including maintenance of the property and payment of real estate taxes. Most ground leases have a term of from 50 to 99 years.

AGRICULTURAL LEASES

A lease of agricultural land involves unique issues. A lessor under an agricultural lease may wish to impose restrictions against the use of pesticides, fertilizers, or of other chemicals potentially hazardous to the environment. A lessor may also seek to limit the types of crops that may be grown on the property to qualify for governmental crop subsidies or to maintain an adequate soil nutrient level. A lessor may wish to reserve the right to terminate the agricultural lease if commercial development of the land becomes a potential. An agricultural lease should address which party is responsible for ensuring that an adequate water supply is provided and maintained for the property and should address the respective parties' responsibilities for growing and harvesting crops and entitlement to any profits from sale of the crops.

COMMERCIAL LEASES

The terms of commercial leases vary significantly, depending upon the type of property and improvements. A lessor under a shopping center lease often collects both a base rent and an additional rent equal to a percentage of the lessee's sales ("percentage rent"). A lessor under an office or industrial commercial lease generally does not collect percentage rent, but may be particularly concerned with other economic considerations. For example, if the lessor is paying for the utility costs, the lessor may seek to place specific limitations upon the types and quantities of electrical equipment that the lessee may operate on the property.

In many cases the lessor may contribute funds to modify, or may actually modify, the leased space in preparation for the tenant's occupation. The most extreme example of this type of lease is the "build to suit" lease in which an entire building is constructed by the lessor to lessee specifications and delivered to the lessee when completed. The cost of the construction usually is amortized over the term of the lease, including a return on investment for the lessor-developer. This arrangement can be particularly useful to a foreign business that requires a unique or unusual facility.

OTHER SIGNIFICANT OWNERSHIP INTERESTS

Occasionally foreign investors may acquire real estate interests other than fee simple ownership or a leasehold. Many such other types of real estate interests exist. The three most common are "easements," "mineral interests," and "water rights."

EASEMENTS

An easement is an interest in real estate that permits one person to use another person's land for a particular purpose. For example, an easement may be given to a telephone company or power company to permit it to place its lines above or under property owned by another party, or an easement may be provided to give a right of access over the property of an adjoining landowner. Easements should be in writing and should be recorded in the county recorder's office of the county in which the property is located to provide notice of the easement to third parties. An easement typically "runs with the land," meaning that the easement continues to encumber the property "burdened" by the easement, even if the property is conveyed to another owner.

Mineral Interests

Mineral interests may be purchased or leased apart from surface rights to real estate. Both the federal and the state governments often "reserve" the mineral rights to many parcels of real estate. These mineral rights may be separately acquired or leased from the U.S. government or from the state of Arizona. Mineral rights reserved by the U.S. government may be acquired through filing mining claims or through purchase applications filed with the U.S. Bureau of Land Management. Mineral rights reserved by the state of Arizona may be acquired by mining claims, exploration permits, and leases issued by the Arizona Department of Mines and Mineral Resources. Mineral rights owned by private parties may be purchased or leased in the same manner as other interests in real estate.

Water Rights

Water rights present special considerations. In some cases, water rights are attached to land ("appurtenant") and cannot be transferred except in connection with a transfer of the land. In other cases, water rights are personal property rights not connected with any particular land and can be transferred independently. Water rights in Arizona are the subject of complex statutory regulation, explained further in the chapter "Water Rights."

State Land

Privately-owned Arizona real estate presents many attractive investment opportunities. In addition, a significant amount of the land in Arizona, including land in prime urban areas, is owned by the state of Arizona and available for purchase or lease. Fee simple ownership of land may be acquired from the state by purchase or by an exchange of private land for the state land. Special conditions govern the acquisition of state land, whether by direct purchase or by exchange. For instance, state land cannot be sold or exchanged for less than its appraised value, and state land in most cases must be sold to the highest bidder at an advertised public auction.

Land owned by the state of Arizona may be leased for agricultural, grazing, or commercial purposes. The term of an agricultural or grazing lease is limited to not more than 10 years, but a lessee of state land has a preferred right to renew an existing agricultural or grazing lease for up to an additional 10 years. A commercial lease of state land may be for up to 99 years, but a commercial lease for a term of over 10 years is subject to competitive bidding at public auction. An application to acquire or lease state land must be made on forms provided by the Arizona State Land Department. An application fee is required and public notice requirements must be satisfied.

THE ROLE OF PROFESSIONALS AND CONSULTANTS

Real estate brokers match a buyer with a seller of real property. Normally, brokers are employed by the seller to locate an interested buyer, but it is not uncommon for a foreign investor to retain a broker for assistance in locating suitable real estate for purchase. The broker or salesperson in some cases may be asked only to identify likely prospects for sale or lease. In other cases the broker or salesperson may be authorized to negotiate contracts for sale and leases. In still others the broker or salesperson may be empowered to sign documents on behalf of an owner.

A broker usually receives a commission for services. In a sale the commission is usually paid by the seller upon the closing of the sale, based on a percentage of the purchase price. In a lease the commission is commonly paid by the lessor at the time of execution of the lease or at the time the tenant occupies the leased space. The amount of a lease commission is determined by various formulas. A common one is a percentage of the rent to be paid over a period of years. Another is a specified amount multiplied by the amount of space leased to the tenant.

A written brokerage agreement is usually signed by the seller or buyer engaging the broker and by the broker. Brokerage agreements can be exclusive, giving a single broker the exclusive right to deal on behalf of an owner. Brokerage agreements can provide that brokers are entitled to a commission only if the transaction is consummated. Unless the agreement expressly says otherwise, a broker will be entitled to a commission on a sale if the broker has procured a ready, willing, and able buyer, even if the sale fails to close. In most cases brokerage agreements must be in writing to be enforceable. Brokerage agreements generally specify the responsibilities of the broker, the amount of the commission to which a broker will be entitled, the conditions that must be satisfied for a broker to earn the commission, the time when the commission will be paid, and the duration or term of the brokerage agreement.

With very limited exceptions, it is unlawful to engage in real estate brokerage activities without a license. It is also unlawful to compensate an unlicensed person for brokerage services. If a party to a real estate transaction, or the party's agent, is a licensed broker or salesperson, this must be disclosed to the other party.

FINANCING REAL ESTATE

INTRODUCTION

When purchasing or developing real estate, the investor will encounter a variety of financing options. There may be existing financing that the investor will have to consider in its own financing strategy. Beyond or in lieu of existing financing, other sources include seller financing, conventional financing, public financing, and private equity participation.

Assumption of Existing Financing

It is not unusual for the investor to find real property encumbered by existing financing. The investor should obtain as much information as possible about such financing. If the investor chooses to purchase property subject to existing financing, which party remains liable for such financing is a negotiated matter. If the investor wants to assume the existing financing, the loan documents need to be reviewed to determine if there are any transfer restrictions or assumption fees that will be incurred. If existing financing is assumed, the investor may choose to use "wraparound" financing. Wraparound financing involves a promissory note promising to pay the existing underlying balance, with interest, as well as the investor's new financing. The wraparound financing documentation should be compared to the underlying financing documentation to ensure that their provisions and payment schedules do not conflict.

Seller Financing

When an investor purchases real estate, the seller frequently will agree to accept at the closing only a portion of the total purchase price as a down payment. The balance of the purchase price is evidenced by a investor's promissory note promising to pay the balance over time, with interest. To secure repayment of the promissory note, the investor typically places a deed of trust or mortgage on the purchased property that encumbers the property with a lien. The property may be sold in foreclosure if the investor fails to make payments on the promissory note. Conventional financing, mentioned briefly immediately below, is discussed in more detail in the following chapter "Financing and Investment" under "Conventional Financing." Notes and related security documents may become "securities" subject to special restrictions and requirements discussed in more detail in the chapter "Securities Laws."

Seller financing covers only the deferred portion of the purchase price for the property. If additional funds are necessary for the development of the property, they must be obtained from other sources, described in this chapter and in the following chapter "Financing and Investment."

CONVENTIONAL FINANCING

The most common sources of borrowed funds for real estate are loans from banks, insurance companies, pension funds, and savings and loan associations. Recent developments in the commercial finance markets have somewhat limited the availability of loans for real estate investments, but commercial financing from institutional lenders, both inside and outside Arizona, continues to play an important role.

PUBLIC FINANCING

Arizona has a unique form of public financing for Arizona real estate projects. The state permits the formation of "community facilities districts" to construct and finance infrastructure improvements for real estate projects, such as roads, sidewalks, drainage facilities, and sewer, water, and utility systems.

A community facilities district has governmental power to tax and issue bonds. Because the interest paid to the holders of the bonds issued by a community facilities district is generally exempt from federal and state income tax, the interest rate on funds made available through the sale of these bonds is often significantly lower than conventional financing rates.

Below-market interest rates may also be available when financing is provided through the sale of industrial development bonds.

DOING BUSINESS IN ARIZONA

PRIVATE EQUITY PARTICIPATION

A foreign investor with significant capital resources may choose to participate in Arizona real estate investments by becoming an "equity participant" in a partnership with a local real estate developer. Such transactions may be structured several ways. One method is for the equity participant to advance to the partnership funds to purchase and develop a particular piece of real estate. The developer contributes time and expertise to the partnership. The equity participant typically is entitled to recover the participant's equity investment and to earn a specified annual return on the investment before any revenues are distributed to the developer. When the equity participant has recovered the equity investment and a specified annual return, any additional revenues are divided between the developer and the equity participant on an agreed percentage basis.

An investor who wishes to participate to a significant degree in the management of the project may elect to be a *general* partner in the venture. As a general partner the investor will be exposed to liability for all losses on the project, even beyond the investor's investment. An investor who wishes to limit exposure on the project to the investor's equity investment and who is willing to assume a more passive role may become a limited partner.

Another alternative for an investor seeking acquisition and development funds is a real estate syndication. A real estate syndication usually involves a limited partnership formed to acquire and develop the project. The syndicate is funded by the sale of limited partnership interests to one or more equity investors. The sale of interests in limited partnerships constitutes a sale of "securities" and is regulated by federal and state securities laws, as discussed under "Securities Laws."

DEVELOPMENT OF ARIZONA REAL ESTATE

In evaluating investment opportunities in Arizona real estate, an investor should consider how the real estate will be put to use. Four areas of concern in real estate development are: public regulations and restrictions on the use of land; private regulations and restrictions on the use of land; management and marketing of Arizona real estate; and construction of buildings.

PUBLIC REGULATION

Local governments seek to assure and promote coherent, orderly growth in a manner that balances the quality of life of its residents with competing and conflicting needs of the community. Because of these and similar concerns, most Arizona counties, cities, and towns, like local governments in other states, have enacted comprehensive land use and zoning regulations. Arizona has a tradition of favoring limited governmental regulation. Local governments in Arizona historically have encouraged economic growth and development. As a result, foreign investors often find the regulatory climate in Arizona for land development more favorable than the regulatory climate in many other states.

ZONING AND LAND USE REGULATIONS

Arizona counties, cities, and towns have broad authority to regulate land uses within their boundaries. Most of these local governmental units have adopted land use plans and zoning ordinances that specify the uses permitted on parcels of land within their jurisdiction. Certain parcels may be zoned by local authorities for agricultural purposes, others for single-family residential uses, and still others for light industrial and manufacturing. A detailed zoning code may specify additional requirements, such as building "set-back lines," parking requirements, landscape requirements, provisions for adequate drainage and flood control, restrictions on building height, and others. No development activity can be commenced on land subject to zoning restrictions unless the requirements of the zoning ordinance are satisfied.

If an owner wishes to develop land with a project not permitted by the existing zoning, the owner may apply to the local government for rezoning of the property or for a variance. If successful, the effect is to change the zoning classification of the affected property to a zoning classification that permits the use desired by the owner-applicant or to permit a particular use as an exception to existing zoning.

The average rezoning takes three to nine months, depending on the nature and complexity of the issues. The process is begun by submission of an application to the local government. The submission is accompanied by detailed plans and drawings for the proposed project. The application is processed by the local government's planning and zoning department, and the procedure usually involves extensive negotiations with the department's staff over preconditions to rezoning approval. Common stipulations may include a requirement to convey additional rights-of-way, or to widen streets to provide better access to the project, or to provide a landscape buffer between the project and an adjoining landowner.

After the zoning staff has processed the application, a preliminary hearing may be held before the local government's planning commission. This body is made up of appointed private citizens who analyze and make recommendations, often very specific, on the application. After the planning commission makes a final decision to approve or reject the application, a formal hearing is then held before the elected governing body, which accepts or rejects the decision of the planning commission. At the hearing, the owner-applicant presents the case for approval. If the application is approved, the rezoning is granted, and the owner can proceed with the proposed project under the new zoning, subject to complying with any stipulations. Any interested person can appear at these hearings to oppose or support the proposed change. The property owner seeking a rezoning is well-advised to meet in advance with the surrounding landowners to answer questions and, if possible, resolve their concerns prior to the hearing.

SITE PLANS AND SPECIAL USE PERMITS

Although a particular project may be a permitted use under existing zoning, zoning codes frequently require the owner to obtain approval of a site plan or a special use permit from the local government prior to development. Site plan and special use permit requirements are required for projects in which the local government, for policy reasons, seeks a more substantial role. The local government may have special concerns with the design of a particular project, or with the detailed uses to be made of the property, because of the potential impact such design or uses may have on surrounding property and the community at large. Projects likely to require site plan approval or a special use permit are high-rise office buildings, shopping centers, resorts, mobile home parks, sports arenas, residential extended care facilities, and warehouses.

The procedures for obtaining special use permits and site plan approval vary greatly from jurisdiction to jurisdiction. In simple cases the procedures may involve only approval of the planning staff. In other cases the procedures may involve a process similar to rezoning approvals, including public hearings and a requirement of final approval by the local governing body.

ANNEXATION

Occasionally an investor acquires land outside the boundaries of an existing city or town, land which is under the jurisdiction of the county. The level of governmental land use regulation in a county is often less than in a city or town, but the level of public services and amenities also is often less. A landowner therefore may want to have the land annexed into a city or town.

In order to annex property into a city or town, the city or town to which the property will be annexed must consent. Consents must also be obtained from a specified number of persons whose real and personal property would be subject to taxation by the city or town in the event of annexation. The precise procedures for annexation are complex, and legal counsel should be consulted.

MUNICIPAL SUBDIVISION REGULATIONS

Each local governmental unit in Arizona has the authority to regulate the subdivision of land within its boundaries. Municipal subdivision regulations often require that a detailed map of the planned subdivision "plat" be prepared, submitted to the local government, approved, and recorded with the county recorder, prior to the sale or lease of the subdivided land. Municipal subdivision regulations address lot design, set-back requirements, street design, placement of public utility lines, drainage, and similar matters. Municipal subdivision regulations are independent from, and in addition to, subdivision regulations administered by the Arizona Department of Real Estate. No subdivision may be approved until adequate assurances, such as performance bonds or standby letters of credit, have been provided to the local governmental unit, assuring that roads, utilities, drainage structures, and other necessary public facilities will be properly installed by the developer.

DEVELOPMENT FEES

As part of obtaining rezonings, site plan approvals, special use permits, and building permits, many Arizona cities and towns collect development fees from the project owner. Development fees are assessed to help the local governmental unit offset its costs of providing necessary public services, such as water, sewers, and roads. Development fees can be substantial and must be taken into account in any economic feasibility analysis.

OTHER REGULATIONS

The uses to which investors put real estate may dictate whether other regulations are applicable. For example, when constructing a building, certain environmental laws may be triggered, as discussed in more detail in "Construction of Buildings" in this chapter below and in the "Environmental Laws" chapter.

Private Regulation

In addition to public regulation of land uses, individual property owners also may restrict and regulate the uses of their land in ways that will bind subsequent owners and lessees of that land. The most common methods of private regulation are deed restrictions, reciprocal easement agreements, and declarations of covenants, conditions, and restrictions.

Deed Restrictions

The use of property can be regulated by private "deed restrictions." These restrictions are covenants or promises expressly stated in recorded deeds. Deed restrictions may benefit certain individuals personally, in which case the restrictions terminate when the benefitted owner transfers the owner's interest in the property. Most deed restrictions, however, "run with the land" and bind not only the original owner of the restricted property but all succeeding owners.

Deed restrictions often are used to restrict the use of property to a particular purpose, such as "for park purposes only," "for church purposes only," or "for single-family residential purposes only." Deed restrictions are enforceable by court action for injunction, by foreclosure of a lien against the property, and sometimes, if the owner "assumes" the obligation, against the owner personally. Deed restrictions also can impose financial obligations. For example, a deed restriction may compel a property owner to maintain a roadway or other amenity.

Deed restrictions generally are enforceable, provided that the person taking title to the property burdened by the restrictions has notice of the existence of the restrictions through active notice or by "constructive notice" which is provided by recording the deed restrictions, together with a legal description of all of the affected properties, in the office of the county recorder of the county where the property is located.

Reciprocal Easements

Adjoining landowners often enter into reciprocal easement agreements by which they grant each other rights to use portions of their respective lands. Reciprocal easement agreements are commonly used in commercial developments to provide mutual parking and rights-of-way over paved parking areas owned by multiple owners. Reciprocal easement agreements address uses of the easement property, including maintenance, insurance, construction, and allocation of expenses. All who have, or who subsequently succeed to, title to the property benefitted by a reciprocal easement automatically, by virtue of the fact of possession or ownership, become entitled to the use and benefit of the easement. Similarly, all who possess, or succeed to, title to the property burdened by the reciprocal easement are compelled to permit the use of their property as authorized by the easement.

Declarations (CC&Rs)

As part of the real estate development process, the owner often records a written declaration of covenants, conditions, and restrictions (CC&Rs), which is a comprehensive plan for the development of property. This type of private development control often is used for large residential developments and planned communities. CC&Rs are recorded in the records of the county where the property is located, giving future owners of the property notice of their existence, because the declarations will bind them. Although similar to deed restrictions, CC&Rs are more extensive and may limit the types of improvements that can be constructed on the property. For instance, a CC&R may require conformance to a certain architectural style.

CC&Rs often provide for the organization of a homeowners' or property owners' association to administer and enforce the declaration. Owners of lots and parcels in the development become members of these associations and have obligations to pay regular assessments to the associations. The members usually have voting rights, although a developer almost always controls the association during the early phases of a project. Associations often have the power to enforce the members' obligations to pay assessments by filing liens against the property of delinquent members.

MANAGEMENT AND MARKETING

If real estate is to be operated for investment use rather than used by an owner in the owner's own business, it is common to retain either professional property managers or brokers to assist with the management and leasing of the project. Real estate brokers are also used to sell the property.

PROPERTY MANAGEMENT

Property managers generally are responsible for the day-to-day operation of a project. Among the functions performed by a project manager are overseeing necessary services, such as maintenance, repair, and security, maintaining tenant relations, supervising project employees, and accounting. A property manager is reimbursed by the project owner for costs incurred by the manager in operating a project and is paid a fee. The fee frequently is based on a percentage of the gross collections received from a project, although sometimes there is a guaranty of a minimum fee.

Many of the activities undertaken by property managers are regulated by the Arizona Department of Real Estate. A property manager must obtain a real estate broker's or salesperson's license before engaging in any regulated activities. The Arizona Department of Real Estate requires all property management agreements to be in writing and to include certain mandatory provisions.

BROKERS

It is common for an owner to retain a real estate broker or salesperson to assist in the sale or lease of real property. The "Real Estate Brokers" section above describes the role of the broker in real estate transactions.

SALE OR LEASE OF SUBDIVIDED LAND

When land is divided into multiple parcels for sale or lease, the seller must take into account special federal, state, and local laws. Unless land divided into six or more parcels is exempt from regulation, it is necessary, prior to offering the land for sale, to register the subdivided land with the Arizona Department of Real Estate and to obtain from the Arizona Department of Real Estate a public report disclosing facts and details about the subdivision. This public report must be distributed to all prospective purchasers. For federal compliance purposes, Arizona is one of only a handful of "certified" states. Being a certified state means that the federal government will accept the Arizona public report as satisfying federal requirements relating to the sale or lease of subdivided lands if certain requirements are met. Sellers of subdivided land in Arizona can thus avoid a second "subdivision" filing with the federal government.

Before assuming that the subdivision registration process is necessary, it is important to determine if any one of numerous exemptions is applicable. There are exemptions for commercial and industrial properties, improved property, property sold to builders and developers, and leases of property for less than one year. Applicability of these exemptions is very technical, and the exemptions differ under federal and state law.

CONSTRUCTION OF BUILDINGS

PUBLIC REGULATION OF CONSTRUCTION

Ordinarily, before any construction work can begin in Arizona, the owner of the building site must obtain a building permit from the city in which the property is located. If the property is located outside the city limits, the building permit is issued by the county in which the property is located.

Building permits are required in order to give the city or county building agency an opportunity to review the plans and specifications to make sure they comply with all building code requirements. These requirements relate to structural safety and integrity, fire safety, water supply, sewage disposal, access to public streets, and zoning restrictions.

In Arizona, a builder is called a "contractor." "General contractors" perform all phases of construction. "Specialty contractors" do only work involving a particular skill, such as plumbing or electrical work. "Subcontractors," who are also often specialty contractors, are engaged by contractors to perform only a part of a larger job for which the contractor was engaged by the owner.

It is unlawful to act as a contractor in Arizona without a contractor's license issued by the Arizona Registrar of Contractors, unless an exemption from licensing is expressly granted by statute. Currently, there are two major exemptions. First, an owner of property who builds or improves structures on the owner's property is exempt from licensing if the structure, or group of structures, is intended for the owner's occupancy and is not intended for sale or for rent. Second, owners of property who build or improve structures on their property are exempt from licensing if they contract for the construction work to be done by a licensed contractor or contractors.

Contractors must be aware of the numerous and complex environmental laws (federal, state and local), that affect construction activities. Construction can cause air, surface water, ground water, and soil contamination. Construction may involve the use and storage of hazardous substances and the disposal and refuse of hazardous wastes. All activities are governed by environmental laws. Some require that governmental permits be issued before commencing the work. For more information on environmental laws, see the chapter on "Environmental Laws."

SELECTION OF CONSTRUCTION PROFESSIONALS

The owner of private property in Arizona is free to choose the architect, engineer, contractor, and other members of the construction team. Such a selection process may include private negotiation or competitive bidding, with the selection going to whomever the owner believes best able to produce the desired result on time and within budget.

Architects, engineers, and other design professionals are required to be registered or licensed by an Arizona regulatory agency, such as the State Board of Technical Registration.

The architect and the engineer are responsible for the design of the building project, for its style, appearance and utility, and for its structural soundness. The architect and engineer usually inspect the progress of construction for compliance with the plans and specifications. Although design and construction are separate phases, experienced developers often choose a professional or team of professionals to produce a building project with responsibility for both the design and construction. Owners must carefully examine the qualifications and experience of such design-build professionals because of the concentration of responsibility in a single person or organization.

CONSTRUCTION CONTRACTS

The most widely-used forms of construction contracts in Arizona are the printed forms prepared by the American Institute of Architects (AIA). These contract forms are frequently modified by the owner and the contractor as the particular construction project may require, or to change or eliminate unacceptable provisions. Typically, contractors will use their own forms of contract with specialty subcontractors.

PAYMENT OF CONTRACTORS

Architects and engineers are usually paid for design work when the plans and specifications are completed and paid for their inspection work after each inspection.

Whether the construction contract calls for payment of a lump sum amount or the contractor's "cost plus a fixed fee," most construction contracts will require the owner to make progress payments to the contractor, usually monthly. Unjustified failure to pay the contractor according to the terms of the contract is usually grounds for suspending or terminating the construction work.

Any failure by the owner to pay the contractor, any failure of the contractor to pay specialty subcontractors, or any failure of the subcontractors to pay their workmen or material suppliers, may result in the filing of "mechanics' liens" against the owner's property. These liens may be foreclosed in a manner similar to foreclosure of a mortgage on the property. To prevent or protect against mechanics' liens, owners may require the contractor to furnish construction bonds that guarantee that the contractor will perform the work according to the terms of the construction contract (performance bonds) and that payment will be made for all labor and materials furnished on the construction project (payment bonds).

Construction Disputes

Most construction disputes are resolved by negotiation, often with the active participation of the architect, who is given much authority under the standard AIA contract forms. "Partnering" is a new approach to prevention of construction disputes, one gaining wide acceptance. Partnering is a process. The parties meet before construction begins to identify potential problems and suggest solutions. The parties establish a mechanism for handling problems at the job site before the problems rise to the level of disputes. The parties pledge themselves to produce a quality construction project, on time, on budget, without litigation.

The favored method of resolving construction project disputes which cannot be settled by negotiation is by arbitration rather than court litigation. Arbitration is designed to be private, less costly than litigation, and often more likely to reach a fair result, because arbitrators are frequently chosen for their special construction industry knowledge. Construction disputes that do reach the courts can be among the most protracted and costly of suits because they often involve complicated facts and require extensive use of expert witnesses.

CONVENTIONAL FINANCING

CHAPTER OUTLINE

SUMMARY

Conventional financing is financing provided by banks, commercial finance companies, savings and loan associations, insurance companies, pension funds, and other *non-governmental* lenders. Conventional financing is typically either commercial financing or real estate financing. The proceeds from commercial financing are customarily used to provide working capital for business or to finance a transaction such as the acquisition of a business. The proceeds from real estate financing are commonly used to finance acquisition of real estate or to provide funds for improvements to real estate. This chapter examines general concepts, the documentation of financing and loan transactions, and the securing of loans by encumbrances, security interests, and guaranties. Financing of real property transactions is also briefly considered in the prior chapter "Real Property." A special kind of financing is treated in the chapter "Tax-Exempt Financing."

In General

Conventional financing may take many forms, but there are several elements common to all conventional financing transactions: the parties, the loan duration, and the interest rate.

Parties

The principal parties to a loan transaction are the lender and the borrower. There may be more than one of each. In a commercial loan the lender is typically a bank or commercial finance company. In a real estate construction loan it is a bank or a savings and loan association. In other real estate loans, such as acquisition loans or permanent loans issued following completion of construction, the lender is usually a bank, a savings and loan association, an insurance company, or a pension fund.

A lender may require additional assurances of repayment as security for repayment of the loan, such as a mortgage or deed of trust. The owner of the property given as security may be someone other than the borrower, in which case the owner of the property will also become a party to the transaction as the encumbrance. A lender may require a guarantor who will also become a party to the loan transaction.

Duration of Loan

A loan is either a "term" loan or a "demand" loan. A term loan is a loan for a specified period. The borrower under a term loan may be required to make periodic payments of loan principal and interest throughout the term or may be permitted to make a single payment of the entire loan balance at the end of the term. The borrower of a demand loan is required to repay the loan within a short period following the lender's demand for repayment, which demand may be made at any time.

Most loans by conventional lenders are term loans. Most commercial loans and real estate construction loans have terms of between one and five years. Other real estate loans, such as "permanent financing," have terms of up to 30 years.

INTEREST

Conventional loans, like other loans, require payment of interest by the borrower. The two most common methods for charging interest are the "flat rate" and the "variable rate." Under a flat rate the borrower pays the same rate of interest on the unpaid principal throughout the term. Under a variable rate, the rate of interest is determined at various intervals throughout the term by reference to an objective rate standard, such as the London Interbank Offered Rate or other "cost of funds" index, or to the "base" or "prime" rate of interest charged by the lender or by a designated institution. As the objective rate standard changes, the interest rate on a variable rate loan changes. Thus, an interest rate equal to the "prime rate of interest charged by the lender plus one percent" results in a periodically adjusted rising or falling interest rate that always exceeds by one percentage point the prime rate of interest charged by the lender.

Additionally, Arizona does not have a general usury statute, unlike many other states. Thus, in most circumstances the interest rate can be any rate the parties agree to in writing. There are certain varieties of loans that do have set interest rate maximums. Consumer loans by small loan companies are an example of a fixed rate.

BASIC LOAN DOCUMENTATION

The major document is a promissory note. In many loans there is also a credit agreement.

PROMISSORY NOTE

A promissory note sets forth the promise or obligation of the borrower to repay the principal amount of the loan plus interest, with provisions concerning the rate and computation of interest. The promissory note also sets forth the dates when payments of principal and interest come due.

The promissory note and any credit agreement will also state "events of default." On the occurrence of an event of default, the lender typically has the right to demand immediate payment of the entire balance of the loan prior to the due date. The lender may have the right to sell in foreclosure, any property securing the loan, and may require any guarantor to make payment. Common events of default are failure to make a payment of interest or principal when due, failure to perform some other promise of the borrower, and discovery of a misrepresentation made by the borrower in obtaining the loan.

CREDIT AGREEMENT

A credit agreement provides the basic terms of the loan and typically includes representations and warranties by the borrower that are relied upon by the lender, such as warranties of the accuracy of borrower's financial condition as set forth in financial statements delivered to the lender. The borrower, if not an individual, will be required to represent that it is duly organized and existing under applicable law and that the borrowing has been duly authorized by its governing body.

A credit agreement also customarily includes various covenants, which are promises by the borrower that the borrower must perform or comply with until the loan is paid in full. An example is a covenant that the borrower will provide financial information at periodic intervals. A credit agreement may contain both affirmative and negative covenants. Negative covenants restrict a borrower's activities; for example, they may provide that the borrower will not engage in any other financing transactions until the loan is paid in full, that the borrower's net worth will not fall below a stated amount, or that the borrower's ratio of debt to equity will not exceed given limits.

A credit agreement commonly specifies events of default, any one of which will authorize the lender to demand payment of the loan, foreclose against security, or take other enforcement action. A credit agreement will usually include specific procedures and conditions for any installment funding or future advances.

LOAN SECURITY

A lender may require security for repayment of the loan. Security may be real property, personal property, or both. Documentation used to evidence real property security differs from the documentation used when personal property is security. The law governing the two types of security differs.

REAL PROPERTY SECURITY

Raw land, buildings, and other improvements to land, and leases may serve as security for a loan. The real property may be owned by the borrower or by another. Under Arizona's community property law, for a valid encumbrance upon community real property, both the husband and wife must sign the encumbrance document.

Mortgages and deeds of trust are used to encumber real property to secure loans. Under either a mortgage or a deed of trust the owner of the property has the right to possess and use the property while the loan is current. Included in any mortgage or deed of trust are borrower representations and warranties, such as warranties of ownership and of authority to encumber the property as security. Covenants also commonly are included, such as that the property will be maintained in good repair, that all applicable insurance will be kept in force, and that the property will not be sold or further encumbered.

Arizona law allows both mortgages and deeds of trust to include fixtures by incorporating or adding a "financing statement" that is filed and recorded. Fixtures are improvements attached to the real estate described in the mortgage or deed of trust.

The mortgage or deed of trust will identify events of default in addition to the events of default specified in the promissory note or credit agreement. The mortgage or deed of trust will describe the actions the lender may take after default, including the right to take possession of the real property, to take action to protect or realize upon the security, and to sell the real property through foreclosure or forfeiture proceedings.

The principal difference between a mortgage and a deed of trust is the remedy available to the lender. Under a mortgage, in the event of a default the lender may accelerate the entire unpaid balance of the loan and may foreclose the mortgage. Foreclosure of a mortgage requires bringing suit for the unpaid amount of the loan and foreclosing against the security. Once judgment is obtained, the lender must request the court to direct the sheriff to sell the real property and use the sale proceeds to pay the loan. This process may take several months, even longer if the borrower contests foreclosure. If the property is sold at a foreclosure sale, the borrower can redeem the property within six months after sale, or within one month after sale if the property has been abandoned and is not farm land. Redemption is made by paying the sheriff the price paid by the purchaser at the foreclosure sale, plus the amount of taxes and assessments paid by the purchaser, plus a redemption charge of 8% of the sale price.

Under a defaulted deed of trust the lender has the option to foreclose by suit, as under a mortgage, or to hold a trustee's sale. A trustee's sale is a private sale without suit. The sale is held by a trustee named in the deed of trust, often a title company. The sale may be held on a day noticed, which must be at least 90 days after the trustee gives notice of the sale. A trustee's sale thus can be held more quickly than a mortgage foreclosure sale. After a trustee's sale, the borrower has no right to redeem the property. The borrower can reinstate the loan and prevent the trustee's sale at any time *prior* to the sale by paying the lender only the amount in default (not the entire unpaid balance) together with statutory costs.

The lender may purchase the real property at a foreclosure sale, or at a trustee's sale, and may credit the unpaid amount of the loan as part of the total payment. Arizona law limits the amount of the "deficiency" that may be collected from the borrower or any guarantor after either a mortgage foreclosure or a trustee's sale under a deed of trust. The recoverable deficiency is the amount, if any, by which the debt exceeds the *higher* of the sale price at either the foreclosure sale or the trustee's sale, or the fair market value of the property on the date of the sale. The lender has 90 days after a trustee's sale to commence a deficiency action. However, if the security for the loan is real property of two and one-half acres or less and used as a single one or two family residence, in most cases the lender is not entitled to collect *any* deficiency after either a mortgage foreclosure sale or a deed of trust trustee's sale.

Arizona limits who may be a trustee of a deed of trust. A trustee of a deed of trust must be a person or entity that is specifically listed in the statute as eligible to hold the position. Banks, real estate brokers, and attorneys are examples of qualified trustees.

Personal Property Security

Equipment and inventory are examples of personal property that may secure a loan. Other personal property often furnished as security includes notes, accounts receivable, securities, and contract rights. The property may be owned by the borrower or by another. In the case of equipment, inventory, or accounts receivable, the party furnishing the property will have the right to possess and use the property as long as the loan is not in default. If the personal property is "documentary" personal property, such as promissory notes, stocks, or bonds, the lender usually must take actual possession of the property and hold it in pledge until the loan is repaid. In 1995, Arizona adopted legislation that changed the way a lender perfects a security interest in stock and other types of financial assets; thus, the lender should review these requirements to determine the necessary documentation.

Two kinds of documentation are used when personal property is security for a loan, a "security agreement" or, in the case of notes, securities, and other documentary personal property, a "pledge agreement."

Provisions similar to a mortgage or deed of trust are common in security agreements and pledge agreements, such as representations that the borrower owns the personal property and is authorized to provide it as security, a covenant to maintain the property in good condition and, if the personal property consists of contract rights, a covenant not to amend, modify, or terminate the contract rights without the approval of the lender. In all cases, the security agreement and pledge agreement will contain promises not to sell the personal property or to grant other security interests in the personal property without the lender's approval.

The security agreement or pledge agreement will also state events of default and the actions the lender may take if an event of default occurs, including the right to sell the personal property security and to use the proceeds of the sale to pay the loan. Arizona has adopted the Uniform Commercial Code, which sets forth mandatory but flexible foreclosure procedures to insure that adequate notice is given and that the foreclosure sale is conducted in a "commercially reasonable" manner.

RECORDING AND FILING

Mortgages, deeds of trust, security agreements, and pledge agreements are between a lender and the person furnishing the security. They give the lender rights in the property enforceable against the party owning the security. To protect its rights in the security against claims by other persons the lender must take additional action. In the case of real property, the lender must record the mortgage or deed of trust with the county recorder of the Arizona county in which the real property is located. Recording is the filing of the document with the recorder, where it becomes public record and notice to the world, as a matter of law, of the existence of the mortgage or deed of trust.

In the case of personal property, the lender must file either the security agreement itself or a "financing statement" with the Arizona Secretary of State or, as to certain property such as farm equipment, with the county recorder of the county in which the personal property is located or where the debtor resides.

Arizona has very strict margin and typeset requirements for recording documents with county records. If the requirements are not complied with, the document will not be recorded. These requirements do not apply to filing financing statements with the Secretary of State. As mentioned, as to certain documentary personal property the lender must actually take possession of the property in pledge in order to protect a lender against claims by third parties against the security.

Loan Guarantees

A guaranty is an agreement made by a person other than the borrower that the loan will be paid or that other actions to be performed by the borrower will be performed. Guaranties are taken when the borrower's credit or security is considered weak or inadequate. For example, in a loan to a small or closely-held corporation the lender will often require guaranties from the shareholders of the corporation. A guaranty may be unlimited, or it may be limited to a specific amount or percentage, or to a single or limited number of transactions, or to obligations incurred within a given period of time.

The obligation of the guarantor comes due upon the borrower's default. If the guaranty so provides, the lender may proceed independently against the guarantor, without first attempting to collect from the borrower or to recover against other security.

TAX-EXEMPT FINANCING

CHAPTER OUTLINE

SUMMARY

Financing for private projects may be available through the issuance and sale of tax-exempt bonds by certain governmental units. The principal benefit is lower-cost financing. Because most purchasers of tax-exempt bonds do not pay federal or state income taxes on the interest received, interest rates on the bonds are typically below the rates generally prevailing in the marketplace. The benefit is passed on to private borrowers in the form of lower interest loans by the governmental unit. Although borrowers in tax-exempt financing transactions may have higher origination costs than with conventional financing, lower interest costs throughout the term of the loan usually produce substantial overall savings.

Tax-exempt financing for private projects in Arizona takes one of two forms: financing provided by the sale of private activity bonds and financing provided by the sale of community facilities district bonds or public improvement district bonds.

Private Activity Bonds

In General

The sale of private activity bonds (PABs), once referred to as "industrial development bonds," is designed to provide both for-profit and not-for-profit entities with an attractive means of borrowing money at low cost for investment in Arizona projects. In Arizona, all counties, all major cities, and many smaller cities and towns have established industrial development authorities with the ability to issue PABs on behalf of private borrowers. No restrictions in Arizona limit the use of PABs financing by foreign businesses. Sales of PABs are governed by both federal and state laws.

Qualifying Projects

In Arizona, PABs are generally used to provide financing for three types of projects: the acquisition or construction of "manufacturing facilities," the acquisition or construction of "qualified residential rental projects," and the acquisition or construction of "facilities for nonprofit corporations."

Manufacturing Facilities

A "manufacturing facility" can be acquired or constructed with financing provided through the sale of PABs. A manufacturing facility is any facility used in the manufacture or production of tangible personal property. Limited on-site office space and warehousing space can be included in a manufacturing facility if functionally related and subordinate to day-to-day manufacturing operations.

Several restrictions under federal law affect the amount that can be used to finance the acquisition or construction of specific manufacturing facilities. Interest on tax-exempt bonds issued to finance a manufacturing facility will become taxable if the aggregate amount of the borrower's capital expenditures, including the expenditures made with bonds proceeds, in the local jurisdiction in which the facility is located during the period beginning three years before the issuance of the bonds and ending three years after the issuance of the bonds exceeds $10 million. A borrower cannot be the recipient of PABs financing for a manufacturing facility if the aggregate of the financing proceeds, plus other outstanding PABs financings of the borrower for acquisition or construction of facilities elsewhere in the United States, exceeds $40 million.

QUALIFIED RESIDENTIAL RENTAL PROJECTS

A "qualified residential rental project" can be acquired or constructed with proceeds from the sale of PABs. A qualified residential rental project is a building or buildings with self-contained residential units that are offered for rent to the general nontransient public. Federal law conditions the receipt of PABs financing for the acquisition or construction of qualified residential rental projects on the agreement by the borrower to reserve a percentage (either 20 or 40 percent) of the rental units for rental to individuals or families whose income is less than a set percentage of the median gross income in the jurisdiction. This condition must be observed for 15 years or, if longer, the period the financing remains outstanding.

FACILITIES FOR NONPROFIT CORPORATIONS

A corporation or partnership that has been determined to be a nonprofit entity for federal tax purposes may finance the construction or acquisition of a headquarters building, health care facilities (hospitals, nursing homes, and related equipment), or other facilities designed to achieve its charitable purposes. In general, such financings are not subject to the following volume limitations.

Restrictions on Use of Financing Proceeds

Federal and state laws impose the following restrictions on the use of financing proceeds from the sale of *any* PAB (other than for a nonprofit entity):

- Not more than 25 percent of the proceeds can be used to acquire land.

- None of the proceeds can be used to acquire an existing building unless an amount equal to at least 15 percent of the acquisition cost is spent on the rehabilitation of the building.

- None of the proceeds can be used to acquire used equipment unless an amount equal to at least 100 percent of the acquisition cost of the equipment is spent on rehabilitation of the equipment.

- Not more than two percent of the proceeds can be used for the payment of various costs associated with the issuance of any PAB, including application costs and the fees for attorneys, accountants, and underwriters involved in the transaction.

Volume Limitations

Federal law limits the dollar amount of PABs that can be issued in any state during any calendar year (other than for nonprofit entities) to the greater of $50 per resident of the state or $150 million. In 1996, the maximum amount of PABs that could be issued in Arizona was approximately $200 million.

The annual monetary limit on the issuance of PABs in Arizona is allocated among various project categories. Specified portions of this limit are allocated annually to projects designated by the Director of the Department of Commerce, to qualified mortgage revenue bonds and qualified mortgage credit certificate programs, qualified student loan programs, qualified manufacturing projects, and miscellaneous projects that are not described or provided for in any of the mentioned categories.

PROCEDURE

An application for PAB financing must be prepared and submitted to the industrial development authority (IDA) with jurisdiction over the area in which the financed project is or will be located. The IDA will consider the application and may, in its discretion, either grant or decline to grant preliminary approval. Preliminary approval is important, because project costs and commitments paid or incurred prior to preliminary approval, generally may not be reimbursed or paid from the proceeds of PAB financing. Therefore, prospective borrowers should avoid significant financial undertakings with respect to any project until preliminary approval is secured.

Once preliminary approval is obtained, a for-profit applicant must apply to the Arizona Department of Commerce for an allocation of the state's volume limit on PAB financing. Because the state's volume limit is generally allocated on a first-come-first-served basis within the relevant project areas and frequently fully allocated early in each calendar year, it is advisable to file applications for allocations on January 1, or as early as possible in the year to improve the chances of securing an allocation.

After preliminary approval has been granted, any necessary allocation of the state's volume limit has been received, and the terms of the financing have been determined, PABs may be sold in a public offering through a municipal investment broker or privately placed with one or more institutional or other purchasers. The terms of financings vary as to critical elements such as length of the obligation (either long-term or short-term), applicable interest rate (either a fixed rate or a variable rate), and the nature of any security (either a mortgage or lien on the project or a bank letter of credit, or both). The financial creditworthiness of the borrower and the amount of financing involved are among the considerations that affect both the method of sale and the terms of the PABs.

Following agreement for the sale of the PABs and the terms of the related financing, and prior to their sale, an application must be made to the IDA for final approval. The final approval is generally preceded by a public hearing, notice of which must be published in a local newspaper. The hearing gives local residents an opportunity to express their opinions. If final IDA approval is obtained, the matter is then presented for ratification by the governing body that organized the IDA, either the board of supervisors of the county or the mayor and council of the city or town. If approved, the financing is thereafter "closed."

COMMUNITY FACILITIES AND PUBLIC IMPROVEMENT DISTRICT BONDS

Arizona law authorizes the owners of real property in an area to petition the city for the organization of a "community facilities district." Similarly, the owners of real property in incorporated or unincorporated areas can petition the city or county, as applicable, for the formation of a "public improvement district." Either type of district is permitted to issue tax-exempt bonds to finance a variety of public improvements intended to benefit the district and ultimately to be owned by the district. Projects for construction of streets and sewers are typical. These districts are also often used in Arizona to finance a portion of the costs of large residential or commercial development projects, such as master-planned communities and industrial parks.

Typically, the bonds issued by such districts are repaid from special assessments on the benefited individual parcels of real property within the district. Assessments are usually spread evenly over 10 years. Alternatively, "community facilities district" bonds may be repaid from annual *ad valorem* (property) taxes levied on the real property within the district.

Disclosure of Foreign Investment

Chapter Outline

Summary

Arizona, unlike certain other states, imposes no specific requirements governing the disclosure of investment or business activities by foreign persons. Nevertheless, certain investment and business activities conducted by foreign persons within Arizona may be subject to disclosure under the laws of the United States.

International Investment and Trade in Services Act

The International Investment and Trade in Services Act (Investment Act) mandates disclosure of various types of business activities involving foreign persons. Enacted for the purpose of compiling data regarding the extent of foreign investment in the United States, the Investment Act makes clear that it is not intended to prevent, delay, or discourage investment by foreign persons.

All of the information gathered under the Investment Act is confidential. Access to reported information is available only to officials and employees of U.S. government agencies for analytical and statistical purposes.

Disclosure of three types of activities engaged in by foreign persons may be required under the Investment Act: "foreign direct investment" in the United States, "foreign trade in services" with U.S. persons, and "foreign portfolio investment" in the United States. For purposes of the Investment Act, the term "foreign person" is defined broadly to include any individual, corporation, partnership, or other organization that is either a resident of a foreign country or subject to the jurisdiction of a foreign country. Failure to disclose the information required under the Investment Act may result in civil and criminal penalties.

Foreign Direct Investment

Definition

The Investment Act requires disclosures with respect to "foreign direct investment" in the United States. "Foreign direct investment" is defined as the direct or indirect ownership or control by any foreign person of 10 percent or more of the voting interest in any U.S. "business enterprise." "Business enterprise" is defined as a corporation, partnership, or other organization that conducts profit-making activities in the United States. Additionally, the ownership of real estate in the United States constitutes a business enterprise under the Investment Act, unless the real estate is held exclusively for personal use, such as a personal residence. As discussed below, regulations issued under the Investment Act exempt from disclosure minimal levels of foreign direct investment.

Parties With Disclosure Responsibility

All required disclosure forms relating to foreign direct investment must be completed by the U.S. business enterprise in which a foreign person acquires the threshold interest. The Investment Act refers to such a U.S. business enterprise as a "U.S. affiliate" of the foreign person who makes such investment. In the situation in which the ownership of real estate constitutes a business enterprise, the required disclosure must be made by the person or persons who acquire beneficial interests in the real estate. Additionally, disclosure may be required by certain persons who assist or intervene in the purchase or sale of direct investment interests made by or to foreign persons, including real estate brokers, accountants, and lawyers.

DISCLOSURE FORMS

Four types of disclosure forms are required in connection with foreign direct investment in the United States: initial reports, quarterly reports, annual reports, and five-year "benchmark" surveys. All required forms must be filed with the Bureau of Economic Analysis of the U.S. Commerce Department. The forms require information relating to the U.S. business enterprise and its foreign owners, although the identity of any foreign individual need not be disclosed. The specific forms are described below.

■ Initial Reporting Forms

Forms BE-13, BE-14, and BE-607 must be filed within 45 days of the date that a foreign person acquires an interest in a U.S. business enterprise. Limited exemptions may apply if the U.S. business enterprise has total assets of $1 million or less *and* owns fewer than 200 acres of land. For purposes of both the assets test and the land ownership test, all assets and land owned by the U.S. business enterprise in the United States must be considered, not merely land and other assets owned in Arizona. If an exemption is claimed, a special exemption form must be completed.

■ Quarterly Reporting Forms

Form BE-605 or form BE-605 Bank, must be filed within 30 days after the close of each fiscal or calendar quarter of the U.S. business enterprise, except for the fourth quarter report, which may be filed within 45 days. However, a U.S. affiliate is exempt from filing either of these forms if the total assets, the annual revenues, *and* the net income of the U.S. business enterprise as of the relevant periods are *each* less than $20 million. If an exemption is claimed, the exemption section on the respective form must be completed.

■ Annual Reports

Form BE-15 must be filed within 60 days after the date the form is made available to the public. However, a U.S. affiliate is exempt from filing Form BE-15 if the total assets, annual revenues, *and* net income of the U.S. business enterprise as of the relevant periods are *each* less than $10 million. If an exemption is claimed, a special exemption form must be completed. The claim for exemption is not an annual filing requirement for U.S. affiliates that remain below the $10 million exemption level from year-to-year.

■ Five-Year "Benchmark" Surveys

Form BE-12 must be filed by a U.S. affiliate if the U.S. business enterprise is owned by a foreign person at the end of the fiscal year preceding the year in which the form is made available to the public. The form is generally required to be filed by May 31, and it is made available two to three months prior to that due date. The next five-year benchmark survey is scheduled for 1998.

FOREIGN TRADE IN SERVICES

Involvement by a foreign person in "foreign trade in services" also triggers disclosure under the Investment Act.

DEFINITION

The term "foreign trade in services" refers to the furnishing or receiving of "services" by foreign persons in transactions with unaffiliated U.S. persons. The term "services" is defined as economic activities that do not involve the production of tangible goods. Specific services subject to disclosure include engineering, real estate management, construction, communications, data processing, management consulting, banking, advertising, accounting, legal, education, and health care.

PARTIES WITH DISCLOSURE RESPONSIBILITY

The U.S. business that either furnished or received the services has the responsibility to file the required disclosure forms.

DISCLOSURE FORMS

Two types of forms are required in connection with the disclosure of foreign trade in services, annual reports, and five-year "benchmark" surveys. All required forms must be filed with the Bureau of Economic Analysis of the U.S. Commerce Department. The forms require information relating to the type of services either furnished or received by the U.S. business and the citizenship of the foreign person involved in such services. The specific forms are described below.

■ Annual Reports

Form BE-22 must be filed by March 31, and the form is generally made available to the public in January. However, a U.S. business is exempt from filing Form BE-22 if the annual aggregate value of services provided to or received from foreign persons is $1 million or less. If an exemption is claimed, only select portions of form BE-22 must be completed. Other forms may be required on an annual basis in connection with specific types of services. For example, Form BE-47 generally must be filed by U.S. businesses that provide construction, engineering, architectural, or mining services to unaffiliated foreign persons.

- **Five-Year "Benchmark" Surveys**

Form BE-20 must be filed by any U.S. business whose aggregate value of services provided to or received from foreign persons exceeded $500,000 with respect to the fiscal year in which the five-year benchmark survey is conducted.

FOREIGN PORTFOLIO INVESTMENT

"Foreign portfolio investment" must also be disclosed under the Investment Act.

DEFINITION

The term "foreign portfolio investment" refers to direct or indirect investment by foreign persons in "U.S. securities." The term "U.S. securities" is defined to include all stocks, warrants, options, bonds, and limited partnership interests issued by any U.S. corporation, limited partnership, trust, or governmental agency.

PARTIES WITH DISCLOSURE RESPONSIBILITY

Disclosure of foreign portfolio investment is required to be made by *issuers* of U.S. securities and *holders of record* of U.S. securities beneficially owned by foreign persons.

DISCLOSURE FORMS

Forms relating to foreign portfolio investment are required in connection with five-year "benchmark" surveys. The next survey is scheduled in 2000. Generally, the forms require the disclosure of information relating to the principal business activities of the issuing company and the percentage of foreign ownership of the company. All required forms must be filed with the U.S. Treasury Department.

Form FPI-2 must be filed by holders of record of U.S. securities, if the fair market value of the securities held by such persons and owned by foreign persons as of the last day of the fiscal year preceding the survey is $20 million or more. The U.S. Treasury Department may request any U.S. issuers of securities to file Form FPI-1 irrespective of whether it has evidence of foreign investment in its securities. U.S. issuers of securities are required to file Form FPI-1 if their total consolidated assets on behalf of foreign persons are $10 billion or more.

AGRICULTURAL FOREIGN INVESTMENT DISCLOSURE ACT

The Agricultural Foreign Investment Disclosure Act (Agricultural Act) requires disclosure of the ownership of certain agricultural land by foreign persons. Disclosure under the Agricultural Act may be necessary in addition to disclosure required under the Investment Act. In contrast to the Investment Act, information disclosed under the Agricultural Act is available for review by the public. Failure to disclose the information required under the Agricultural Act may result in civil penalties.

TYPE OF INVESTMENTS REQUIRING DISCLOSURE

Disclosure is required under the Agricultural Act if any foreign person acquires any interest in "agricultural land." "Agricultural land" refers generally to U.S. land currently used, or used at any time within the preceding five-year period, for farming, ranching, forestry, or timber production. The definition of agricultural land excludes, and, hence, disclosure is not required with respect to, land that does not exceed 10 acres and that produces annual gross revenues of less than $1,000, nor to an interest in land that is limited to a security interest, nor to a leasehold interest of shorter than 10 years, nor to a contingent future interest, nor to an interest solely in mineral rights.

The term "foreign person" is defined as any individual who is not a citizen or national of the United States, or which is any corporation, partnership, or other organization organized under the laws of a foreign jurisdiction. The term "foreign person" also includes a U.S. corporation, partnership, or other organization if at least 10 percent of the interests are held by single non-U.S. citizen or foreign entity (or any group of non-U.S. citizens or foreign entities acting in concert). "Foreign person" also includes any such organization if at least 50 percent of the interests therein are held by any number of non-U.S. citizens or foreign entities, even though not acting in concert.

PARTIES WITH DISCLOSURE RESPONSIBILITY

Disclosure under the Agricultural Act is the responsibility of the foreign person who acquires direct ownership of the agricultural land. If the threshold interest in the land is acquired by a U.S. organization classified as a foreign person, disclosure must be made by the U.S. organization.

DISCLOSURE FORMS

Form FSA-153 must be filed not later than 90 days following the date on which a foreign person acquires an interest in U.S. agricultural land. The form requires information pertaining to the identity of the foreign person, the purchase price paid to acquire the land, the date of acquisition, and the purpose intended for the land. The form must be filed with the Consolidated Farm Service Agency office in the county in which the land is located.

SECURITIES LAWS

CHAPTER OUTLINE

SUMMARY
DEFINITION OF "SECURITY"
REGISTRATION
    IN GENERAL
    TRANSACTIONS NOT SUBJECT TO UNITED STATES
        LAWS GOVERNING REGISTRATION
    TRANSACTIONS NOT SUBJECT TO ARIZONA LAWS
        GOVERNING REGISTRATION
    EXEMPTIONS FROM REGISTRATION REQUIREMENTS
        PRIVATE PLACEMENT EXEMPTION
        REGULATION D EXEMPTION
        OTHER EXEMPTIONS
DISCLOSURE AND ANTIFRAUD PROVISIONS
BROKER OR DEALER REGISTRATION
OTHER STATE "BLUE SKY" LAWS

SUMMARY

Various commercial transactions that involve offers or sales of "securities" are subject to regulation by the United States and by Arizona. Designed to protect investors who invest money or other property in corporations, partnerships, limited liability companies, and other enterprises, the securities laws impose three principal requirements. First, the offer or sale of the relevant securities must be "registered" with the appropriate governmental bodies, unless exempt. Second, adequate disclosure must be made to potential investors regarding the securities and the issuer of the securities. Third, generally the persons or entities who engage in the business of offering or selling securities must be registered or licensed.

Failure to comply with applicable securities laws can result in serious penalties. Investors may be entitled to return of the money or other property invested. Criminal fines and imprisonment can be imposed for certain violations.

DEFINITION OF "SECURITY"

The securities laws apply only if a "security" is involved. "Security" is broadly defined to include *any* arrangement in which a person invests money or other property in a common enterprise with the expectation of earning profits primarily through the efforts of others. Conventional investment vehicles, such as stocks and bonds issued by a corporation, constitute securities. Less traditional investment vehicles, such as various oil and gas interests, depository receipts, voting trust certificates, and certain promissory notes also fall under the definition. Even investments in franchises, condominiums, real estate, gold and silver bullion, diamonds, and furs have sometimes been held to be securities.

Various interests in partnerships may also constitute securities. The purchase of an interest in a *limited* partnership is treated as a purchase of a security; so a syndication of limited partnership interests requires compliance with the securities laws. An interest in a *general* partnership usually is *not* characterized as a security, because a general partner ordinarily enjoys full and equal control over partnership affairs with all other general partners. However, if the general partnership agreement leaves a partner with insignificant power or control, the partner is so dependent on the other partners that he or she is incapable or unable to exercise meaningful management powers, a general partnership interest may be treated as a security.

Similarly, an interest in a limited liability company may constitute a security, depending upon the amount of management control or power held or exercisable by the investors.

REGISTRATION

IN GENERAL

"Registration" is required in connection with an offer or sale of any security unless an exemption exists. Registration requires that a special disclosure statement or "prospectus" be filed by the issuer of the security with the Securities and Exchange Commission (SEC) and with the Arizona Corporation Commission (ACC). There are different registration forms for various types of securities offerings, including forms for foreign issuers.

A registration statement must set forth detailed information regarding the issuer's business, including financial data. The statement must describe the securities to be offered for sale and the proposed method of sales and distribution. The SEC and the ACC review the registration statement to ensure that all required information is adequately set forth. The security can be offered for sale only after the review process is completed and after the SEC and the ACC approve the statement. Registration at both the federal and state levels can be time consuming and expensive, and often subjects the issuer to ongoing quarterly and annual reporting requirements that may compel the disclosure of confidential information.

TRANSACTIONS NOT SUBJECT TO UNITED STATES LAWS GOVERNING REGISTRATION

Not every offer or sale of securities is subject to registration under U.S. securities laws. An offer and sale may be exempt as outside the scope of the SEC registration requirements. Regulation S, which is of particular interest to the foreign investor, provides that certain offers and sales of securities conducted abroad are not subject to SEC registration, and Rule 144A, which provides that certain sales of securities to qualified institutional buyers are exempt from SEC registration.

Two conditions must be met for the Regulation S exception. First, each offer and sale of the relevant securities must be made in an "offshore transaction." To constitute an offshore transaction, each offer and the mechanics of each sale must take place outside the United States. Second, no "directed selling efforts" can be made in the United States in connection with the offering. Directed selling efforts are activities undertaken to create a market or otherwise to generate public interest in the securities, whether undertaken by the issuer, a distributor, or any party acting on behalf of either of them.

Regulation S procedures also must be followed to ensure that the securities offered "come to rest" outside the United States. These are designed to prevent the securities from being re-offered and resold in the United States. The procedures vary based upon the nationality and reporting status of the person or entity issuing the securities and upon the degree of U.S. market interest in the securities. Foreign issuers do not have to comply with these procedures if they do not report to the SEC on a regular basis and if they have no substantial U.S. market for their securities.

Compliance with Rule 144A permits a sale of eligible securities to large institutional investors to be accomplished as a "private placement" that is not subject to standard SEC registration requirements. A securities offering qualifies for exempt status under rule 144A if the securities involved are not "fungible" and are offered only to "qualified institutional buyers." The SEC defines a "qualified institutional buyer" in terms of the total value of an institution's portfolio. An institution must exceed certain threshold values, which vary according to the type of institution, in order to qualify a transaction under Rule 144A. Under the rule, "fungible securities" are securities that, when issued, are part of a class of securities that are listed on a U.S. stock exchange.

Transactions not Subject to Arizona Laws Governing Registration

Certain offers or sales of securities may not involve sufficient contacts in Arizona to be subject to registration under Arizona law. Arizona securities laws apply only to transactions in securities offered or sold "within or from" Arizona. The issuance of a security is more likely not to require compliance with Arizona securities laws if:

- The issuer is organized under the laws of another country or another state,

- None of the brokers and underwriters involved in selling the securities are Arizona residents,

- Offers and sales are not made to Arizona residents,

- Purchase agreements are not negotiated or executed in Arizona,

- The securities are properly registered in other jurisdictions where the purchasers reside, and

- The offering materials disclose that the transaction has not been registered with the ACC.

If *all* of these factors exist, the fact that the securities relate to an investment in Arizona generally will not require registration of the securities with the ACC.

Exemptions from Registration Requirements

Although a particular transaction may involve a security and may involve sufficient contacts in Arizona to be subject to both

U.S. and Arizona securities laws, an exemption may nevertheless exist. The "private placement" exemption and exemption under Regulation D are the most frequently used exemptions.

PRIVATE PLACEMENT EXEMPTION

The private placement exemption is one of the exemptions most utilized under both U.S. and Arizona Laws. The private placement exemption is derived from the concept that securities registration protection is not needed for limited offerings to sophisticated individuals capable of understanding the risk of an investment. An offering of securities will generally be exempt from registration under the private placement exemption if:

- The offering is made to a limited number of people who are known to the offeror,

- The offering is made without the use of advertising, public meetings, or other means of public solicitation,

- The offerees receive, or are provided access to, the kind of information that would otherwise be contained in a registration statement,

- The offerees are "sophisticated" and can be reasonably expected to understand the merits and risks of the investment offered, and

- Certain restrictions are adopted limiting resale of the securities.

Regulation D Exemption

Exemption under Regulation D is available for offerings that do not exceed certain aggregate dollar amounts and that are confined to a limited number of people. Regulation D exemption is also available for offerings made solely to "accredited" investors, such as banks, insurance companies, investment companies, and certain wealthy individuals and entities. The Regulation D exemption is from the U.S. securities laws. There is a similar exemption under Arizona law, but the exemptions provided by Regulation D and the Arizona exemptions are not identical. Care must be taken to ensure that each element of the exemption is met for both U.S. and Arizona purposes.

The conditions for exemption under Regulation D are better defined than the conditions for the private placement exemption. Accordingly, most offerings that may qualify for the private placement exemption are also structured so as to meet the conditions of Regulation D.

Other Exemptions

Other exemptions from registration are also available. Transactions in securities that occur in only one state are exempt from SEC registration. Certain transactions are exempt from both U.S. *and* Arizona registration requirements. For instance, sales of promissory notes and other commercial paper that constitute securities are exempt if they have a maturity of less than nine months. Certain exchanges of securities between an issuer and existing security holders are exempt, such as when an issuer proposes to exchange one form of securities for another. Certain limited resales of securities are also exempt if they are made by the owner without the involvement of the issuer or a broker or dealer.

Disclosure and Antifraud Provisions

Even though a securities transaction may not be subject to U.S. or Arizona securities registration laws, the disclosure and "antifraud" provisions of the U.S. and Arizona securities laws may still apply. The antifraud laws are designed to prohibit fraud, devices, deceptions, and other schemes to defraud or mislead an investor, and to prohibit any untrue or inaccurate statement of material fact, or failure to state a material fact, in any offer or sale of securities.

Because of the difficulty in demonstrating that a person has made complete and correct oral representations, a written disclosure document is frequently prepared in connection with a securities offering. A disclosure document must be prepared even though registration may not be required. When a disclosure document is prepared for an exempt unregistered private placement, the document is often referred to as a "private placement memorandum" or "private offering memorandum" and is not reviewed by a governmental body. Care must nevertheless be taken in its preparation to ensure its accuracy and completeness.

Promoters and others involved in offering and selling securities should provide investors with complete and accurate information. The offering materials should include all information that a reasonable investor would take into account in making an investment decision. Inconsistent statements should not be made in any of the offering materials, nor by any broker or promoter. If the offering of a security takes place over a period of time, the information should be kept current.

The antifraud provisions of U.S. securities law are generally interpreted more broadly than the registration provisions. They may apply to transactions outside the scope of the U.S. securities registration laws. The antifraud provisions have been applied to protect investors when significant conduct occurs within the United States and also when the relevant conduct occurs outside the United States but has a significant impact either within the United States or on the interests of U.S. investors. In determining whether the antifraud laws apply, courts have considered the following:

- the location of the various negotiations and the execution of the relevant documents

- the location of the use of the proceeds

- the degree of use of the U.S. mails

- the proportion of the conduct inside the United States as compared to outside the United States

- the proportion of the damage to investors and the market within the United States as compared to the damage outside the United States

Unlike the U.S. antifraud laws, the application of the Arizona antifraud laws is determined on the same basis as the application of the Arizona registration laws. Thus, Arizona's antifraud laws apply only if the transaction is made "within or from" Arizona.

BROKER OR DEALER REGISTRATION

Both U.S. and Arizona securities laws require that persons engaged in the business of selling securities be registered as "brokers" or "dealers." A person may be considered to be "engaged in the business" and thereby subject to broker-dealer registration if involved in as few as two securities offerings during a 12-month period.

Broker-dealer registration is separate and distinct from the registration of securities. Certain exemptions from broker-dealer registration exist. In some situations, an exemption from securities registration may exist, but an exemption from broker-dealer registration may not exist, or vice versa.

Registered broker-dealers are independently subject to detailed recordkeeping and reporting requirements. Registered broker-dealers under U.S. law must be members of a registered association of securities dealers. Personnel of broker-dealers engaged in sales activities in Arizona must also be licensed as salesmen or agents by the Arizona Corporation Commission and must pass an examination.

OTHER STATE "BLUE SKY" LAWS

If a security is offered or sold within or from, or involves contacts with, states other than Arizona, the securities laws of those states may also apply, based on the degree of contacts in each particular state. The various state securities laws are frequently referred to as "blue sky" laws, a reference to the intent of the laws to ensure that buyers not be defrauded and sold worthless "deep blue sky."

An offering that is made, for instance, to offerees in 10 states may be required to comply with the applicable requirements under the laws of all 10 states, as well as the securities laws of the United States and Arizona. Evaluation of a proposed offering should consider not only the securities registration provisions, but also the disclosure and antifraud provisions and the broker-dealer registration requirements. A state-by-state blue sky survey is frequently prepared by legal counsel to summarize the availability of exemptions from securities and broker-dealer registration provisions under the various state blue sky laws.

IMMIGRATION

CHAPTER OUTLINE

SUMMARY

Foreign persons conducting business operations in Arizona may seek an extended stay in the state for themselves or for other foreign persons they seek to employ in Arizona. Admission of foreign persons into the United States is governed exclusively by the U.S. immigration laws. Individual states, such as Arizona, have no immigration authority.

Generally, a foreign person can be admitted into the United States under one of two broad categories, immigrant or nonimmigrant. Immigrant status is an appropriate goal for persons seeking to become permanent residents of the United States. Individuals with immigrant status have the right to live in the United States indefinitely and to pursue virtually any investment or business objective. Obtaining permanent residency status as an immigrant is commonly referred to as obtaining a "green card."

The number of foreign persons who can obtain immigrant status in any year is limited, and there are preferences that favor relatives of U.S. citizens. However, the 1990 amendments to the U.S. Immigration Act create an important new way for investors to attain immigrant status.

The majority of foreign persons who enter the United States do so through nonimmigrant visas. A nonimmigrant visa allows a foreign person to reside temporarily in the United States for a given period of time and, depending upon the particular visa classification, to engage in specific permitted activities.

EMPLOYMENT-BASED INVESTOR IMMIGRANT CLASSIFICATION

The 1990 amendments to the Immigration Act created another employment-based investor "immigrant" classification. Individuals who invest $1 million in capital in a new commercial enterprise or troubled business and who employ 10 or more persons in the United States can receive permanent residence status in the United States. The amount of investment required is adjusted downward if the investment is made in certain targeted high unemployment areas. Congress has authorized 10,000 immigrant visas under this classification with 3,000 set aside for investors in the targeted areas. Application for this immigrant visa classification is made on Form I-526, which is accompanied by substantial supporting documentation. The cumbersome labor certification process does not apply to this category, *i.e.,* the petitioning company does not have to demonstrate that qualified U.S. workers are unavailable to perform the job in question or that the foreign person's employment will not adversely affect the wages or working conditions of similarly-employed U.S. workers.

Type B-1 (Business Visitor) Visa

The B-1, "Business Visitor," visa is designed for foreign persons whose presence in the United States will be limited to a few months. Activities associated with international trade or commerce are among the activities permissible under a B-1 visa. For example, a recipient of a B-1 visa can enter the United States to sign contracts and open bank accounts. However, active management of an investment or business while in the United States is *not* authorized under a B-1 visa. Furthermore, employment in the United States is *not* permitted. The normal rules for B-1 activities have been revised for Mexican and Canadian business persons under terms of the North American Free Trade Agreement (NAFTA). Under NAFTA, Mexican and Canadian business persons have more liberal terms of entry with regard to some B-1 activities than do nationals of other countries.

Requirements for B-1 Visa

Among the requirements for the issuance and maintenance of a B-1 visa are:

- The foreign person must intend to depart the United States at the expiration of the term of the visa.

- The foreign person must possess sufficient financial resources to travel to and depart from the United States.

- The foreign person must maintain a foreign residence throughout the person's stay in the United States.

Procedure for Obtaining B-1 Visa

In General

An application for a B-1 visa is made at a U.S. consulate abroad. An applicant is not required to file any paperwork with the U.S. Immigration and Naturalization Service (INS), the agency that administers the immigration laws.

United States Visa Waiver Program

The U.S. "Visa Waiver Program" is an expedited method for nationals of certain countries to visit the United States for up to 90 days to engage in activities permitted under a B-1 visa. Instead of applying for a B-1 visa at a U.S. consulate and meeting the B-1 visa requirement, foreign nationals of countries that participate in the Visa Waiver Program must satisfy the following criteria: the foreign person must acquire a nontransferable round-trip ticket from an approved airline, he or she must be traveling on a passport issued by one of the participating countries, and before arriving in the United States, the foreign person must sign a form (INS Form I-94W) in which the person acknowledges understanding the terms of the Visa Waiver Program, including the absence of any right to a hearing pending deportation if the person stays in the United States over 90 days. As of October 1, 1994, recipients of the Visa Waiver Program are permitted to apply for adjustment to permanent residence status, but only upon the payment of a penalty in addition to the filing fee. As of April 1995, the following countries were participants in the Visa Waiver Program:

Andorra	Japan
Argentina	Liechtenstein
Australia	Luxembourg
Austria	Monaco
Belgium	The Netherlands

Brunei	New Zealand
Denmark	Norway
Finland	San Marino
France	Spain
Germany	Sweden
Iceland	Switzerland
Ireland	United Kingdom
Italy	

The Immigration Act of 1990 has authorized the U.S. State Department to expand participation in the Visa Waiver Program. In 1994, Congress provided the authority for the designation of "probationary" participants in the Visa Waiver Program, based on criteria less restrictive than those applied to full participants. When the "probationary" designation expires, a country's participation in the program will either be terminated or made permanent. On the basis of the criteria for "probationary" participation, citizens of additional countries may soon have the opportunity to enter the United States under this expedited process.

TYPE E (TREATY TRADER/INVESTOR) VISA

The E, "Treaty Trader" or "Treaty Investor," visa category is intended for foreign persons seeking entry into the United States for extended periods of time. An initial stay of one year is granted to holders of E visas, which can be extended almost indefinitely. Two types of E visas are issued. A holder of an E-1 (Treaty Trader) visa is permitted to oversee or work in an enterprise engaged in substantial trade with the United States. A holder of an E-2 (Treaty Investor) visa is authorized to engage in activities relating to a substantial investment in the United States. Separate requirements govern the issuance of E-1 and E-2 visas.

Requirements for E Visas

Requirements for E-1 Visa

The following requirements must be satisfied to obtain an E-1 visa:

- A treaty containing treaty-trader provisions must exist between the United States and the country in which the foreign person has citizenship. A current list of countries with which the United States has outstanding treaties with such provisions can be found in the *Visa Bulletin* of the U.S. Department of State, Bureau of Consular Affairs.

- If the foreign person is an employee, majority ownership of the foreign person's employer must be held by nationals of the treaty country.

- The principal trader and employees of the treaty enterprise must have the same nationality as the treaty enterprise.

- The foreign person or the person's employer must be engaged in ongoing "trade," which, for this purpose, is the exchange, purchase, or sale of goods, services, or technology.

- The trade engaged in by the foreign person or the person's employer must be "substantial." At present, no minimum dollar amount is used in determining whether a specific amount of trade is substantial. Instead, the evaluation is made on the basis of such factors as the quantity of transactions and the volume, nature, and duration of the trade.

- More than 50 percent of the trade conducted by the foreign person or the person's employer must be between the United States and the treaty country.

- The foreign person must either exercise supervisory or executive duties or possess skills not generally available in the United States.

REQUIREMENTS FOR E-2 VISA

The following requirements must be satisfied to obtain an E-2 visa:

- A treaty containing treaty-investor provisions must exist between the United States and the country in which the foreign person has citizenship. A current list of countries with which the United States has treaties with such provisions is in the *Visa Bulletin*, U.S. Department of State, Bureau of Consular Affairs.

- If the foreign person is an employee, majority ownership of the foreign person's employer must be held by nationals of the treaty country.

- The principal investor and employees of the treaty enterprise must have the same nationality as the treaty enterprise.

- The foreign person or the person's employer must be engaged in an "active" investment in the United States. To be characterized as active, the business underlying the investment must represent a real operating enterprise productive of some service or commodity. For example, an investment in a manufacturing facility would be an active investment, but an investment in undeveloped land for its potential appreciation in value would not be an active investment.

- The investment of the foreign person or the person's employer must be "substantial." An investment is substantial if the investor personally has at risk, sufficient funds to establish or develop the enterprise. Although no particular dollar amount is required, in a small to medium-sized business, the investor should have personally at risk approximately one-half of the funds necessary to commence operations. The amount at risk can be proportionately smaller for larger businesses. However, the Immigration Act of 1990 authorized the U.S. State Department to establish an amount of investment that will be treated as substantial.

- The business invested in by the foreign person or the person's employer must either employ U.S. workers or be capable of creating job opportunities for U.S. workers.

- The foreign person must fulfill an essential role in the enterprise. If the foreign person is not an employee, the person must own a majority ownership interest, *i.e.*, at least 50 percent of the enterprise. If the foreign person is an employee, the person must serve in a managerial capacity or in a technical capacity for the U.S. enterprise or must supervise persons in technical positions with respect to the U.S. enterprise.

PROCEDURE FOR OBTAINING E VISA

An application for an E visa is usually made at a U.S. consulate abroad. The basic procedure is to submit an official application (Form OF-156) with a passport and supporting documentation reflecting the applicant's qualifications under the desired E visa category. It is also possible to apply for an E visa through the INS. The INS application process usually takes longer to complete. The INS and U.S. consulates do not always reach the same conclusion on granting E visas.

Type H-1 B (Distinguished Merit and Ability) Visa

The H-1 B, "Distinguished Merit and Ability," visa is often used by companies temporarily to employ foreign persons who qualify as persons in "specialty occupations." An H-1 B visa is usually granted for periods of up to three years. When need is demonstrated, an extension of up to an additional three years, for a total maximum stay of six years, is possible.

Requirements For H-1 B Visa

The following two requirements must be satisfied to obtain an H-1 B visa:

■ The foreign person must be engaged in a "specialty occupation." Specialty occupations are defined as those requiring theoretical and practical application of a body of highly specialized knowledge or attainment of a bachelor's or higher degree in a specific field.

■ The position to be filled in the United States must be of sufficient complexity that it requires a person with specialized knowledge.

Procedure For Obtaining H-1 B Visa

An employer seeking to employ a foreign person in a specialty occupation in Arizona must file Form I-129 and its H supplement with the INS. The form must be accompanied with documentation demonstrating the applicant's qualifications for the H-1 B visa and with proof of filing a Labor Condition Attestation, *i.e.,* that the applicant will be paid the prevailing (average) wage for that position in a particular geographic area.

Type L-1 (Intra-Company Transferee) Visa

The L-1, "Intra-Company Transferee," visa enables companies with operations abroad to transfer employees temporarily to the United States to assist in local operations. If the foreign company is commencing activities in the United States, an L-1 visa is granted for one year. If the company has existing operations in the United States, an L-1 visa may be initially granted for up to three years. Certain extensions of the term of an L-1 visa may be available.

Requirements for L-1 Visa

The following requirements must be satisfied to obtain an L-1 visa:

- The foreign person sought to be transferred to the United States must have been employed abroad in an executive or managerial capacity or in a capacity involving "specialized knowledge" on a full-time basis for at least one of the last three years preceding the visa application. Specialized knowledge refers to particular knowledge of the employer's product, service, and equipment, and to their application in international markets.

- The company that will employ the recipient of the L-1 visa must be the same company for whom the employee has worked abroad, or a parent, subsidiary, or affiliate of that company.

- The foreign person's employment in the United States does not have to be in a capacity similar to that in which the person was employed abroad.

- Both the U.S. company and its parent, subsidiary, or affiliate abroad, must be engaged in active business operations throughout the period the employee remains in the United States. The mere presence of an agent or office either in the United States or abroad is not sufficient.

PROCEDURE FOR OBTAINING L-1 VISA

An employer seeking to obtain an L-1 visa on behalf of an employee in connection with employment in Arizona must file Form I-129 and its L supplement with the INS. The form should include supporting documentation demonstrating the applicant's qualifications for the L-1 visa. If the U.S. operation is commencing activities, the employer must provide additional information, including evidence that a physical location for the operation has been secured, evidence of preliminary contracts that demonstrate that the new operation has customers, and evidence that the foreign employer or affiliate has invested sufficient funds to pay the wages of the transferred employees.

An expedited procedure to obtain L-1 visas is available to an employer that seeks to transfer a number of employees to the United States. Rather than submit individual L-1 applications on behalf of each employee, the employer may submit a "blanket application" on behalf of all of the employees. To be eligible for a blanket application, the employer must currently maintain operations at a minimum of three sites in the United States or abroad, the U.S. operation must have been conducted for at least one year, and the employer must have obtained 10 L-1 visas in the past year, have had annual U.S. sales of at least $25 million, or have employed a work force in the United States of at least 1,000 employees.

Other Visas

A number of other visas may be available in connection with entry into the United States by foreign persons contemplating investment or business activities. Information regarding these additional visa classifications can be obtained by contacting the INS, a U.S. consulate abroad, or legal counsel with experience in the field of immigration law.

MAQUILADORA OPERATIONS

CHAPTER OUTLINE

SUMMARY
BENEFITS OF MAQUILADORA OPERATION
OPERATIONAL ASPECTS
    MEXICAN CUSTOMS DUTIES
    U.S. CUSTOMS DUTIES
    FORM OF ORGANIZATION
    REAL ESTATE
    RESTRICTIONS ON THE EMPLOYMENT OF
FOREIGNERS
    TAXES
    GOVERNMENT APPROACHES
    ENVIRONMENTAL APPROVALS
    SALES IN MEXICO

SUMMARY

Arizona's proximity to Mexico offers manufacturers that locate in Arizona an opportunity to participate in Mexico's "maquiladora" program, which provides substantial savings in labor and operational costs. The decree for the Development and Operation of the Maquiladora Export Industry, as amended (the Maquiladora Decree), was established by the Mexican government to counteract unemployment. The maquiladora program is designed to encourage U.S. and other foreign enterprises to establish manufacturing facilities in Mexico that can profitably utilize Mexican labor. United States and other foreign investors are permitted to own up to 100 percent of the interests in qualifying manufacturing facilities in Mexico.

A typical venture under the maquiladora program involves the delivery of product components to Mexico by a U.S. manufacturer. The product components are then assembled at a Mexican manufacturing facility operated by the U.S. manufacturer. Following assembly, the finished products are exported from Mexico to the United States or to a third country for distribution and marketing. Another common arrangement under the maquiladora program involves the transportation to Mexico by a U.S. manufacturer of finished products that are packaged at a Mexican facility and then transported back to the United States for distribution and marketing.

The maquiladora program has been affected by the passage of the North American Free Trade Agreement, effective January 1, 1994, among the United States, Canada, and Mexico (NAFTA), Pursuant to NAFTA, all restrictions on trade among member countries will be phased out over different periods of time applicable to different products and services. With respect to maquiladora operations, imports of raw materials and equipment used in the maquiladora process, and domestic sales and export of maquiladora products, will be free of custom duties and tariffs by January 1, 2001.

BENEFITS OF MAQUILADORA OPERATION

The principal benefit of maquiladora operations in Mexico by a U.S. manufacturer is the savings in operational costs because of the relatively low costs of labor, utilities, and overhead. Wages paid to Mexican workers are much lower than wages paid to workers in the United States. In 1990, the typical wage paid to workers in maquiladora plants near the U.S.-Mexican border was approximately 15 percent of the U.S. minimum wage. Although fringe benefits required by Mexican law add approximately 80 percent to the cost of basic wages, overall labor costs in Mexico remain considerably lower than labor costs in the United States.

Also, a benefit of maquiladora use by an Arizona manufacturer that locates in Arizona is the low cost of transporting goods to and from Mexico.

OPERATIONAL ASPECTS

MEXICAN CUSTOMS DUTIES

Mexican law authorizes the duty-free import of equipment, materials, and supplies for assembly or packaging of products intended for subsequent export from Mexico. Goods are generally classified by Mexican customs regulations as either raw materials and product components, or as manufacturing equipment, including tools and spare parts. Items within the first classification are permitted to remain in Mexico, duty-free for two years following the date of entry. Items within the second classification may remain in Mexico as long as the corresponding maquiladora program remains in effect. An initial application for import into Mexico is called a "pedimento de importación," and is required before any article can be imported into Mexico.

U.S. CUSTOMS DUTIES

U.S. customs laws also provide incentives in connection with maquiladora operations. No duty is required on products imported into the United States from a Mexican maquiladora facility when the Mexican operation is confined to packaging. When the maquiladora operation involves assembly of products, the import duty is limited to the enhancement of the value of the products by assembly in Mexico. Thus, an import duty is not paid on the underlying value of the product components.

FORM OF ORGANIZATION

Maquiladora operations in Mexico are usually conducted through a Mexican corporation, a "sociedad anónima de capital variable," commonly abbreviated S.A. de C.V., which can be a subsidiary of a U.S. or other foreign corporation. An increasingly popular method for companies to enter Mexico is through a "subcontractor" (or similar contractual relationship), pursuant to which a local Mexican company assembles semi-finished goods supplied by non-Mexican entities into finished goods for export. This arrangement, also sometimes referred to as a "shelter plan," permits a company to receive the same beneficial treatment afforded to other foreign investors, and the same technical and managerial authority over operations of the domestic Mexican company as the company would have through its own subsidiary Mexican corporation. Use of a shelter arrangement also permits a U.S. or foreign investor to avoid the initial costs of acquisition or construction of a manufacturing facility in Mexico.

REAL ESTATE

Maquiladora operations may require the use of real estate in Mexico. As a general rule, companies with any foreign ownership are precluded under Mexican law from owning real estate or improvements situated within 100 kilometers of the U.S.-Mexican border or within 50 kilometers of any coastline. However, the Mexican Constitution and the Mexican Foreign Investment Law permit companies whose by-laws include a provision in which shareholders of such companies consider themselves Mexican nationals and will not invoke the protection of their governments in matters relating to their activities in Mexico to own real property located in the restricted zone that is intended for business activities. In addition, Mexican law permits designated banks to serve as trustees for "land trusts" established to hold land within the restricted areas. A foreign investor does not have a property right in the real property held in a land trust, but does have the rights to the use, benefit, and enjoyment of such real property. The maximum term of such a trust is 50 years, but may be renewed on request by the interested party for a similar term.

RESTRICTIONS ON THE EMPLOYMENT OF FOREIGNERS

Mexican law requires that 90 percent of the employees of any company operating in Mexico be Mexican citizens. This does not apply to directors, administrators, and general managers (Art. VII Ley Federal del Trabajo). The immigration of foreign individuals for managerial or other positions is usually permitted only if qualified Mexicans are unavailable. Entry into Mexico by foreign individuals for employment generally requires a visa, which may be obtained at a Mexican consulate located in any foreign country.

TAXES

Profits earned by a maquiladora facility are taxed in Mexico at a rate of 34 percent. These taxes may be creditable against taxes payable in the United States or other countries. Maquiladoras are required to report their profits in accordance with "arm's-length" principles. Under these "arm's-length" principles, the appropriate transfer price set by related companies is the amount that would have been charged or paid if the transaction had occurred between unrelated companies. The failure to comply with transfer pricing rules could subject the maquiladora to certain sanctions and penalties in Mexico, and the parent company may not be able to credit certain amounts against taxes payable in the jurisdictions in which it has to file tax returns.

GOVERNMENT APPROVALS

Operation of a maquiladora facility in Mexico is subject to approval by Mexico's Ministry of Commerce and Industrial Development (the Ministry). To obtain approval, an applicant must provide the Ministry with a detailed description of intended operations, including the nature of the industrial processes to be used and the machinery and equipment required. The application must be submitted on forms issued by the Ministry.

ENVIRONMENTAL APPROVALS

In addition to the basic governmental approval necessary to conduct maquiladora operations in Mexico, approvals may be required from the Mexican Environmental Ministry. Manufacturing facilities must obtain an "environmental operating license." A license is issued only after it is determined that the relevant facility will not have an adverse environmental impact on the local area. Waste and other by-products of manufacturing operations in Mexico determined to be hazardous by the Environmental Ministry must be removed from the country. Periodic reports must be filed with the Environmental Ministry regarding the quantity of waste and its disposal.

SALES IN MEXICO

Pursuant to NAFTA, the products manufactured under a maquiladora program can be sold in the Mexican market under a phaseout program in which, by January 1, 2001, all maquiladora production may be sold in Mexico without restrictions or additional tariffs. Pursuant to the Maquiladora Decree, in 1998, a maquiladora operation may sell up to 75 percent of the total value of its annual exports for the preceding year. The ability to market products in Mexico is conditioned on meeting several requirements.

Among them, a maquiladora must demonstrate a favorable currency balance. A favorable currency balance is met when a maquiladora's revenues from sales or exports of products abroad exceed its costs of importing materials into Mexico. A maquiladora intending to sell products in Mexico must furnish a guaranty, payment bond, or other security for the payment of all applicable customs duties. Although customs duties are not levied when products are intended for ultimate export from Mexico, duties are charged on products intended for sale in Mexico.

ANTITRUST LAWS

CHAPTER OUTLINE

COMPETITIVE EFFECTS OF PROPOSED MERGER
HORIZONTAL MERGERS
DEFENSES
COMPLIANCE WITH HART-SCOTT-RODINO ACT

SUMMARY

U.S. antitrust laws have evolved in recent years to become more favorable to business. The principal antitrust laws are federal, such as the Sherman and Clayton Acts, although there is an Arizona antitrust law. Penalties for antitrust violations can be severe, including fines, imprisonment, and triple damages. Antitrust violations include illegal agreements among competitors (horizonal restraints), illegal agreements between manufacturers and dealers (vertical restraints), and attempts to monopolize. Certain agreements are always (*per se*) illegal; others are tested by the "rule of reason" as to whether they unreasonably restrain trade.

BACKGROUND

Interpretation and enforcement of U.S. antitrust laws have undergone a significant transformation in recent years. The initial antitrust legislation was enacted during a period of public concern about the aggregation of economic power. More recent interpretations of the antitrust laws have focused on economic efficiency. The "Chicago School" of economics argues that only those trade practices that harm consumer welfare through reductions of output should be prohibited. This philosophy is reflected in current governmental enforcement policies and judicial interpretations of the antitrust laws, which are increasingly favorable toward business and the unrestricted operation of the free market. Many restrictive former antitrust rules have been abandoned.

Only a few businesses locating in Arizona will have a size or market impact that would create antitrust concerns, but for such businesses, analysis of potential antitrust implications is essential.

In Arizona there are two sources of antitrust regulation: federal antitrust laws, including the Sherman Act, the Clayton Act, and the Robinson-Patman Act, and, at the state level, the Uniform State Antitrust Act. Enforcement of federal laws is the responsibility of the U.S. Justice Department and the U.S. Federal Trade Commission. Enforcement of state laws is the responsibility of the Arizona Attorney General. Private citizens can also bring civil suits under both federal and state antitrust laws.

Although reduced in recent years, the scope of the antitrust laws remains extensive, and even anti-competitive conduct that occurs abroad may violate federal antitrust laws if it has a "direct, substantial, and reasonably foreseeable effect on U.S. commerce."

Penalties for violations of the antitrust laws can be significant. Large monetary fines can be imposed under federal and state law and criminal sanctions under federal law. In civil suits, private parties may recover three times the actual damages suffered, plus attorneys' fees.

HORIZONTAL RESTRAINTS - AGREEMENTS AMONG COMPETITORS

IN GENERAL

Not all agreements among competitors (horizontal agreements) are illegal under the antitrust laws, only those that "unreasonably" restrain trade within the meaning of Section One of the Sherman Act or its counterpart section under the Arizona act. Some agreements are regarded by the courts as so plainly anti-competitive, that no proof of their unreasonableness is necessary. These are conclusively (*per se*) illegal. No inquiry is made as to the precise harm a *per se* illegal agreement may cause, and no business justification is a defense.

The legality of other horizontal agreements is analyzed under the "rule of reason" to determine whether, on balance, the agreement constitutes an unreasonable restraint of trade. Under the rule of reason all relevant circumstances are weighed, both the positive and negative effects on competition. If the agreement is determined to have an insignificant effect on competition and to have a legitimate business justification, the agreement will be found to be legal.

HORIZONTAL AGREEMENTS AFFECTING PRICE

Agreements among competitors that affect price present the greatest risks. Section One of the Sherman Act prohibits not only agreements among competitors that directly raise prices, but also combinations formed for the purpose, and with the effect, of raising, depressing, fixing, pegging, or stabilizing prices. An agreement setting minimum or maximum prices is illegal *per se*. Agreements among competitors that indirectly affect price, such as agreements to restrict price advertising or to prohibit premiums or discounts, are also illegal *per se*.

TERRITORIAL DIVISIONS AND CUSTOMER ALLOCATIONS

It is illegal for competitors to divide markets among themselves by agreeing not to compete with each other in certain geographical areas or not to compete for certain customers. Such agreements to divide markets, whether by territorial division or customer allocation, are illegal *per se*.

COVENANTS NOT TO COMPETE

A covenant is often included in an agreement for sale of a business that prohibits the seller from entering into competition with the purchaser of the business in a particular area for a particular time. Even though most agreements among competitors not to compete in certain geographical areas are illegal *per se*, a covenant not to compete that is an element of a sale of a business is evaluated under the "rule of reason." The covenant not to compete in the context of the sale of a business is regarded as part of a larger agreement that has a legitimate objective as its principal goal, and the public interest in facilitating a transfer of a business is deemed to justify the rule of reason approach. If the covenant is not unreasonably broad in geographical scope and is not unreasonably long in duration, the covenant is legal.

GROUP BOYCOTTS

A group boycott is an agreement among competitors to refuse to deal with another competitor or to refuse to deal with a supplier or customer. The objective of such an agreement is to force another party out of business or to force the acceptance of some condition. A group boycott undertaken by a group with market power, which has the intent or effect of driving another competitor out of business, is generally illegal *per se*. Other group boycotts are tested under the rule of reason.

JOINT VENTURES

A joint venture is a partnership formed for a particular purpose, such as to perform research and development or to produce and market a new product. The legality of joint ventures among competitors is usually determined under the rule of reason.

Many factors are considered under a rule of reason analysis of any joint venture to determine whether the anti-competitive effects of the venture are outweighed by competition-enhancing features. Among them are the size of the joint venturers, their share of their respective markets, the contributions of each party to the venture, the reasonableness of their relationship to the purposes of the venture, and the likelihood that one or all of the parties would undertake a similar project in the absence of the joint venture. Other factors include the scope and duration of the venture, the nature of the functions transferred by the members of the joint venture to the joint venture itself, the efficiencies created through the formation and function of the joint venture, whether a pattern of joint ventures has emerged in the particular industry, and whether the joint venture builds new productive capacity or utilizes existing capacity.

The principal factor is the magnitude of the venture. An "over-inclusive" venture is of concern, because it reduces the number of potentially competing parties. Nevertheless, an extremely large venture may be justified if only a venture of that size could successfully achieve the objectives of the venture.

Joint venture status does not insulate otherwise impermissible behavior. Price fixing, illegal group boycotts, and territorial or customer allocations are illegal *per se* even though engaged in by a joint venture.

Under the National Cooperative Research Act of 1984, there is a special statutory relaxed rule of reason standard for research and developmental joint ventures. A joint research and development venture is one for theoretical analysis, development of testing or basic engineering techniques, experimental production of prototypes, equipment, or processes, exchange of research information, or establishment and operation of research facilities.

VERTICAL AGREEMENTS - RESTRAINTS BETWEEN MANUFACTURERS AND DISTRIBUTORS OR RETAILERS

Manufacturers or other producers may seek to enter into agreements with distributors and retailers of their products (vertical agreements). Under federal law, the legality of vertical agreements is determined under Section One of the Sherman Act. Certain vertical agreements are unlawful *per se*. Other vertical agreements are analyzed under the rule of reason.

Exclusive Dealing Arrangements

An agreement by two businesses to deal exclusively with one another is a common form of vertical agreement; one which often arises in a distributorship arrangement, because an exclusive distributorship typically provides a distributor with the right to be the exclusive outlet for a manufacturer. Agreements of this kind are judged under the rule of reason. Such exclusivity provisions are generally upheld as not violating the antitrust laws, as long as they do not restrain an undue percentage share of either the manufacturer's or the distributor's market. Thus, where numerous distributors compete with one another, each with its own exclusive product line, the antitrust laws do not make such arrangements illegal.

Territorial and Customer Restrictions

Territorial and customer restrictions may be sought by a manufacturer. For example, a manufacturer may limit a dealer's sale of the manufacturer's product to a particular geographical area and time, prohibit other dealers from selling the manufacturer's product in the same area, or restrict sales by dealers to certain customers. In contrast to horizontal agreements among competitors involving territorial divisions and customer allocations that are illegal *per se*, vertical agreements of this kind between manufacturers and distributors are tested under the rule of reason. The justification is that although vertical agreements limit competition among dealers in the same brand, they may enhance competition among dealers of different brands. But vertical agreements relating to territorial or customer restrictions must not be used as a subterfuge to accomplish prohibited horizontal price-fixing or territorial arrangements.

Resale Price Maintenance

It is illegal for a manufacturer to fix the prices at which its products can be resold by wholesalers and retailers (resale price maintenance). Resale price maintenance agreements generally are held to be *per se* unlawful. The rule of *per se* illegality applies to agreements to set maximum, as well as minimum, resale prices. The general *per se* rule of illegality does not apply to a manufacturer that issues "suggested" retail prices, provided that the manufacturer does not compel a retailer to follow the suggestions.

A manufacturer may attempt to terminate a distributorship with a dealer that refuses to comply with suggested resale prices. When other complaining retail dealers induce the manufacturer to threaten the price-cutter with termination, a difficult question of liability arises. Although the manufacturer cannot compel the retailer to cease price-cutting and maintain the suggested standards, which would be *per se* illegal resale price maintenance, a manufacturer generally can terminate its relationship with a price-cutting retailer, because the U.S. Supreme Court has said that, absent any purpose to create or maintain a monopoly, the Sherman Act does not restrict the right of a manufacturer to exercise its own discretion as to parties with whom it wishes to deal. There are circumstances, however, in which a manufacturer may be found to be in violation of the rule against resale price maintenance, should it terminate a distributor who does not maintain minimum resale prices, particularly when the termination is accompanied by an agreement with remaining retailers that they will maintain or fix resale prices.

Monopolization and Attempts to Monopolize

Monopolization Defined

Section Two of the Sherman Act prohibits monopolization and attempts to monopolize.

Monopolization, under Section Two of the Sherman Act, is the possession of "monopoly power," plus some conduct that demonstrates intent to exercise or maintain the monopoly power. Monopoly power refers either to the "power to control prices" or the "power to exclude competition." The power to control prices exists if a business can establish appreciably higher prices than those charged by competitors for equivalent goods without a substantial loss of its business to its competitors. The power to exclude competition exists if a business can dominate a market by eliminating existing competition from the market and preventing new competition from entering.

A business that does not have monopoly power can nevertheless be guilty of attempted monopolization if it has sufficient market power so that there is a "dangerous probability" that the business will be successful in attaining monopoly power. Attempted monopolization requires a specific intent to monopolize.

Proof of monopolization, or of attempt to monopolize, is a two-step process. First, it must be demonstrated that the alleged offender has monopoly power in the relevant market or a dangerous probability of attaining market power. Second, there must be proof of some type of monopolistic conduct showing a willful intent to acquire or maintain that power.

Determination of Relevant Market

The first step in a Section Two Sherman Act case is to determine the relevant market in which the monopoly power allegedly exists. The relevant market is the area of effective competition in which the alleged monopolist operates. This market has two separate dimensions, the products or services included in the market and the geographic area covered.

RELEVANT PRODUCTS

The relevant products in the market include all products or services that are reasonably interchangeable with the products that the alleged offender produces. Some of the factors that courts consider in determining whether products are "reasonably interchangeable," and therefore in the same market, are whether the products have the same or similar characteristics or uses, whether the products are sold to similar customers, and whether the products are distributed and sold by the same kinds of distributors or dealers. Products do not have to be identical to be in the same product market, but they must meaningfully compete with each other.

RELEVANT GEOGRAPHIC MARKET

The relevant geographic market is the geographic area in which the sellers of a relevant product or service operate; the area in which the alleged monopolist faces competition from suppliers of competing products and to which purchasers can practically turn for such products or services. The relevant geographic area can be as large as the entire world or as small as a single city.

PROOF OF MARKET MONOPOLY POWER

Once the relevant market is determined, the next inquiry is whether the alleged offender actually has monopoly power in the relevant market. One way to demonstrate market power is direct proof of the alleged offender's actual control over prices or of exclusion of competitors. But direct evidence is often lacking. In the absence of direct proof, the courts focus on two other considerations: "Market share statistics and barriers to entry."

Market share statistics are often used to determine market monopoly power. Market share statistics show the percentage of the market that the alleged monopolist controls. If the market share is sufficiently large, a court will generally conclude that the alleged offender has the power to control prices.

Barriers to entry are also often used. Barriers to entry are obstacles that a new business would face if it tried to enter the same market. Barriers to entry may exist when significant capital would be necessary to fund the new business or when the new business would require specialized training or technology. If entry barriers are low, a business with a high market share may not necessarily have market monopoly power, because if such a business should raise its prices, minimal entry barriers would likely motivate other businesses to enter the market.

PROOF OF MONOPOLY CONDUCT

An alleged offender's monopoly power, by itself, does not constitute unlawful monopolization. The monopoly power must be coupled with conduct showing intent to exercise or maintain that power. This conduct is referred to as "predatory" or anticompetitive conduct. The courts have not fully defined what constitutes predatory conduct, but two of the more common types are "predatory pricing" of products and "refusals to deal."

PREDATORY PRICING

Predatory pricing occurs when a firm prices its products so low that the intended effect is to discipline or eliminate competition and thereby allow the firm to later charge higher prices. The obvious problem is to distinguish prices that constitute legitimate competitive behavior from prices that are predatory. The courts do not want to discourage low prices if the result is more competition. Courts are skeptical of predatory pricing claims and usually will not uphold them unless it is clearly shown that the alleged offender can both eliminate competition and preclude others from reentering the market once the offender is able to charge monopolistic prices.

In determining whether a price is predatory, courts consider the alleged offender's costs in producing the product. If a firm prices its products below its marginal or average variable costs, there is a presumption of predatory pricing. An alleged offender can rebut this presumption by showing that its pricing policy is the result of a legitimate competitive response to market conditions.

REFUSALS TO DEAL

It is often difficult to distinguish between legitimate business practices designed to increase market share and practices that are exclusionary or predatory, especially regarding refusals to deal with competitors. Many believe that a business has an absolute right to choose the parties with whom it deals, but this is not always true. A monopolist's refusal to deal with a business or a competitor is predatory and illegal if the refusal is intended to eliminate competition.

PRICE DISCRIMINATION UNDER THE ROBINSON-PATMAN ACT

The Robinson-Patman Act prohibits a seller engaged in commerce from discriminating in price between two or more buyers. A violation of the Robinson-Patman Act requires that there be at least two sales, one of which is interstate in character, and that there be actual discrimination in sales of goods. In other words, there must be at least two sales to different customers at different prices. A sale, plus only an offer to sell at a higher price, does not constitute illegal price discrimination. The Robinson-Patman Act also makes it unlawful for a buyer knowingly to induce or receive a discriminatory price, but in such case a buyer cannot be found liable unless the seller is also liable.

EXCEPTIONS

The prohibition against price discrimination in the Robinson-Patman Act does not prohibit "functional discounts," price reductions granted by sellers to purchasers based on the position of the purchaser in the distribution chain. An example is a favorable price charged by a manufacturer to a wholesaler, which is less than the price the manufacturer would charge a retailer or a consumer, provided that the functional discount offered to the one wholesaler is available to all other wholesalers.

There is also an exemption from the Robinson-Patman Act for "delivered pricing" that reflects the costs of transportation. A manufacturer that quotes one price for products available at the factory may quote a higher delivered price for products delivered elsewhere. Although some delivered pricing has been found illegal as being nothing more than a subterfuge to diminish price competition, a legitimate delivered pricing structure does not violate the Robinson-Patman Act.

DEFENSES

There are a number of defenses to a claim of price discrimination. Where a seller acts "in good faith to meet an equally low price of a competitor," there is no illegal price discrimination. It is also not a Robinson-Patman Act violation if the price differential is made in response to changing conditions affecting the market or marketability of the product. This defense permits, for example, price cuts on obsolete or seasonal goods. Another defense authorizes price differentials attributable to differences in the cost of manufacture or sale, such as a quantity discount attributable to lower costs achieved by economics of scale.

MERGERS

Section 7 of the Clayton Act prohibits a merger if the effect of such merger may be to lessen competition. Merger may be by way of consolidation, stock acquisition, or asset acquisition. A merger may be a horizontal merger, which is a merger between direct competitors, a vertical merger, which is a merger between a product producer and a product distributor, or a conglomerate merger, which is a merger between producers of different products or between producers in different geographic areas. Although all three categories of mergers have generated government challenges in the past, present enforcement of the Clayton Act is generally limited to horizontal mergers.

MARKET POWER

As in monopolization cases, the starting point of horizontal, vertical, or conglomerate merger analysis is to define the appropriate product and geographic markets. Market definition often plays a major role in merger litigation. If the product or geographical market is narrowly defined, the competitive impact of the merger will be more pronounced than in a broader market. Generally, a market is determined by the "interchangeability" of use. Thus, for example, if customers can readily turn to other products or to other geographic areas, those products and geographic areas are within the relevant market.

COMPETITIVE EFFECTS OF PROPOSED MERGER

Once the relevant markets have been defined, a merger analysis requires an examination of the likely anti-competitive effect of the merger. That analysis differs depending on the precise type of merger involved, but in this chapter only the anti-competitive effects of horizontal mergers are discussed, because vertical and conglomerate mergers are seldom a problem in practice.

HORIZONTAL MERGERS

Horizontal mergers present a greater risk of anti-competitive harm than either vertical or conglomerate mergers. The principal concern with a horizontal merger is potential for market concentration, a market that is substantially controlled by four or fewer companies. The courts have never determined precisely how competitive impact is to be measured in a horizontal merger. At least two standards have been employed for this purpose.

One standard is to examine sales revenue within the relevant market and to rank the various competitors by percentage share of such sales. Although no single formula has been accepted by the courts, any merger among major competitors in a market in which the top four firms control more than 75 percent of that market is a market concentration having a significant risk of illegality under the Clayton Act.

Courts have also recently looked to some extent to a set of arithmetic measurements used by the Justice Department that attempts by mathematical formula to evaluate market concentration, both in markets dominated by large equally-sized leading competitors and in markets dominated by one or two large firms. Although these standards have not been entirely accepted by the courts, they offer some guidance as to federal enforcement policy.

DEFENSES

In an action challenging a merger, the merging firms often assert defenses or justifications for behavior that appears to be anti-competitive. One is the "failing company defense." The applicability of the failing company defense is limited. The parties must show that the failing acquired company faced a grave probability of business failure and that it made a good faith effort to find other less anti-competitive purchasers.

Another defense is that of "beneficial consequences." Although the U.S. Supreme Court has stated that an otherwise anti-competitive merger is not permitted because it promotes competition elsewhere or because it advances a social objective, the economies promoted by a merger may be relevant. If it can be demonstrated that the merger will result in cost savings that could not have been obtained without the merger and that the savings clearly outweigh any increase in market power, such efficiencies may constitute a defense.

COMPLIANCE WITH THE HART-SCOTT-RODINO ACT

The Hart-Scott-Rodino Antitrust Improvements Act requires notice to the Justice Department and the Federal Trade Commission at least 30 days before certain mergers can be consummated. Unless the transaction is otherwise exempt from the notification requirement, the notification, and a payment of a $45,000 fee are required in any case in which the proposed merger meets all of the following three tests:

The first is the "commerce" test. This test is met if at least one of the parties to the merger is engaged in commerce or in any activity affecting commerce.

The second is the "size-of-the-parties" test. This test is met if either party to the transaction has at least $100 million of annual net sales or total assets and the other party has at least $10 million of annual net sales or total assets. If a non-manufacturing company is being acquired, the total assets test alone is used.

The third is "size-of-the-transaction" test. This test is met if the acquiring party will obtain voting securities and assets in excess of $15 million or if the acquiring party will obtain 15 percent or more of the voting securities or assets of the acquired party.

After receipt of the prescribed premerger notification, the Justice Department or Federal Trade Commission may request additional information. If additional information is requested the merger cannot be consummated until 20 days after the Commission's receipt of the additional information.

EMPLOYMENT LAWS

CHAPTER OUTLINE

SUMMARY

Employers in the United States historically have had significant discretion as to employment matters, including hiring, discharge, and working conditions. However, in recent years the working place has become increasingly regulated and the discretion of employers limited by federal and state legislation. Arizona, for the most part, has not participated in this trend. For example, some states now require payment of a minimum wage higher than the federal minimum wage, but in Arizona only the federal minimum wage and overtime law applies.

Representation of employees by a union — an organization formed to represent the collective rights of employees — often has an impact. Federal laws generally encourage union representation. Many state laws in the United States also encourage union representation. Most states permit "union security agreements," that compel employees to join a union. Arizona is one of a minority of states that have enacted "right-to-work" laws that protect the jobs of employees who wish to remain non-union. This may account, at least in part, for the fact that Arizona unions have less influence than in other states. Fewer than one in five employees are represented by a union in Arizona.

GENERAL REGULATION OF EMPLOYMENT

Legislation in recent years has increased regulation of the workplace in four principal categories: equal rights in hiring, firing and promotion; wages and hours; job safety; and miscellaneous issues, such as veterans' rights, the duty to provide advance notice of plant closings, and restrictions against the use of polygraphs and other lie detector devices.

CIVIL RIGHTS LAWS

FEDERAL LEGISLATION

- **Title VII of the U.S. Civil Rights Act of 1964, as amended in 1991 (Title VII)**

Title VII prohibits discrimination in employment on the basis of race, color, religion, sex, or national origin. The prohibition applies to all elements of the employer-employee relationship, including hiring, firing, wages, promotion, and transfer. Title VII applies to every employer that has 15 or more employees engaged in any business affecting interstate commerce.

Title VII is enforced by the federal Equal Employment Opportunity Commission (the EEOC). Employees or job applicants can file charges of discrimination with the EEOC. The EEOC itself may also file charges against an employer on behalf of employees or job applicants. Following an investigation and attempts at resolution, the EEOC, employees, or job applicants may file a suit against the employer. Remedies available include compelled employment, reinstatement, back pay, compensatory damages, punitive damages and equitable relief and attorneys' fees. Employees are entitled to a jury trial.

■ Age Discrimination in Employment Act (ADEA)

The ADEA protects individuals who are at least 40 from employer discrimination based on age with respect to hiring, firing, wages, promotions, transfers, and other terms, conditions, or privileges of employment. The ADEA applies to any employer engaged in business affecting interstate commerce that has 20 or more employees. An exception permits age discrimination when age is a "bona fide occupational qualification" reasonably necessary to the normal operation of the employer's business. Selection of a younger employee over an older one is permitted if reasonably based on factors other than age.

Age discrimination claims must be filed with the EEOC. Thereafter, the EEOC, employees, or job applicants can file suit against the employer. Remedies available include compelled employment, reinstatement, back pay awards, liquidated damages, and attorneys' fees.

■ The Rehabilitation Act

The Rehabilitation Act prohibits employers from discriminating against "qualified handicapped persons" and also requires employers to take affirmative steps to provide employment opportunities to handicapped persons. Employers subject to the Rehabilitation Act are federal contractors and subcontractors and recipients of federal financial assistance.

A "qualified handicapped person" is a handicapped person who can do a particular job. The employer must make reasonable accommodation to the person's handicap, unless doing so would cause the employer undue hardship. A "handicapped person" is defined as any person who has a physical or mental impairment that substantially limits one or more major life activities, who has a history of such impairment, or who is perceived as having as such an impairment. Examples of handicapped persons are persons suffering from blindness, heart disease, or epilepsy. Whether an accommodation is reasonable in a particular circumstance depends upon a number of factors, including the size and financial ability of the employer, the type of business, the number of persons to be accommodated, and the nature and cost of the accommodation required.

The U.S. Department of Labor enforces the Rehabilitation Act. Violations can result in cancellation of existing contracts with the U.S. government and disqualification from future contracts.

■ Americans with Disabilities Act of 1990 (ADA)

The ADA prohibits discrimination against "qualified individuals with disabilities." The prohibition extends to hiring, firing, wages, promotions, transfers, and all other terms, conditions, or privileges of employment. A "qualified individual with a disability" is one who meets the definition of a "qualified handicapped person" under the Rehabilitation Act. The ADA applies to an employer engaged in a business affecting interstate commerce that has 15 or more employees. The ADA is enforced by the EEOC. Rights of action and remedies under the ADA are similar to the remedies under Title VII described above.

- **Equal Pay Act (Pay Act)**

The Pay Act prohibits discrimination in employee wages on the basis of sex. It requires employers to pay equal wages for work at a single site of employment requiring equal skill, effort, and responsibility, regardless of sex. Differences in wage rates are permissible if attributable to operation of a seniority system, a merit system, a system that measures earnings by the quantity or quality of production, or any other system based on factors other than sex. The Pay Act applies to any employer with two or more employees. The Pay Act is administered by the EEOC. Either the EEOC or the employee may file a lawsuit to enforce the provisions of the Pay Act. Remedies include back pay awards, damages, and attorneys' fees.

- **Section 1981 of the Civil Rights Act of 1870 (Section 1981)**

Section 1981 prohibits discrimination based on race or membership in an ethnic group. Any employer engaged in business affecting interstate commerce is subject to Section 1981. Unlike Title VII, a job applicant or employee is not required to file a charge with the EEOC before suing the employer for a violation of the statute. Remedies under Section 1981 include requiring employment, back pay, compensatory damages, punitive damages, and attorneys' fees.

STATE LEGISLATION

- **Arizona Civil Rights Act (Arizona Act)**

The Arizona Act mirrors the federal civil rights laws and applies to Arizona employers with 15 or more employees. (Note: The Act's prohibition against sexual harassment applies to employers with one or more employees.). The Arizona Act is administered by the Civil Rights Division of the office of the Arizona Attorney General.

WAGE AND HOUR LAWS

FEDERAL LEGISLATION

■ Fair Labor Standards Act (FLSA)

The FLSA requires payment of minimum wages and overtime. The FLSA also limits the employment of children. Virtually all employers are subject to FLSA. Under the FLSA employers must pay employees not less than the prescribed minimum wage. The minimum wage is currently $5.15.

Under the overtime provisions of the FLSA most employees must be paid one and one-half times their regular rate of pay for all hours worked in excess of 40 hours per week. There are exceptions to the minimum wage and overtime standards for certain employees, including executive, administrative, and professional personnel, as well as outside sales employees.

The FLSA is administered and enforced by the Wage-Hour Division of the U.S. Department of Labor. The Labor Department may bring an action against an employer to compel compliance with the FLSA, or employees can sue for unpaid wages, liquidated damages, injunctive relief, and attorneys' fees.

■ Davis-Bacon Act

The Davis-Bacon Act requires employers that contract with the federal government to pay their employees a special minimum wage, i.e., the "prevailing wage" rate for corresponding classes of employees employed on projects of a similar character in the area in which the contracted work is to be performed. The Davis-Bacon Act is enforced by the Labor Department. Failure to pay the required "prevailing wage" can result in termination of the underlying contract and back pay obligations. If the contract is canceled and the work completed by another contractor, the employer may be liable for any excess costs incurred by the government.

■ Walsh-Healy Act

The Walsh-Healy Act mandates a special "prevailing minimum" wage which must be paid to employees of employers that supply goods or materials to the U.S. government. Enforcement and sanctions are similar to those applicable under the Davis-Bacon Act.

■ Family and Medical Leave Act of 1993 (FMLA)

The FMLA applies to workers who have been employed at least twelve months when the employee works at a site employing at least 50 people (within 75 surface miles of the workplace). It entitles eligible employees to twelve weeks of unpaid leave during a twelve month period (1) to care for a newly born or adopted child, (2) due to the employee's serious health condition, or (3) to care for a spouse, child, or parent with a serious health condition. When the leave expires, the employee is entitled to be restored to the same or equivalent position with equivalent pay, benefits, and other conditions of employment. The employer must continue the existing health insurance coverage during the leave, but may have the right to recover the premiums if the employee fails to return to work.

A serious health condition is generally defined under the FMLA as one that requires hospitalization, lasts more than three days, or is chronic and incapacitating. Employers may request documentation detailing the employee's eligibility for FMLA leave and verification from the employee's health care provider. Employees must also make a reasonable effort to provide the employer with at least 30 days notice of a foreseeable leave of absence, or, if the leave is unanticipated, as soon as practicable.

DOING BUSINESS IN ARIZONA

The FMLA authorizes the Wage and Hour Division of the U.S. Department of Labor to investigate and resolve complaints. Employees may also file suit to enforce their rights under the law without filing an agency complaint. Employers who violate the FMLA or discriminate against employees exercising their rights under it are liable for lost compensation, compensatory damages, and attorneys' fees.

STATE LEGISLATION

Arizona laws relating to wages and hours generally govern the payment of wages. An employer in Arizona is required to designate at least two days each month as fixed pay days, not more than 16 days apart. Discharged employees must be paid all wages due within three working days of the date of discharge or by the end of the regular pay period in which they are discharged, whichever is sooner. Employees who quit must be paid all wages due by the end of the regular pay period in which they terminate. Violations can result in employer liability of three times the amount of wages due.

SAFETY LAWS

FEDERAL LEGISLATION

- **The Occupational Safety and Health Act (OSHA)**

OSHA imposes a duty on employers to provide employees with a safe and healthful place to work. OSHA requires all employers to furnish employees with a workplace free from recognized hazards causing, or likely to cause, death or serious physical harm. OSHA is administered by the U.S. Labor Department, which from time to time issues mandatory safety standards. The Labor Department is authorized to conduct inspections of the workplace to determine compliance with these standards. Violations of OSHA can result in civil and criminal penalties. In some hazardous situations an employer can be ordered to shut down its operations.

- **Mine Safety and Health Act (MSHA)**

MSHA prescribes standards governing working conditions of employees employed in mining operations. Sanctions for violations of MSHA are similar to the sanctions imposed under OSHA.

STATE LEGISLATION

- **Arizona Occupational Safety and Health Act (Arizona OSHA)**

Although OSHA is a federal law enforced by the U.S. Labor Department, OSHA provides that an individual state may assume responsibility for safety and health within its jurisdiction, provided that the state has a federally approved OSHA plan. Arizona has assumed responsibility for workplace safety in the state in accordance with standards set by the U.S. Labor Department.

OTHER SIGNIFICANT LAWS

FEDERAL LEGISLATION

- **Uniformed Services Employment and Re-employment Rights Act (USERRA)**

USERRA requires employers to grant employees time off to fulfill temporary military obligations, and to rehire individuals who leave work to serve full time in the U.S. Uniformed Services for up to five years. The Act also prohibits discrimination against individuals who apply for, perform, or have performed military service. In addition to re-employment, covered employees have pension rights and the right to continued health insurance coverage for up to 18 months while in the military.

Employees must notify their employer in advance of the need for military leave, and also must reapply for employment after their service. The time limits for reapplication vary depending on the length of service. Once re-employed, the employee may not be discharged except for good cause for up to one year, again depending on the length of service. Damages recoverable for violation of USERRA include re-employment, lost wages and benefits, liquidated double damages for "willful" violation, and attorneys' fees.

■ Worker Adjustment Retraining and Notification Act of 1988 (WARN)

WARN requires employers of 100 or more employees to provide advance notice to employees and to local and state officials before implementing a plant closing or a mass layoff. A "plant closing" is a shutdown of facilities at a single site that results in a loss of jobs for 50 or more employees for at least 30 days. A "mass layoff" is a reduction in the work force of 50 or more workers at a single site, provided that the reduction affects at least one-third of the total work force. A reduction in the work force of 500 or more at a single site is a mass layoff, regardless of the percentage of the work force affected. An employer is not obligated to provide advance notice of a mass layoff if the work force reductions will last for less than six months. A mass layoff which, contrary to initial expectations, extends beyond six months will violate WARN, unless the extension beyond six months is due to business circumstances not reasonably foreseeable and notice is given as soon as it becomes apparent that work force reductions will extend beyond the six-month period. Employers that violate the notice requirements of WARN are liable to each unnotified employee for back pay and benefits for a period of up to 60 days. Employers that violate the notice requirements may also be fined by local governmental units.

■ Employee Polygraph Act of 1988 (Polygraph Act)

The Polygraph Act prohibits employers from using polygraphs, "lie detectors," or similar devices to screen job applicants or current employees. The Act prohibits an employer from taking any adverse employment action based solely on the results of a polygraph test or based on an employee's refusal to submit to such a test. The Polygraph Act applies to any employer engaged in interstate commerce, but certain government contractors are exempt. Employers may be fined up to $10,000 for each violation. Employees or prospective employees have the right to sue for damages, including reinstatement, back pay, benefits, and attorneys' fees.

■ Immigration Reform and Control Act of 1986 (Immigration Act)

The Immigration Act prohibits employers from employing aliens who are not authorized to work in the United States. An alien is not authorized to work in the United States unless the person is either an immigrant lawfully admitted into the United States under a permanent resident classification or a non-immigrant lawfully admitted into the United States under a special visa classification. The Immigration Act requires employers to verify the right of each employee to work in the United States and to attest to receipt of documentary evidence of the right. Virtually all employers are subject to the Immigration Act. Violations of the Immigration Act are punishable by civil and criminal penalties. See also the "Immigration" chapter.

■ Drug-Free Workplace Act (Drug Act)

The Drug Act requires federal contractors and grantees to implement anti-drug programs. Employers are required to provide information to employees regarding the dangers of drug abuse in the workplace. If an employee is convicted under a criminal drug law for a violation that occurs at the workplace, the employer must notify U.S. authorities. The employer must also impose sanctions against the convicted employee or require the employee to satisfactorily complete a drug abuse or rehabilitation program. The Drug Act does not require drug testing of employees. Employers covered by the Drug Act are those that hold contracts with the U.S. government in excess of $25,000 and recipients of federal financial assistance. Violations of the Drug Act may result in the termination of existing federal contracts and disqualification from future contracts.

STATE LEGISLATION

■ Workers' Compensation Act

Arizona has workers' compensation insurance laws, as do most states. The law requires employers to maintain insurance that provides specified benefits to employees for job-related accidents causing injury. The cost of the insurance is paid by employers through payment of premiums into a state fund or to a private insurance carrier. Some employers qualify to be self-insured.

■ Arizona Economic Security Act (AESA)

AESA provides for the payment of benefits for specified periods to individuals who become unemployed through no fault of their own. The cost of the benefits is provided by employers, who are required to make periodic contributions to a state unemployment insurance fund.

- **Arizona Drug Testing of Employees Act (Drug Testing Act)**

While the Drug Testing Act neither requires nor prohibits employee drug screening, it grants legal protection to employers who conduct drug or alcohol impairment tests that conform to the requirements of the Act. Compliance protects the employer from liability for actions taken in good faith relating to positive test results, failure to test or detect a specific drug or condition, or the elimination of a prevention or testing program.

In order to comply with the Drug Testing Act, the employer must publish and distribute a written statement to employees describing the drug and alcohol testing policy. The Act contains specific requirements, and each policy must describe which employees are subject to testing, under what circumstances, the substances for which the employee is tested, the methods and procedures of testing, and the consequences of positive test results or of failure to participate. The employer also must pay for employee testing, compensate the employee for his or her time, ensure that it is done in a reasonable and sanitary area, keep all communications relating to the testing confidential, and provide employees with the opportunity to explain a positive test.

- **1996 Arizona Employment Protection Act**

This Act strengthens the employment-at-will doctrine, allowing employers or employees to terminate the employment relationship at any time for any reason unless there is a written contract to the contrary. In order to overcome the presumption that the employment relationship is at-will, the contract must be signed by both the employee and the employer, or be set forth in an employee handbook that identifies itself as a contract, or be signed by the party to be charged. Under this law, implied contracts are not enforceable.

The Act also limits "wrongful discharge" suits based on public policy. Before this law, courts allowed lawsuits alleging that a termination was "morally wrong," even if it did not violate a specific law. Now these claims are not allowed. The employee must base the claim on a specific Arizona statute or the state constitution. The Act also protects "whistle blowers" against terminations in retaliation for a refusal to violate Arizona law.

The Act limits remedies in some areas. If the statute provides for a specific remedy, a successful plaintiff may receive no more than that remedy. An employee may not base a claim on the statute to obtain a greater award than the one contained in the statute itself, such as damages for emotional distress, humiliation, or punitive damages in a discrimination action. However, such damages can be awarded in a proper case. The Act also shortens the statute of limitations for wrongful termination. In order to pursue a claim, the employee must file suit within one year of termination.

■   **Other Matters**

ARBITRATION

Many employers are increasingly adopting arbitration provisions into employment contracts. These provisions typically require employees to arbitrate any disagreements arising in the course of employment. Both employers and employees often prefer arbitration to litigation because of its lower cost and quicker resolution of claims. Courts also view arbitration agreements favorably. Recently, courts have sent employment discrimination lawsuits based on Title VII, the ADEA, and the ADA to arbitration when an arbitration clause required it.

UNIONIZATION OF EMPLOYEES

The unionization of employees can affect an employer's discretion in employment matters. Briefly examined below are how a union is recognized, the effect of the union recognition and the impact on unionization of Arizona's right-to-work law. Also discussed is the impact when a business is sold upon collective bargaining with unions and upon existing union collective bargaining agreements.

UNION RECOGNITION

Unions generally obtain recognition through one of two means, voluntary recognition by the employer or an election under the supervision of the National Labor Relations Board (NLRB). In a voluntary recognition, an employer agrees to a "card check" by an impartial third party to verify that a majority of employees wish to be union represented. A card check is an examination of union authorization cards signed and dated by employees indicating their desire to be represented by the union. This avenue to union recognition is not common today.

More often an employer will refuse to recognize the union and declare its doubt of the union's claim of majority status. The employer is entitled to place the burden on the union to prove its claim of support by an uncoerced majority of employees. In response the union or an employee will file a petition with the NLRB seeking an NLRB-conducted election by secret ballot. The NLRB petition must be supported by a showing of interest of at least 30 percent of the employees. The showing of interest is usually made by union submission to the NLRB of authorization cards signed and dated by the requisite percentage of employees.

If there is a petition supported by the required showing of interest, the NLRB will schedule a hearing to address the NLRB's jurisdiction and the status of the parties. The principal issue at the hearing is often the determination of an appropriate "unit," the grouping of all employees, or of some particular class of employees, who will be eligible to vote for or against the union.

The election is customarily held on the employer's property. The election ballot usually reads, "Do you wish to be represented for purposes of collective bargaining by [the labor union]?" The actual counting of ballots is done by the NLRB personnel, but both the employer and employee may be represented at the election by observers. To prevail the union must obtain a majority of all valid votes cast.

Post-election questions may be raised and a hearing held as to the validity of the election or as to conduct affecting the results of the election. Threats, promises of benefits, surveillance, or interrogation are examples of conduct that can provide a basis for overturning an election result.

EFFECT OF UNION RECOGNITION

Once a union has achieved recognition, the employer is required to "collectively bargain" with representatives of the union as to wages, hours, and other terms and conditions of employment. The employer must bargain with representatives of the union, which then exclusively represents *all* employees in the bargaining unit. After union recognition an employer cannot negotiate with any individual employees within the unit, including those opposed to the union.

Neither the employer nor the union is obligated to make concessions. Each side merely has a duty to "bargain in good faith." Good faith on the part of the employer generally requires that the employer have an open mind and a sincere desire to reach an agreement, and that it make a sincere effort to do so. If an agreement is reached, a binding contract must be signed for the agreed term, most often from one to three years.

IMPACT OF RIGHT-TO-WORK LAWS

In some states all employees are obligated to join a union or to pay dues to a union, either to obtain employment or to retain their positions, once the union and the employer have signed a collective bargaining agreement. However, the National Labor Relations Act enables individual states to prohibit compulsory union membership. Arizona is one of a minority of states that has adopted such a "right-to-work" law. No employee in Arizona is required to join a union or to pay dues to a union as a condition of employment.

EFFECT OF UNION OR BARGAINING AGREEMENT UPON SUCCESSOR EMPLOYER

The question of union representation often is involved in the context of the sale of a business. If employees of the business are represented by a union, the issue may arise of whether the successor employer must bargain collectively with the union or of whether it must abide by the terms of an existing collective bargaining agreement made between the union and the seller.

Generally, the buyer of a business is not bound by the seller's union contract nor required to bargain collectively with an existing union, unless there is "substantial continuity" of work force between the successor employer and the predecessor employer. Whether substantial continuity exists depends on a number of factors, the most important of which is whether a majority of the employees of the successor employer were employed by the predecessor employer. Even if a duty to bargain is found, a successor employer is not obligated to comply with the terms of an existing collective bargaining agreement, unless the successor employer expressly or implicitly adopts the agreement or if the successor employer is the "alter ego" — essentially the same party — as the predecessor employer.

EMPLOYEE BENEFITS

CHAPTER OUTLINE

Summary

Although wages are primary compensation for services, various non-cash benefits are also usually an integral part of total compensation. Salaried employees, often called "rank-and-file employees," are generally the recipients of basic benefits, including medical and retirement. "Management employees" (executive personnel) commonly receive basic benefits supplemented by such items as deferred compensation, stock options, restricted stock, and other stock-based arrangements. Benefit payments are governed principally by federal laws.

Regulation of Employee Benefits

Employee benefits are subject to significant regulation under U.S. law. The Employee Retirement Income Security Act (ERISA) and the Internal Revenue Code (the Code) are the principal federal statutes. State laws generally are superseded (preempted) by federal law.

ERISA

ERISA is a comprehensive regulatory scheme. Under ERISA, employers must meet reporting and disclosure requirements, including annual reports to the U.S. Department of Labor, the agency which administers ERISA. ERISA also imposes minimum standards on certain types of plans to assure that basic benefits are provided to rank-and-file employees, rather than being confined to management personnel. ERISA also imposes standards for the administration of employee benefit plans.

ERISA can be enforced through proceedings brought by the Labor Department, employees, beneficiaries of employees, or plan fiduciaries, such as a plan administrator or a plan trustee. The Labor Department in some cases can impose fines for violations of ERISA.

The Internal Revenue Code

The Code's impact on employee benefit plans is primarily through requirements imposed as a condition of obtaining favorable tax treatment. Failure to satisfy the Code's requirements can result in loss of employer tax deductions for the plan contributions made by the employer or of employer deductions for costs of plan benefits paid by the employer. Violations of the Code can also result in loss of favorable tax treatment for employees as to receipt of benefits from a plan and the taxation of an otherwise tax-exempt trust. For example, for public companies in the United States, compensation in excess of $1 million is not deductible, unless certain conditions are satisfied. One of the most common exceptions is for "performance-based" compensation.

Impact of State Law

ERISA generally preempts state laws that relate to employee benefit plans. However, state insurance laws as they apply to insured plans are expressly exempted from preemption under ERISA. Accordingly, insured employee benefit plans (but not self-insured plans) are subject to Arizona's laws regulating insurance, including laws requiring that specific benefits be provided by medical plans.

Specific Benefit Arrangements

A variety of benefit arrangements may be provided by employers to employees. Among the most common arrangements are medical plans, qualified retirement plans, nonqualified plans, stock-based compensation arrangements, and performance unit plans.

Medical Plans

Adequate medical coverage is an increasingly important consideration for workers. The availability of employer-provided medical benefits is an important part of employee compensation. Medical coverage can be provided by an employer in several ways, including through insured and self-insured plans, health maintenance organizations, preferred provider organizations, and medical reimbursement arrangements. Under the Code, certain medical plans must not discriminate in favor of highly-compensated employees.

Medical benefits are usually provided to employees and their dependents only during employment. However, an employer who employs 20 or more employees and who maintains a group medical plan must allow certain former employees and their dependents to continue plan coverage, at the employee's expense, for a minimum of 18 months. Collective bargaining agreements often require longer continued health coverage for former employees.

Qualified Retirement Plans

Retirement benefits can be provided through a wide-range of qualified plans. A retirement plan is a "qualified plan" if it satisfies detailed Code requirements. A number of favorable tax consequences result from status as a qualified plan. An employer is entitled to a current deduction for contributions made to such a plan. Employees are not taxed on their plan benefits until benefits are actually received. The trust established under a qualified plan to receive contributions is not taxed on its earnings, which permits tax-free compounding. Six of the most common types of qualified retirement plans are the following:

Profit-Sharing Plans

Under a profit-sharing plan employer contributions can be contingent on the employer's profits. More likely, the employer is permitted to make contributions in its discretion, whether or not the employer makes a profit. Contributions made by an employer are allocated to individual accounts established for eligible employees. Upon retirement or other termination of employment, an employee is entitled to benefits based upon the employee's account balance.

Money Purchase Pension Plans

A money purchase pension plan is similar to a profit sharing plan except that it requires fixed annual contributions by an employer without regard to profits.

Defined Benefit Pension Plan

Under a defined benefit pension plan an employee is promised a fixed pension at retirement, the amount being determined by the employee's salary, years of employment, or both. The employer is required annually to contribute an amount actuarially sufficient to fund pension benefits.

Section 401(K) Plans

A Section 401(k) plan is a profit-sharing or stock bonus plan under which employees make pre-tax contributions that are not taxed until the employee retires. Employee contributions may be matched by tax-deductible contributions from the employer.

Stock Bonus Plans

A stock bonus plan is similar to a profit-sharing plan, except that the benefits are generally distributed in stock of the employer. Under certain stock bonus plans employees are authorized to exercise voting rights with respect to shares allocated to their accounts.

Leveraged Employee Stock Ownership Plans

A leveraged employee stock ownership plan is a specific type of stock bonus plan under which the plan borrows funds to invest primarily in the employer's stock. Employees who participate in a leveraged stock ownership plan have the right in certain cases to vote the shares allocated to their accounts.

Nonqualified Plans

Nonqualified plans play an important role as a tax and retirement planning device for executives. The principal attraction of nonqualified plans is that they are not subject to many of the onerous requirements of ERISA and the Code. Such plans can provide benefits to executives without providing corresponding benefits to rank-and-file employees. Two of the most common forms of nonqualified plans are excess benefit plans and deferred compensation plans.

Excess Benefit Plans

An excess benefit plan provides an executive with a supplemental pension equal to the difference between the pension that the executive would have received under the employer's qualified retirement plan if there were no limitation on benefits imposed by the Code and the limited pension that the executive will actually receive under the qualified plan.

Deferred Compensation Plans

A deferred compensation plan permits covered executives to avoid current income tax by deferring current compensation for a specified period or until retirement. Interest on the deferred amounts during the deferral period may be credited to the executive as a further benefit. In order to avoid adverse tax consequences to covered executives, and to avoid ERISA regulation, nonqualified deferred compensation plans are neither funded nor secured. Executives generally have no greater right to payment than do other unsecured creditors. Although there are ways in which the employer's promise can be secured, there is no way to give executives priority over their employer's other creditors without an adverse tax result.

Stock-Based Arrangements

The theory underlying stock-based arrangements is that the executive who has the right to acquire the employer's stock, or to receive compensation based upon the performance of the stock, will have an incentive to work more diligently for the company's success. Among the most common forms of stock-based arrangements are stock options, restricted stock, and stock appreciation rights.

Stock Options

A stock option is a right granted by an employer to an employee that permits the employee to purchase shares of the stock of the employer at a fixed price within a specified time. The option permits the employee to share in the appreciation in the stock of the employer while avoiding the risk of depreciation in value. Stock options are of two kinds, incentive stock options and nonqualified stock options.

■ Incentive Stock Options

Incentive stock options (ISOs) are creations of the Code and must satisfy the Code's requirements. One requirement is that the exercise price of the option (the amount payable by the employee to acquire the stock) cannot be less than the fair market value of the underlying stock on the date of the grant of the ISO. Also, an ISO must be exercised within ten years after the date of grant.

The principal benefit of an ISO is the tax treatment available to an employee. An employee is not taxed either at the time of the *grant* of an ISO or at the time of the *exercise* of the ISO, unless the employee is subject to the special alternative minimum tax. If the stock acquired upon exercise of an ISO is not sold or disposed of until after a mandated holding period, any gain to the employee from the sale is capital gain. No deduction is available to an employer in connection with an ISO unless the employee sells the ISO stock before the holding period.

■ Nonqualified Stock Options

A nonqualified stock option (NQSO) is any option that does not qualify as an ISO. Unlike ISOs, NQSOs are not required to meet specific requirements. However, as a result of state and federal tax and securities laws, NQSOs tend to have common features. Typical NQSOs permit the employee to purchase stock at a fixed price for a specified period of time at a price at or below the fair market value on the date of grant. Most NQSOs cannot be exercised until a specified period has expired, and most expire upon termination of employment, except by death, retirement, or disability.

The employee's tax treatment under an NQSO is not as favorable as under an ISO. Although the employee is generally not taxed upon grant of an NQSO, the employee will realize taxable ordinary income at the time of exercise of the option. Also, the favorable exercise price paid by the employee is the employee's "basis" in the stock in the event of a subsequent sale. Any amount realized on a subsequent sale that is in excess of the employee's basis is taxable at capital gain rates.

An employer does obtain more favorable tax treatment in connection with an NQSO than with an ISO. Although no deduction is available to an employer that issues an ISO, an employer that issues an NQSO is entitled to a deduction upon the employee's exercise of an NQSO to the extent of the amount taxed as ordinary income to the employee.

RESTRICTED STOCK

Restricted stock is stock of the employer issued to an employee for the performance of services. Restricted stock is subject to restrictions on the employee's stock ownership rights. For example, the employee's ownership of some or all of the shares may be made contingent on continued employment by the employer for a specified period. Restricted stock is often issued to an employee without cost to the employee or at a significant discount.

An employee is not subject to tax on restricted stock until all of the stock restrictions lapse. When the stock restrictions lapse the employee realizes ordinary income in an amount equal to the excess of the fair market value of the stock as of the date the restrictions lapse over the amount, if any, paid for the stock. Any appreciation in the stock that occurs after the restrictions lapse generally is eligible for capital gain treatment.

An employee can elect to be taxed immediately upon the receipt of the restricted stock. In such case, the employee realizes ordinary income equal to the excess of the fair market value of the stock on the date of receipt over the amount, if any, paid for the stock. Any appreciation in the stock occurring after the date of receipt is then eligible for capital gains treatment.

STOCK APPRECIATION RIGHTS

A stock appreciation right (SAR) is a right to be paid an amount equal to the difference between the value of a share of an employer's stock on the date the SAR is granted and the value of that share on the date the SAR is exercised. SARs are frequently granted in conjunction with stock options and often require that the underlying option be exercised as a condition for the exercise of the SAR. Payments under SARs can be made in cash or in employer stock. The tax treatment of SARs is generally the same as the tax treatment of NQSOs.

PERFORMANCE UNIT PLANS

Awards under performance unit plans are usually contingent upon the attainment of corporate performance goals within a specified period of time, such as a specified increase in the market share of the employer or improvement in the performance of the employer relative to a group of competitors.

Participation in a performance unit plan generally is limited to senior executives in a position to have a direct impact upon the employer's success. Eligible employees are awarded a specified number of units valued at a designated dollar amount. The period for measuring performance usually ranges from three to five years. If the goals of the plan are achieved, the employee receives the difference between the value of the unit on the date that it was awarded to the employee and the value of the unit at the end of the performance period. Payment is usually made in cash. An employee granted a performance unit is generally not subject to tax until amounts are actually paid out under the plan.

OTHER BENEFIT ARRANGEMENTS

Other employee benefits may be provided by an employer, including additional incentive arrangements for executives such as bonus plans, phantom stock plans, junior stock plans, delta stock plans, and convertible debenture plans.

Intellectual Property

Chapter Outline

Summary

Businesses often own valuable intangible assets referred to as "intellectual property." These assets may consist of trade secrets, trademarks, and patentable or copyrightable technology. Federal and state laws provide protection to owners of intellectual property in various circumstances. The following chart summarizes the protections of trade secrets, trademarks, patents, and copyrights.

CHART: SUMMARY OF INTELLECTUAL PROPERTY

	Protectable Subject Matter	**Available Protections**
Trade Secrets	Virtually any information, including ideas	Right to prevent disclosure or use of information
Trademarks	Words, names, symbols, or devices	Right to prevent others from using same or similar marks to identify merchandise
Patents	Machines, processes, or compositions of matter	Right to exclude all others from making, using, importing, offering to sell, or selling patented invention
Copyrights	Literary works, musical works, artistic works, and computer software	Right to prevent others from reproducing copyrighted work; exclusive right to distribute copyrighted work

Eligibility for Protection	Commencement of Protection	Duration of Protection
Information must not be known or must not be readily ascertainable by proper means by other persons; information must also be the object of reasonable efforts under the circumstances to maintain its confidentiality	On creation	Until legitimate and proper discovery by another
Use of the mark to adequately distinguish one's goods or services; registration may provide enhanced protectability	On use of the trademark	So long as properly used as a trademark
Novelty, nonobviousness, and utility	When granted by the U.S. government	20 years from filing date of patent application; with respect to design patents, 14 years from date granted
Tangible form of expression and originality	On creation	Life of the author plus 50 years as respect to works made for hire, 75 years from publication, or 100 years from creation, whichever expires first

TRADE SECRETS

IN GENERAL

Manufacturing businesses and other businesses may possess commercially sensitive information. The ability to benefit from such information and yet keep the information secret from competitors is a common business objective. Substantial protections are available if the information is a "trade secret."

REQUIREMENTS OF A "TRADE SECRET"

Among items of information characterized as trade secrets have been manufacturing processes, product specifications, employee training manuals, computer programs, data bases, marketing plans, financial statements, and customer lists.

There are two requirements for business information to qualify as a "trade secret." One essential is that the information must not be generally known or readily ascertainable by proper means by other persons.

The second requirement is that reasonable efforts must be made to maintain the secrecy of the information. The holder of the trade secret must take affirmative steps to safeguard confidentiality. There are no specific actions that must be taken, but the following should be considered:

- Advise employees through an employee manual or other writing of the employer's policy regarding protection of trade secrets

- Require employees who have access to trade secrets to sign confidentiality agreements

- Physically separate trade secret information from other information

- Install locks on gates and doors leading to areas where trade secrets are housed

- Label trade secret documents clearly with a proprietary notice and instruct employees as to the significance of the notice

- Restrict access by use of password codes to access computer systems used to store trade secrets

UNIFORM TRADE SECRETS ACT

Arizona and approximately 30 other states have adopted the Uniform Trade Secrets Act (the Act). Under the Act a person who obtains a trade secret through improper means such as theft, bribery, misrepresentation, or espionage, or a person who obtains a trade secret from another, if such person has reason to know that the trade secret was obtained by improper means, can be enjoined or sued for substantial damages. Legal action may be taken under the Act against competitors, employees, suppliers, partners, and virtually any other person or entity who seeks to disclose or use another's trade secret improperly.

TRADEMARKS

IN GENERAL

A trademark is often used by a manufacturer to identify its merchandise and to distinguish its merchandise from items manufactured by others. A trademark can be a word, a name, a number, a slogan, a symbol, a device, or a combination.

A *trademark* should not be confused with a *tradename*. Although the same designation may function as both a trademark and a tradename, a tradename refers to a business title or the name of a business; a trademark is used to identify the goods manufactured by the business.

SELECTION OF TRADEMARK

A manufacturer should carefully consider the trademark selected for its merchandise. The level of protection against infringement of a trademark varies with the "strength" or "uniqueness" of the trademark. "Descriptive" marks are the weakest and least defensible. A descriptive trademark is a name that describes some characteristic, function, or quality of the goods. A "fanciful" mark, the strongest type of mark, is a coined name that has no dictionary definition.

Evaluation should also include consideration of the likelihood of success in obtaining federal and state registrations of the trademark. For example, a trademark that is "merely descriptive" cannot be registered under either federal or Arizona law.

Selection of a trademark should be accompanied by a trademark search to determine whether another manufacturer has already adopted or used a mark that is the same or similar to the one desired. Publications provide lists of existing trademarks, registered and unregistered, and there are businesses that specialize in trademark searches. Actual and potential trademark conflicts should be avoided, lest the manufacturer become involved in an expensive infringement lawsuit. Of even greater concern is the potential loss of the right to use a mark after considerable expenditure in advertising merchandise bearing the mark.

Advantages of Trademark Registration

Under the trademark laws of the United States and Arizona, the principal method of establishing rights in a trademark is actual use of the trademark. "Registration" of a trademark is not legally required but can provide certain advantages.

Federal registration of a trademark is presumptive evidence of the ownership of the trademark and of the registrant's exclusive right to use of the mark in interstate commerce, strengthening the registrant's ability to prevail in any infringement action. After five years of continued use of the mark following federal registration the registrant's exclusive right to use the trademark becomes virtually conclusive. Federal registration may assist in preventing the importation into the United States of foreign goods that bear an infringing trademark. There are also other less tangible advantages of registration, such as the goodwill arising out of the implication of government approval of the trademark.

State registration provides some advantages, not as extensive as federal registration. State registration is usually advisable, particularly in situations in which a manufacturer's sales will occur only in Arizona.

Federal Registration Application Process

Federal trademark registration requires that a trademark application be filed with the U.S. Patent and Trademark Office. The application must identify the mark and the goods with which the mark is used or is proposed to be used and must be accompanied by payment of the requisite fee. After the application is filed it is reviewed by an examiner who evaluates, among other matters, the substantive ability of the mark to serve as a valid mark and the possibility of confusion with existing marks. If the examiner rejects the application, the examiner's decision can be appealed to the Trademark Trial and Appeals Board. An adverse decision by that body can be appealed to federal court.

If the application is approved, the mark is published in an official publication of the Patent and Trademark Office. Opponents of the registration have 30 days after publication, or such additional time as may be granted, to challenge the registration. If no opposition is raised, or if the opponent's claims are rejected, an applicant whose mark is already in use receives a "certificate of registration." An applicant whose trademark is proposed before use receives for future use a "notice of allowance."

An applicant who receives a notice of allowance must within six months of the receipt of the notice furnish evidence of the *actual use* of the trademark. The applicant then is entitled to a certificate of registration. Failure to furnish evidence of the actual use of the mark within the time allowed results in rejection of the application.

POST-CERTIFICATE FEDERAL PROCEDURES

A certificate of trademark registration issued by the Patent and Trademark Office remains in effect for 10 years. Registration expires at the end of six years unless the registrant furnishes evidence of continued use of the trademark. The initial 10-year term of a certificate of registration can be renewed within the term's last six months for an additional 10-year term by furnishing evidence of continued use of the mark and paying a fee.

After at least five years of continuous use of a trademark following the receipt of a certificate of registration, a registrant can seek to have the status of the trademark elevated from "presumptive" evidence of the registrant's exclusive right to use of the trademark to virtually conclusive evidence of an exclusive right. To do so the registrant must furnish the Patent and Trademark Office with evidence of continuous use of the trademark for at least five years. Additionally, there must not be any outstanding lawsuit or claim that challenges the registrant's rights to use the mark.

State Registration Application Process

Arizona trademark registration law requires that a trademark application be filed with the Arizona Secretary of State. The application must identify the mark and the goods with which the mark is used and must be accompanied by the requisite fee. In contrast to registration of a mark under federal law, the mark must actually be in use before an Arizona registration application can be filed. If the trademark application is approved, the applicant receives a certificate of registration. A certificate of registration has an initial 10-year term and can be renewed indefinitely for successive 10-year terms.

Markings

Before receipt of a certificate of registration the designation "TM" can be used in association with the trademark. After a federal certificate of registration has been obtained, merchandise can be marked "Reg. U.S. Pat. Off.," or with "Registered in the U.S. Patent and Trademark Office," or with an encircled "R" or some similar designation to reflect that the trademark has been federally registered. Marking is not required, but proof of marking may be necessary to recover damages in an infringement action.

Tradenames

Arizona provides separate registration of tradenames with the Arizona Secretary of State. The application is simple. The registration remains in effect for five years and may be renewed for successive five year terms. The Secretary of State will not register any tradename if it might mislead the public or is not readily distinguishable from names, titles, or designations previously registered and still in effect, or if it is the same as, or deceptively similar to, an existing corporate name or corporate name which has been reserved.

PATENTS

IN GENERAL

One who invents or discovers a new machine or device or a new manufacturing process may be able to obtain a U.S. patent. A U.S. patent provides the inventor with the exclusive right for a specified time to make, use, import, offer to sell, or sell in the United States the patented invention. A patent provides the holder with a limited monopoly on the use of the patented invention. A valid patent forecloses use of the patented invention by any other party, even if another party independently conceives the identical invention.

A utility patent, which generally covers the functional aspects of a machine, manufacturing process, or composition of matter is enforceable beginning at the grant of the patent and ending 20 years (plus up to 5 more years for certain delays) after the filing date of the regular patent application. A design patent, which covers the design or appearance of an article of manufacture, is enforceable for 14 years from the granting date of the patent. A provisional patent, which is filed before a regular patent application, establishes a priority filing date and provides up to twelve months to further develop the invention without filing a regular patent application. Anyone without authority from the patent holder who makes, uses, imports, or sells in the United States the patented invention during the life of the patent is considered to "infringe" the patent and may be liable for damages.

Effect of Foreign Patents

A foreign patent is generally not enforceable in the United States. Furthermore, an invention that is the subject of a foreign patent cannot be the subject of a U.S. patent, unless an application for a U.S. patent is filed within one year following issuance of the foreign patent. Accordingly, an inventor who holds a foreign patent and who fails to apply for a U.S. patent within one year from the date of the issuance of a foreign patent will usually have no recourse against others who use the invention in the United States.

Requirements of Patentability

Three requirements govern patentability in the United States of a particular invention. First, an invention must be "novel." An invention is novel if it has not previously been known or used by others in the United States, nor patented, nor described elsewhere. Second, the invention must be "nonobvious." An invention is nonobvious if it could not have been conceived by a person with ordinary skill in the field to which the invention pertains. Third, the invention must have "utility." An invention has utility if it is useful and is capable of performing the function claimed by the patent.

In order to determine novelty and, hence, patentability of an invention, it is often useful to search the records of the U.S. Patent and Trademark Office. There one may examine all U.S. patents, many foreign patents, and a large number of technical publications. A patent search is customarily performed by a patent attorney or by an individual with similar technical training, sometimes referred to as a patent agent. A patent attorney or patent agent may be asked to render an opinion regarding the patentability of a particular invention. An inventor can then make an informed decision as to whether to proceed with the cost of an actual patent application.

Patent Application Process

A U.S. patent application must be filed with the U.S. Patent and Trademark Office. A complete patent application includes four elements. First, the application must include the "specification." The specification is a description of what the invention is and what it does. The specification can be filed in a foreign language, provided that an English translation, verified by a certified translator, is filed within a prescribed period. Second, the application must include an oath or declaration. The oath or declaration certifies that the inventor believes himself or herself to be the first and original inventor. If the inventor does not understand English, the oath or declaration must be in a language that the inventor understands. Third, the application must include drawings, if essential to an understanding of the invention. Fourth, the appropriate fee must be included.

After a proper application is filed, the application is assigned to an examiner with knowledge of the particular subject matter. The examiner makes a thorough review of the application and the status of existing concepts in the relevant area to determine whether the invention meets the requirements of patentability. The patent review process takes from 18 months to three years.

Rejection of a patent application by the examiner may be appealed to the Board of Patent Appeals. Decisions of the Board of Patent Appeals may be appealed to the federal courts.

Provisional patent application requirements are less stringent than a regular patent application. The oath or declaration of the inventor and claims are not required and the application is held for the 12 month period without examination.

Markings

After a patent application has been filed, the product made in accordance with the invention may be marked with the legend "patent pending" or "patent applied for." After a patent is issued, products may be marked "patented" or "pat.," together with the

U.S. patent number. Marking is not required, but it may be necessary to prove marking in order to recover damages in an infringement action.

Rights to Patented Inventions

Disputes sometimes arise between employers and employees over the rights to inventions made by employees during the course of employment. Because of this, employers often require employees to execute formal agreements under which each signing employee agrees that all rights to any invention made by the employee during the term of employment will belong to the employer.

Copyrights

In General

Copyright law provides the author of a copyrightable work (or such person's employer in the case of a "work made for hire") with exclusive rights to use, distribute, modify, and display the work. Generally, works are entitled to copyright protection for the life of the author plus 50 years. However, as to works made for hire, copyright protection is for the shorter of 75 years after publication or 100 years after creation. Anyone who without authority exercises the rights reserved exclusively to the copyright owner is considered to infringe the copyright and may be liable for damages.

Copyrightable Works

Works of authorship that qualify for copyright protection include literary works, musical works, pictorial, graphic and sculptural works, sound recordings, and architectural works. The Computer Software Copyright Act of 1980 expressly made computer software eligible for copyright protection, a point previously in doubt. The precise scope of copyright protection for computer software has not yet been fully defined. Constantly developing technology is likely to present many new issues, presently unforeseen.

All works eligible for copyright protection must meet two specific requirements. First, the work must be fixed in some tangible form; there must be a physical embodiment of the work so that the work can be reproduced or otherwise communicated. Second, the work must be the result of original and independent authorship. The concept of originality does not require that the work entail novelty or ingenuity, concepts of importance to patentability.

ADVANTAGES OF COPYRIGHT REGISTRATION

Copyright protection automatically attaches to a work the moment that the work is created. However, "registration" of the work with the U.S. Office of Copyrights provides advantages. A certificate of registration is prima facie evidence of the validity of the copyright, provided registration occurs not later than five years after first publication. With respect to works whose country of origin is the United States, registration is a prerequisite to an action for infringement. With respect to all works, regardless of the country of origin, certain damages and attorneys' fees relating to the period prior to registration cannot be recovered in an infringement action. Registration also is a useful means of providing actual notice of copyright to those who search the copyright records.

COPYRIGHT REGISTRATION APPLICATION PROCESS

In order to obtain registration of copyright, an application for registration must be filed with the U.S. Copyright Office. The application must be made on the specific form prescribed by the Register of Copyrights and must include the name and address of the copyright claimant, the name and nationality of the author, the title of the work, the year in which creation of the work was completed, and the date and location of the first publication. In the case of a work made for hire, a statement to that effect must be included. If the copyright claimant is not the author, a brief statement regarding how the claimant obtained ownership of the copyright must be included. An application must be accompanied by the requisite fee, and a copy of the work must be submitted.

COPYRIGHT NOTICE

Until 1989, all publicly distributed copies of works protected by copyright and published by the authority of the copyright owner were required to bear a notice of copyright. A copyright notice is no longer mandatory, but a copyright notice is still advantageous. For example, the defense of "innocent infringement" is generally unavailable to an alleged infringer if a copyright notice is used.

If a copyright notice is used, the notice should be located in such a manner and location to sufficiently demonstrate the copyright claim. The notice should consist of three elements. First should be the symbol of an encircled "C," or the word "copyright," or the abbreviation "copr." Second should be the year of first publication. Third should be the name of the copyright owner.

WORKS MADE FOR HIRE

In a "work made for hire" the employer is presumed to be the author. Authorship is significant because a copyright initially vests in the author. The parties can rebut the presumption of employer authorship by an express written agreement to the contrary.

The term "work made for hire" applies to any work created by an employee in the course and scope of employment. On occasion there is dispute as to whether a work created by an employee arose from the employment. Employers often require execution of a formal employment agreement under which the employee expressly agrees that all copyright rights will belong to the employer. A similar agreement is also advisable in connection with the engagement of an independent contractor to perform copyrightable services for a business.

COPYRIGHT PROTECTION FOR FOREIGN AUTHORS

Copyright protection is available under U.S. law for foreign authors until the copyrightable work is published. If the work has been published, the availability of continued U.S. copyright protection is dependent upon the location of the publication and the nationality or domicile of the author. Copyright protection continues in the United States subsequent to publication if publication by the foreign author occurs in the United States, or occurs in a country that is a party to the Universal Copyright Convention or to the Berne Convention, or occurs in a country named in a Presidential copyright proclamation. If the work is first published by a foreign author outside the United States, continued copyright protection in the United States is available only if the foreign author is either a domiciliary of the United States or a national or domiciliary of a country that is a party to a copyright treaty to which the United States is also a party. A person is generally a domiciliary of the country in which the person resides with the intention to remain permanently.

PRODUCT LIABILITY

CHAPTER OUTLINE

SUMMARY

Arizona's product liability law developed through the common law until 1978, when the Legislature enacted a package of product liability statutes. The discussion that follows is a summary of basic Arizona product liability law.

THEORIES

In Arizona, a product liability action can be pursued under theories of strict liability, negligence, and breach of warranty. The strict liability theory is rooted in the Restatement (Second) of Torts, § 402(A). The negligence theory is an outgrowth of the traditional negligence tort. The breach of express warranty theory is still available, but the breach of *implied* warranty theory has been replaced by the strict liability theory. Because strict liability is typically the plaintiff's theory of choice, the discussion that follows focuses primarily on strict liability.

Arizona statutes broadly define the claims that can be asserted in a product liability action:

> 'Product liability action' means any action brought against a manufacturer or seller of a product for damages for bodily injury, death or property damage caused by or resulting from the manufacture, construction, design, formula, installation, preparation, assembly, testing, packaging, labeling, sale, use or consumption of any product, the failure to

warn or protect against a danger or hazard in the use or misuse of the product or the failure to provide proper instructions for the use or consumption of any product.

The American Law Institute is currently drafting the Restatement (Third) of Torts: Product Liability. Although the Restatement is not itself law, Arizona courts usually follow the Restatement when not inconsistent with Arizona statutes or public policy. Arizona courts are likely to follow the Restatement (Third). If Arizona courts do so, some of the following information will be materially changed or modified.

PARTIES POTENTIALLY LIABLE

Potentially liable parties include manufacturers, sellers, and commercial lessors. A "manufacturer" is a person or entity that designs, assembles, fabricates, produces, constructs, or otherwise prepares a product or component part of a product prior to its sale to a user or consumer, including a seller owned in whole or significant part by the manufacturer, or a seller owning the manufacturer in whole or significant part.

A "seller" includes a person or entity, including a wholesaler, distributor, retailer, or lessor engaged in the business of leasing any product or in the business of selling any product for consumption, use, or resale. Those potentially liable include sellers of used products. A successor corporation may be held liable for "all the liabilities and obligations" of corporations merged or consolidated.

A trademark licensor can be held strictly liable for personal injuries caused by a defective product put into the stream of commerce by a trademark licensee. While not all licensors would be subject to strict liability, the courts closely examine the degree of control possessed by the trademark licensor in deciding whether to apply strict liability to a licensor.

Type of Defects

There are three general types of defects that form the basis for most product liability actions in Arizona, "manufacturing defects," "design defects," and "informational defects." Each of these alleged defects can be presented under either a negligence or a strict liability theory.

Manufacturing Defect

A product has a manufacturing defect if it "contains a danger which the manufacturer did not intend and the customer did not expect." Typically, a manufacturing defect claim involves an aspect of the product that does not meet the manufacturer's specifications.

Design Defect

Arizona has a "two prong" test for design defects. The Arizona approach is very similar to the approach followed in several other states. A difficult issue is determining which test should apply.

The "Consumer Expectation" Test

The first approach for determining whether a product may have a design defect analyzes the safety of the product based on the expectations of the "average consumer." This test of defectiveness provides that the product is defective and unreasonably dangerous if it fails to perform as safely as an ordinary consumer would expect when the product is used in a reasonably foreseeable manner.

A problem with determining when this test should be applied is the question of whether the average consumer has enough knowledge to form a reasonable expectation concerning how safe the product should be.

The consumer expectation approach is generally considered to be "pro-plaintiff." Nevertheless, the test has been criticized by plaintiffs because it would bar recovery in cases in which the danger is within the reasonable expectations of the consumer, even though the manufacturer could have reasonably reduced or eliminated the risk. Arizona arguably follows the rule that a plaintiff may not recover when the danger was known to plaintiff, even though the product could feasibly have been made safer, a rule considered "pro-defendant."

THE "RISK-BENEFIT" TEST

The second test for defectiveness focuses on the design from the viewpoint of the manufacturer and examines the reasonableness of the design choice by the manufacturer rather than examining the expectations of the consumer. In those cases when the consumer expectation test fails to provide a complete answer, Arizona law permits the use of either a combined test or the risk-benefit test alone.

Under the risk-benefit test the jury is instructed that it must determine whether a reasonable manufacturer or seller who had knowledge of the dangerous characteristics of the product would continue to market the product without changing the design. The jury is also told that the manufacturer or seller is presumed to know the harmful characteristics of the product, whether it actually knows them or not.

Arizona jury instructions provide the following list of specific factors to consider under the risk-benefit analysis. The jury may consider these factors in evaluating the reasonableness of the manufacturer's design choice:

- The usefulness and desirability of the product

- The availability of other and safer products to meet the same need

- The likelihood of injury and its probable seriousness

- The obviousness of the danger

- Common knowledge and normal public expectations of the danger

- The avoidability of injury by care in use of the product, including the effect of instructions or warnings

- The ability to eliminate the danger without seriously impairing the usefulness of the product or making it unduly expensive.

The jury is permitted to decide what is a reasonable design, based on common experience, if the factual issues are within the common understanding of jurors. But expert testimony is almost always required to support a plaintiff's strict liability or negligence claims because of the engineering expertise involved in product design that goes beyond common understanding.

If the case is presented to the jury as a *strict liability* case, the manufacturer or seller is charged with knowledge of "the facts the trial has just revealed about the harmful characteristics of the product's design." The effect is that the reasonableness of the manufacturer's design choice is measured not only by the information available at the time the product was designed and distributed (as in a negligence case), but also by the field experience of the product *since* that time, including other injuries, claims, and lawsuits. In essence, everything known about the product through the trial is presented to the jury, and the jury is instructed to consider the product's entire history in deciding whether the product is adequately safe to be sold today. If the answer is "yes," then the product is not defective. If the answer is "no," then the product is defective, unless the manufacturer proves that the knowledge of design alternatives has occurred subsequent to the date the product was manufactured due to technological advances in the "state of the art."

If, however, the case is presented as a *negligence case*, the manufacturer's design choices are examined under the state of knowledge which existed at the time the product was *designed*. This fundamental difference between the two theories results in the plaintiff usually choosing a strict liability theory rather than a negligence theory.

INFORMATIONAL DEFECT

A warning is required if without the warning the use of the product for its intended or reasonably foreseeable use causes the product to be dangerous to an extent beyond that contemplated by the ordinary consumer possessing the knowledge common to the community of the product's characteristics. The product may be found to be defective even though faultlessly made, if the product is unreasonably dangerous to sell without a suitable warning.

At one time it was thought to be inconsistent for a complaint to allege both that the product was defective because it was not properly designed and also that it was properly designed but defective because it lacked adequate warnings. The inconsistency was found by the Arizona Supreme Court to be acceptable pleading. Today a plaintiff is not required to make an election but may proceed "in the alternative," even though the claims are inconsistent.

There are three elements that must be proven by the plaintiff in a "warnings" (informational defect) case: first, that the defendant had duty to warn of the dangerous propensity of the product (that it was defective and unreasonably dangerous without the warnings); second, that the product lacked the warnings; third, that the failure to give required warnings caused the injuries.

When a warning is required it must be reasonably readable and it must sufficiently apprise a consumer, exercising reasonable care under the circumstances, of the existence and seriousness of the danger to enable the consumer to protect against it. Instructions for use are not an adequate substitute for warnings. Warnings are required if failure to follow instructions may pose a substantial risk of harm to the user.

When a warning is required a manufacturer has a duty to warn all reasonably foreseeable users of the product. This requires that a manufacturer use care not only to anticipate who might likely be exposed to the dangers of its product but also to provide a warning that will be effective as to those users. In the pharmaceutical context, a manufacturer of certain drugs has the duty to warn prescribing physicians of the risks of the drug.

The Arizona appellate courts have been among the more liberal courts in extending liability in warning cases. A defendant may be liable even if the evidence indicates that a warning would not have been read and heeded by the injured plaintiff, if there is evidence that warning might have caused some other person (such as the plaintiff's employer) to take action that would have lessened the danger to the plaintiff.

In Arizona the duty to warn is a continuing duty that extends past the time of sale and includes an obligation to warn of dangers that the manufacturer discovers after the initial sale of the product.

DEFENSES

THE PRODUCT IS NOT DEFECTIVE UNDER REASONABLY FORESEEABLE USES

A manufacturer has no duty to make a product that incorporates only the ultimate in safety features. However, the product must not be unreasonably dangerous for reasonably foreseeable use. The fact of an injury, death, or other damage arising from the use of a product does not, standing alone, establish that the product is defective. In order for the defendant to be liable, the product must be found to be both defective and unreasonably dangerous under either the consumer-expectations or the risk-benefit test. The fact that a different type of design or safeguard is available does not, by itself, establish that the product is defective.

The Defect Did Not Cause the Accident or the Injury

A defect in a product does not render the manufacturer or seller liable for the plaintiff's damages unless the defect caused either the accident or the damages. Product defectiveness can act in combination with other causes to be the proximate cause of the injury. A defendant is not relieved of liability simply because the defendant could not have foreseen the manner in which the accident occurred, even though there may have been negligent intervention of third parties.

The Accident or Injury Was Caused by Unforeseeable Alteration or Modification of the Product

A defendant is not liable if the defendant proves that the proximate cause of the incident giving rise to the action was an alteration or modification of the product, not reasonably foreseeable, made by a person other than the defendant after the product was first sold by the defendant. A reasonably foreseeable alteration or modification of a product is one expected of an ordinary and prudent purchaser, user, or consumer and one that an ordinary and prudent manufacturer should have anticipated.

Once a defendant comes forward with evidence of substantial change, the burden shifts to the plaintiff to show that the change did not cause the accident. Evidence of a substantial change raises a fact question for the jury as to whether the change was a superseding intervening cause of the plaintiff's injuries.

The Accident or Injury Was Caused By Unforeseeable Misuse

Another defense in a product liability action is "misuse," which involves proving that the proximate cause of the incident giving rise to the action was a use or consumption for a purpose, in a manner, or in an activity, other than that which was reasonably foreseeable, or was a use contrary to express and adequate instructions or warnings appearing on, or attached to, the product or on its original container or wrapping, if the injured person knew, or with the exercise of reasonable and diligent care should have known, of such instructions or warnings.

Because the "misuse" defense is an affirmative defense, the burden of proof is on the defendant. This defense is not a complete defense; it is subject to the comparative fault system. A plaintiff's misuse of a product is a fault apportioned by the jury. However, the jury may still allocate part of the damages to the manufacturer even if the product was misused. Not all abnormal uses of the product constitute legal misuse. In order for the defense to apply, the misuse must be of a nature that was not reasonably foreseeable. The defense of misuse should not be confused with the defense of contributory negligence. Misuse is an available defense to a strict liability action; contributory negligence is not.

The Design of the Product Complied With the State of the Art

A defendant is not liable if the defendant proves that the plans or design for the product and the methods and techniques of manufacturing, inspecting, testing, and labeling the product conformed to the state of the art at the time the product was first sold by the defendant.

The "state of the art" defense in certain cases provides an escape hatch from liability for injury from a product that would be judged defective through use of a hindsight test. This defense prevents a product from being found defective when it could not have been made any safer under the state of technology that existed at the time the product was manufactured. "State of the art" is defined as:

> The technical, mechanical and scientific knowledge of manufacturing, designing, testing or labeling the same or similar products which was in existence and reasonably feasible for use at the time of manufacture.

State of the art is not the same standard as "industry custom." Industry custom refers to the practices and standards of an industry at a particular time. State of the art is concerned with what feasibly could have been done in light of available technology and scientific knowledge at the point in time when the product was put into production. Evidence of industry standards, customs, and practices is admissible, as is evidence of compliance with federal and other regulatory standards, to assist in determining the state of the art at a given time, but, without more, such evidence does not necessarily establish the state of the art at the time of original manufacture.

In many jurisdictions compliance with the state of the art is only non-conclusive evidence on the issue of whether the product was defective. However, in Arizona compliance with the state of the art is a complete defense. For this reason it is particularly important that the defendant always be prepared to prove, if possible, that the product was designed as safely as the technology permitted at the time of manufacture.

THE PLAINTIFF ASSUMED THE RISK OF INJURY

Unlike contributory negligence, assumption of the risk remains a valid defense to a product liability action in Arizona. However, evidentiary standards weaken this defense. In order to prove that a plaintiff "assumed the risk," there must be clear evidence not only that plaintiff had specific knowledge of the danger but also that plaintiff knew the specific foreseeable consequences of using the product in the manner which caused the injury. This question is virtually always a question for the jury. Additionally, there are many cases which hold that even when the danger of a product is appreciated circumstances may cause it to be momentarily forgotten.

Because the "assumption of the risk" defense is an affirmative defense, the burden of proof is on the defendant. Additionally, although no Arizona court has explicitly held that "assumption of the risk" is a comparative defense in lieu of a complete defense, language from an Arizona Supreme Court decision lends support to this conclusion.

"Assumption of the risk" is not the same as "product misuse." Assumption of the risk focuses on the conduct of the plaintiff. Product misuse focuses on the product. Product misuse may well exist even though the defense of assumption of the risk cannot be established.

PROCEDURE AND EVIDENCE

STATUTE OF LIMITATIONS

Product liability tort actions must be commenced within two years after the cause of action accrues. Arizona courts have held that a cause of action for personal injury "accrues" when a plaintiff discovers, or by the exercise of reasonable diligence should have discovered, that the injury was related to a defendant's conduct. Consequently, the principal statute of limitations issue is whether the plaintiff had notice of a possible relationship between the injury and a product defect more than two years before filing suit.

STATUTORY INDEMNIFICATION

A manufacturer may be required to indemnify a product seller. Indemnification includes the amount of any judgment and reasonable attorneys' fees and costs incurred by the seller in defending the action. The rationale is that a seller which merely "passed through" the product to the consumer should not bear ultimate liability for injury due to a defect caused by the manufacturer.

Indemnification is not required if the seller had knowledge of the defect in the product, or if the seller without the manufacturer's authorization altered, modified, or installed the product, and the alteration was a substantial cause in the resulting injury.

When the seller is indemnified by the manufacturer, the plaintiff must first attempt to satisfy its judgment directly against the manufacturer. Failure of the manufacturer or its insurance carrier to satisfy the judgment upon demand will satisfy the plaintiff's duty to attempt first to collect from the manufacturer.

Similarly, a seller may be required to indemnify the manufacturer if the seller provided the product plans or specifications and they were a substantial cause of the product's alleged defect. A manufacturer cannot obtain indemnification from the seller if the manufacturer had knowledge or, with the exercise of reasonable and diligent care should have had knowledge, of the defect in the product.

COMPARATIVE FAULT AND SEVERAL LIABILITY

Arizona has adopted the "pure" comparative fault concept. To reduce the defendant's liabilities, wrongful conduct of non-parties may be considered by the jury. A finding of fault against

a non-party is considered only in determining the extent of the defendant's fault; it has no binding effect on the non-party.

Self-Critical Analysis Privilege

In 1995, Arizona passed a statute that makes evidence of product safety analyses or reviews, and any reasonable remedial measures taken pursuant to such analyses or reviews, inadmissible to prove negligence, that the product was defective or unreasonably dangerous, or other culpable conduct. Additionally, a plaintiff may not use such evidence to prove punitive damages unless the product safety analyses or reviews or reasonable remedial measures were done in bad faith or solely to affect litigation. However, a plaintiff may use the same evidence to prove feasibility of precautionary measures, to impeach, or to controvert any position taken by a defendant in litigation that is inconsistent with the contents of a product safety analysis, review, or reasonable remedial measures.

A product safety analysis or review is any investigation, inquiry, review, evaluation, or other means by which a person or entity seeks to determine, calculate, predict, estimate, evaluate, or report the safety or health effects of the use of any of its products, systems, services, or processes. Included within the definition is an analysis or review of component parts conducted by a component manufacturer. "Reasonable remedial measures" are actions, including recalls and changes in quality assurance procedures, taken as a result of a product safety analysis or review and intended to improve safety or to lessen the likelihood of safety-related accidents.

Other Accidents

Evidence of other accidents is inadmissible unless plaintiff proves that the other occurrence occurred under the "same or similar circumstances." This requires a substantial similarity between the products and circumstances surrounding each incident. Evidence of other similar "post accident" accidents through the date of trial is admissible.

Damages

Punitive Damages

An award of punitive damages is an extraordinary civil remedy, imposed only when a defendant's conduct falls into the "limited class of consciously malicious or outrageous acts of misconduct where punishment and deterrence is both paramount and likely to be achieved - it is the 'evil mind' that distinguishes actions justifying the imposition of punitive damages."

To justify the award of punitive damages, the plaintiff must prove by clear and convincing evidence both aggravated and outrageous conduct on the part of the defendant and that the defendant had an evil mind.

The "conduct" element requires plaintiff to establish that the defendant's conduct was aggravated or outrageous or that the harm suffered was significant. To satisfy the "evil mind" requirement, a plaintiff must establish either that the defendant actually intended to injure the plaintiff or that the defendant consciously pursued a course of conduct knowing that it created a substantial risk of harm to others. A manufacturer's failure because of profit considerations to make a design change that would have reduced the risk to human life has been held to be sufficient to support a punitive damage verdict.

Collateral Sources

As a general rule, evidence that a person was or was not insured against liability is not admissible evidence on the issue of whether the person acted negligently or otherwise wrongfully. Also, there is no credit or award reduction of any kind for insurance payments or other collateral source payments or benefits to the injured plaintiff. Evidence of the defendant's furnishing or offering to pay plaintiff's medical, hospital, or similar expenses occasioned by the injury is also not admissible. This bar includes all private insurance and workers' compensation payments.

Workers' Compensation

Employers who have paid workers' compensation benefits are not subject to suit by an employee injured by a job-connected accident, except under two specific exceptions. The first is when the injury is caused by the employer's willful misconduct, an act knowingly and purposely done with the direct object of injuring another. The second is when the employee rejects the compensation provided by workers' compensation and, as the law permits, retains the right to sue the employer.

Unless an employer is subject to suit under one of the exceptions, workers' compensation is the employee's exclusive remedy against the employer and bars employee recovery against the employer defendant in a product liability action. However, when the employee sues a third party, such as a manufacturer, the employer can still be named as a "non-party" for the purposes of determining the relative degrees of fault, thereby potentially reducing the manufacturer's exposure.

Even if the employee accepts workers' compensation coverage, if the employee is injured by a third party, other than the employer or a co-worker, the employee may proceed against the third party and receive compensation for medical, surgical, and hospital benefits. An insurer that pays workers' compensation benefits to an employee has a lien on the amount actually collected by the employee from the third party in order for the insurer to recapture compensation benefits the insurer paid the employee and so prevent double recovery by the employee.

Survival and Wrongful Death Actions

In Arizona, a personal injury action survives the death of either the injured person or the wrongdoer, except that upon the death of the injured person damages for pain and suffering are not allowed. Wrongful death actions are brought by the surviving spouse or by the decedent's personal representative probate. Either parent may maintain the action for the death of a child, and a guardian may do so for the death of a ward. Damages are distributed to the surviving spouse, children, or parents in proportion to their damages. A child unborn at the time of the death of the parent is included in the term "children" for whose benefit a wrongful death action may be maintained.

LOSS OF CONSORTIUM

Either spouse may maintain an action for loss of the other's consortium due to injuries caused by the defendant's fault. Arizona also allows parents to sue for the loss of an injured minor or adult child's consortium. In order for a parent to maintain this cause of action, the child must suffer a severe, permanent, or disabling injury that substantially interferes with the child's capacity to interact with the parents in a normally gratifying way. Although evidence of a significant interference in the parent-child relationship must exist, an injury need not be the functional equivalent of death, nor even be catastrophic.

Children can also maintain an action for the loss of an injured parent's consortium. In order for a child to recover, the parent's injury must be severe, permanent, or disabling.

LOSS PREVENTION & PROACTIVE LITIGATION MANAGEMENT

CHAPTER OUTLINE

SUMMARY

The preservation of company assets, the prevention of litigation, and the cost effective management of a lawsuit are fundamental objectives of any business enterprise. Loss prevention programs targeting information management, intellectual property, product safety, and litigation discovery are effective in achieving these objectives for the established business or the start up company. Corporate compliance programs aimed at preventing and detecting violations of applicable laws, regulations, and policies also further the loss prevention goals.

INFORMATION MANAGEMENT

INFORMATION RECORDING PRACTICES

An increasing number of lawsuits are "hot document" cases. Typically, it is the improvidence of the writer in the careless selection of a word, the use of jargon, insertion of a cliche, or mischaracterization of an event that becomes the central theme of the case. The first step to avoiding such a "haphazard paper trial" is the adoption of information recording practices that avoid the creation of hastily prepared documents. Similarly, to protect certain confidential documents and communications from public disclosure, even with the issuance of legal process, the use of appropriate information recording and document distribution practices is vital.

RECORD RETENTION PROGRAMS

Essential to every company is an effective and efficient system for managing company information to address business needs and satisfy legal obligations. A comprehensive and consistently applied record retention program, designed to fit the work environment, improves the storage, protection, retrieval, and disposition of paper and electronic business records.

Legal duties are imposed on a company from statutes, regulations, and the common law requiring the retention of business records. Specifically, the federal government regularly publishes a 500 page collection of record retention requirements. Every state, including Arizona, also has recordkeeping requirements that affect a wide range of business activities. Finally, the courts have developed standards governing the retention of certain types of information. For example, case law has extended record retention requirements for certain documents that are subject to civil discovery.

The manner in which documents are stored, the period of retention, the cost of storage, and retrieval are issues that affect efficiency and the bottom line. Record retention impacts these concerns by reducing the time and costs associated with space requirements, staff time, and equipment investment. Simply, while certain material must be stored, the warehousing of records no longer required for operational or legal purpose is an unnecessary and a wasteful expense.

A record retention program also offers a number of benefits during litigation. Initially, such a program ensures that the company has retained the documents necessary to support its position in the event of litigation. Furthermore, the courts have held that a record retention program is a defense to the allegation of discovery abuse and the claim that a company inappropriately discarded documents sought in litigation. In this regard, the law provides that a consistent, comprehensive, and reasonable record retention program is an acceptable explanation for the absence of otherwise relevant material.

PRE-LITIGATION DISCOVERY RESPONSE PLAN

The federal court and the Arizona state court have adopted civil litigation discovery disclosure rules that require the affirmative disclosure of documents by a party in a civil suit. This means that a company must be in a position to disclose documents that are relevant to the claims and defenses shortly after litigation is filed. Significant time and costs can be saved with a pre-litigation discovery response plan, developed in concert with the company's record retention program, to address the document disclosure obligations efficiently before litigation commences. Because this plan is integrated with existing company document practices, business interruption is minimized, and the time and expense required for document collection is reduced.

INTELLECTUAL PROPERTY AUDIT

INTELLECTUAL PROPERTY RIGHTS

In the rapidly expanding intellectual property arena, a company may not appreciate fully the value of its intellectual property assets or recognize the dilution of those rights by others. The first step in fully exploiting intellectual property holdings is a review of the company's patent, trade secret, copyright, trademark, and service mark holdings.

CORPORATE AGREEMENTS

A number of corporate agreements impact the intellectual property rights and liabilities of a company. A review of the employment, confidentiality, franchise, distributor, manufacturing, marketing, joint venture, licensing, option, and other commercial agreements bearing upon intellectual property or the rights they contain starts the process to ensure that the rights are protected.

INTELLECTUAL PROPERTY LIABILITIES

Conduct that potentially infringes upon the intellectual property rights of others may not be known to the company. To avoid claims of infringement or breach of contract, it is essential to determine if the intellectual property rights of others are being compromised, and if the company is being exposed to liability.

ACTION PLAN

To complete the audit cycle, an action plan that addresses how to maximize intellectual property assets, stop infringement by others, recoup damages, strengthen contractual intellectual property rights, and reduce liability exposure is essential.

PRODUCT SAFETY GUIDELINES

The "processes" employed by product manufacturers typically are attacked as deficient in product liability litigation. An analysis of the processes and resources employed during product design, development, marketing, and sales and the implementation of Product Safety Guidelines will protect these litigation targets.

PRODUCT DESIGN AND DEVELOPMENT

The design and development process is often scrutinized in product liability litigation. To avoid challenges to the adequacy of the process used to evaluate product safety, each step of the product development process should be analyzed carefully.

Product Warnings and Literature

Virtually every product liability lawsuit includes claims of defective warnings or instructions. An analysis of product owner's guides, maintenance manuals, and on-product warnings is prudent to repel attacks upon the product literature and the process through which product warnings and literature are developed.

Product Safety Related Communications

A carelessly recorded statement is powerful evidence in a product liability case. To enhance the accurate recording of opinions and corporate positions, a pre-publication review process for position papers, articles, speeches, service bulletins, recall notices, and dealer letters defuses this tactic.

Marketing and Advertising

Marketing and advertising materials are common sources for data, opinions, and slogans to argue that a company knew of certain risks or targeted inappropriate product consumers. To defeat these allegations, guidelines for the review of marketing and advertising materials are invaluable. The development of illustration and advertising guidelines help ensure uniformity.

Claims, Complaints & Concern Evaluations

Other accidents and claims form the foundation of "defect notice" that allegedly is ignored by the company. These charges can be addressed with guidelines for the processing and maintenance of product claim material and a feedback system to the engineering community to assure proper investigation of the claims.

Resource Library Assessment

Failure to follow mandatory regulations, standards, and voluntary recommended practices are the standard attacks upon a product design. An up-to-date resource library of government regulations, private standards or recommended practices, product-related publications, and safety-related reference materials can enhance product development and avoid these allegations.

Discovery Management

Effective Discovery Management

The efficient prosecution and defense of civil litigation requires the application of proven and practical state-of-the-art discovery services to meet ever-changing discovery challenges.

Disclosure Statements

Substantial savings can be realized if the document disclosure process is integrated with document management practices. This approach effectively minimizes business disruption, time, and the expense required for appropriate document identification and comprehensive collection. This use of a record retention program also furthers the accuracy of the disclosure statement and supports the contention that responsive information is properly disclosed.

Document Production

A significant reduction in document production costs and improved response consistency are essential in aggressive or complex litigation. State-of-the-art software and imaging technology linked together ensures efficient document retrieval, tracking, organization, analysis and production. The failure to take advantage of these technology advances places a company at a significant disadvantage.

WRITTEN RESPONSE PREPARATION

Consistent corporate discovery responses are mandatory to counter the warehousing and sharing of these responses by adverse networking organizations. The integration of document, testimony, and written discovery databases ensure response uniformity at reduced cost.

PRIVILEGED INFORMATION

The protection of privileged communications and confidential information requires the assertion of specific claims and evidentiary support. Proven techniques are available to present these claims to the court in a concise and legally sound posture. Failure to properly assert privileges can result in their waiver and the release of the confidential communication.

DISCOVERY TRACKING SYSTEM

Successful discovery preparation requires accuracy, consistency, and timeliness. The filing of discovery responses, production of documents, and submission of discovery motions should be monitored for timely completion. The courts will impose sanctions if discovery is untimely without sound justification.

Corporate Compliance Programs

Goals of Program

The term "Corporate Compliance Program" is used to describe an organization's formal statement of ethics, law, or policy to be followed by its employees and agents. Violations of these standards by employees or agents can result in civil lawsuits for an organization. Additionally, under the Federal Organizational Sentencing Guidelines enacted in 1991, criminal penalties may be imposed upon corporations, as well as their officers and directors, based upon the misconduct of the organization's employees or agents. An effective Compliance Program will increase the likelihood that an organization will prevent or detect acts of noncompliance. It also has the potential to reduce criminal penalties that an organization may face if problems do arise.

Development of Effective Compliance Program

The Federal Sentencing Guidelines outline the components of an effective compliance program. These elements, described below, must be addressed in a program for best practical results.

- **Scope and Objectives**

The first steps in creating an effective compliance program is to develop the scope and specific objectives of the program. The appropriate scope and objectives of the program can be determined through a needs assessment based on interviews with, or surveys of, pertinent individuals in the corporation.

- ## Written Code of Conduct and Administrative Procedures

The next step is to develop a written code of conduct and written administrative procedures for the corporation. The code should be easily comprehensible to all employees and agents. In particular, the definition of, and penalties for, misconduct should be clearly stated so that they are easily understood. All significant areas of law or regulation that could result in liability for the corporation should be addressed in the code.

- ## Supervision

The development of an infrastructure to support the compliance program once it is in place also is critical to its success. Compliance officers or committees should be organized to facilitate and enforce the compliance program. The compliance officer should be appointed to disseminate information to employees and agents and to answer their questions, monitor employees' and agents' activities, discipline employees and agents, update and revise the compliance program, and investigate and/or report acts of non-compliance.

- ## Reporting Mechanisms

Compliance programs must include clearly defined procedures by which employees and agents can report questionable conduct to management or law enforcement officials. They also should provide for internal investigation procedures and procedures for cooperating with any government investigations.

■ Monitoring and Auditing

Finally, the corporation should monitor and audit the program on an ongoing basis. Monitoring involves day-to-day review and oversight, and auditing involves project-oriented and periodic review by either internal or external auditors. Compliance programs must be reviewed and updated regularly to take account of new developments in the law or new activities in the corporation. If these steps are taken, a compliance program provides an effective loss prevention tool by allowing the corporation to detect or prevent employee or agent misconduct before problems arise.

ENVIRONMENTAL LAWS

CHAPTER OUTLINE

TANK CLOSURE REQUIREMENTS
LOCAL FIRE CODES
EMPLOYEE HAZARD COMMUNICATION
   LABELING OF HAZARDOUS CHEMICALS
   MATERIAL SAFETY DATA SHEETS
   EMPLOYEE INFORMATION AND TRAINING
   WRITTEN HAZARD COMMUNICATION
     PROGRAM
   EMERGENCY PLANNING AND COMMUNITY
   RIGHT-TO-KNOW ACT
   EMERGENCY PLANNING REPORTING
   CHEMICAL INVENTORY
   EMERGENCY NOTIFICATION
   TOXIC CHEMICAL RELEASE REPORTING
SUPERFUND LAWS
   IN GENERAL
   INNOCENT PURCHASER DEFENSE
ENVIRONMENTAL ASSESSMENTS AND
   ALLOCATION OF LIABILITIES

SUMMARY

The diversity and vitality of Arizona's natural environment are key elements of the quality of life in the state. Arizona is widely recognized as having an efficient and workable balance between environmental and developmental objectives. The state's environmental agency works closely with business to foster growth with minimal environmental impairment.

There are three sources of environmental regulation in Arizona: federal, primarily through the U.S. Environmental Protection Agency (EPA); state, through the Arizona Department of Environmental Quality (ADEQ); and local, through certain cities and counties.

AIR POLLUTION CONTROL

GENERAL REQUIREMENTS UNDER THE CLEAN AIR ACT

Under the Clean Air Act (as substantially amended in 1990) the EPA has established air quality standards and timetables for achieving compliance with those standards. The EPA sets minimum air quality levels for "regulated pollutants," which include "criteria pollutants" such as particulates, carbon monoxide, ozone, nitrogen dioxide, lead, and sulphur dioxide, and "hazardous pollutants," such as asbestos and other toxic air emissions.

A variety of programs have been adopted under the Clean Air Act to achieve and maintain air quality standards. A permit must be obtained before a business can construct or modify a plant or other facility that emits regulated pollutants into the air. Standards governing the issuance of air quality permits differ, depending upon whether or not the specific area of the plant or facility has achieved compliance with applicable air quality standards. Areas that have met these standards are referred to as "attainment areas." Areas that have not are referred to as "non-attainment areas."

ATTAINMENT AREAS

In attainment areas a permit is required before a business can construct or modify a facility with the potential to emit one hundred or more tons per year of a regulated pollutant. To obtain a permit the owner or operator must provide for control of emissions by the "best available control technology." The owner or operator must also perform a preconstruction review that demonstrates that the operation of the facility will not result in a significant deterioration of air quality. Whether a facility will "significantly deteriorate" air quality is determined under a classification system that divides attainment areas in the United States into various regions with differing standards of permissible emissions. Increases in pollution are severely restricted in "Class I" regions, which are regions with pristine wilderness or national parks. In Arizona, the Grand Canyon area is a Class I region in which development is effectively precluded. Increases in pollution to facilitate "moderate growth" are permitted in "Class II" regions. All attainment areas in Arizona other than the area surrounding the Grand Canyon are Class II regions.

Non-Attainment Areas

In non-attainment areas the goal is to prevent new or modified construction from interfering with the achievement of air quality standards. Issuance of a permit to construct or modify a plant or facility in a non-attainment area is subject to more rigorous standards than the standards applicable in attainment areas. Issuance of a permit in a non-attainment area is conditioned upon the installation of pollution control equipment that results in the "lowest achievable emissions rate." The owner or operator of a proposed major plant or facility in a non-attainment area must demonstrate that the benefits of the proposed plant or facility "significantly" outweigh environmental and social harms.

The state's most populous county, Maricopa County, which includes the city of Phoenix, has been classified as a non-attainment area for carbon monoxide, particulates, and ozone. The state's second most populous county, Pima County, which includes the city of Tucson, has been classified as a non-attainment area for carbon monoxide and particulates.

New Source Performance Requirements Under the Clean Air Act

The Clean Air Act provides "source performance standards" that apply to new plants or facilities. Although all major sources of air pollution are required to meet minimal air quality standards, the new-source performance standards, which apply in attainment areas as well as non-attainment areas, are designed to ensure that new facilities are built with state of the art pollution control technology. Each source performance standard sets performance criteria for a specific source. To date there are approximately 60 source performance standards, including standards for incinerators, stationary gas turbines, fossil fuel-fired steam generators, and asphalt concrete plants.

State Requirements

Arizona administers and enforces the Clean Air Act under standards approved by the EPA. In addition to standards relating to "criteria pollutants" and "hazardous pollutants," ADEQ has adopted standards for various "non-criteria pollutants," including dust and odors. ADEQ has also adopted standards for the issuance of permits. For example, an installation permit is required before installation of a device that may cause or contribute to air pollution, and an operating permit must be obtained before beginning operation of the device, after performance tests demonstrate that applicable emission standards will be satisfied. The permit process requires that an applicant submit a detailed compliance plan and strict notice requirements must be followed. A public hearing will be held if requested by the public.

Local Government Requirements

Each county is authorized to regulate local air pollution sources. Several counties, namely Maricopa, Pima, and Pinal, have established air pollution control programs under which installation and operating permits must be obtained from a county air pollution control board. The standards governing the issuance of these permits are substantially similar to the federal and state standards.

Water Pollution Control

Water quality in Arizona is regulated under federal, state, and local laws. Primary regulation is through a permitting program intended to limit discharges of pollutants. Generally, water pollution control in Arizona falls into two categories: surface waters (such as water in streams, rivers, lakes, ponds, and springs) and subsurface groundwater.

Surface Water

In General

Under both the federal Clean Water Act and Arizona statutes, water quality standards have been established for all surface water bodies in Arizona. Discharges into surface waters must meet these standards. Every river and stream in Arizona has been inventoried according to its present and potential uses, such as recreational, agricultural, or livestock. Discharges into surface waters may not interfere with these designated uses.

PERMITS TO DISCHARGE INTO SURFACE WATERS

A National Pollutant Discharge Elimination System (NPDES) permit must be obtained before any facility can discharge regulated pollutants into surface waters of the United States. An application for an NPDES permit must demonstrate that regulated pollutants in the discharges will not exceed specific standards. Presently, the permits are issued by the EPA after substantial input from ADEQ, although Arizona may eventually seek authority from the EPA to administer and enforce the NPDES permit program.

DREDGE AND FILL PERMITS

The Clean Water Act prohibits the deposit of dredge or fill materials into the waters of the United States and adjacent wetlands without a permit from the Army Corps of Engineers. Issuance of a dredge and fill permit is conditioned upon state certification that the applicant's discharge will not contravene existing water quality standards. The term "waters of the United States" is broadly interpreted to include tidal waters, streams, and lakes. The definition of "wetlands" includes normally dry arroyos and stream beds that are part of a water tributary system.

Certain activities are exempt from the dredge and fill permit requirements. Exempt activities include normal farming and ranching, construction or maintenance of stockponds or irrigation ditches, and construction of farm or forest roads.

Industrial Pretreatment Regulation

Publicly-owned sewage treatment systems that ultimately discharge their effluents into surface waters, and industrial facilities that discharge into surface waters or into publicly-owned sewage treatment systems are regulated under the Clean Water Act. Such facilities must comply with specific EPA pretreatment standards and, under certain conditions, must obtain facility-specific discharge permits. These standards are intended to limit discharges of regulated pollutants into surface waters and to protect the systems and their operators from dangerous pollutants, such as corrosive materials. Such systems may also be regulated under county or municipal ordinances.

Groundwater

In General

All underground strata in the state that yield usable quantities of potable water are characterized as "aquifers." Strict standards are imposed by ADEQ to preserve the drinking quality of groundwater from the aquifers. Any discharge into an aquifer that would violate these standards is prohibited.

Aquifer Protection Permit Program

The primary means of protecting groundwater quality in Arizona is the Aquifer Protection Permit (APP) Program. Any discharge of a pollutant that has a reasonable probability of adversely affecting groundwater quality is prohibited unless the discharge first receives a permit issued by ADEQ. The term "pollutant" is broadly defined to include any solid, liquid, or gaseous waste, and no pollutant can be discharged into water or upon the ground without a permit.

To obtain an APP an applicant must demonstrate that it will limit the discharge of pollutants (to zero if possible) through the "best available demonstrated control technology, processes, or operating methods." The applicant must also demonstrate financial and technical ability to comply with any condition imposed by ADEQ for the issuance of the permit.

HAZARDOUS MATERIALS

Various federal, state, and local laws address the use and effects of hazardous materials. These laws have three principal purposes: one is to establish specific performance standards for the generation, transportation, storage, handling, and disposal of various hazardous materials; another is to inform workers and the public about the dangers of hazardous materials, to reduce accidents and coordinate responses in emergencies; and the third is to impose liability upon persons responsible for improper handling of hazardous materials.

RESOURCE CONSERVATION AND RECOVERY ACT

Under the Resource Conservation and Recovery Act, the EPA has established standards for the protection of the environment and human health from materials specifically identified as "hazardous waste." The comprehensive regulatory program adopted by the EPA regulates waste materials from generation through final disposal. ADEQ administers and enforces the hazardous waste program in Arizona. Regulations address three broad aspects: generation; transportation; and treatment, storage, and disposal.

GENERATION OF HAZARDOUS WASTE

A facility that generates hazardous waste must advise ADEQ on an annual basis of the level of its generating activities and must comply with specific recordkeeping, handling, and disposal requirements. Before transporting or offering hazardous waste for transportation to an offsite location, the facility must comply with packaging, labeling, and marking requirements. If a generating facility stores waste in excess of 90 days, it is subject to the more stringent regulations described below for facilities that store hazardous waste.

TRANSPORTATION OF HAZARDOUS WASTE

Transporters of hazardous waste must comply with reporting and recordkeeping requirements. Among other requirements, a transporter of hazardous waste in Arizona must obtain a special license from the Department of Transportation before moving such materials.

TREATMENT, STORAGE, AND DISPOSAL OF HAZARDOUS WASTE

A facility that treats, stores, or disposes of hazardous waste is subject to extensive regulation. Strict requirements govern the design, construction, maintenance, operation, and closure of such a facility in order to minimize the possibility of fire, explosion, or unplanned releases of hazardous wastes that could threaten the environment or human health. Among other requirements, personnel at treatment, storage, and disposal facilities must be trained to respond effectively to emergencies. Closure of such facilities must take place in accordance with an approved plan that minimizes the need for further maintenance and the possibility of post-closure escape of hazardous waste. Specific requirements are determined on a facility-by-facility basis.

UNDERGROUND STORAGE TANK REGULATION

Underground storage tanks are subject to federal and state regulations enforced by ADEQ. An underground storage tank is defined as a tank used to store regulated substances, at least 10 percent of the volume of which is located underground. Regulated substances include petroleum and hazardous pollutants but do not include hazardous waste regulated under the Resource Conservation and Recovery Act. An owner of an underground storage tank must notify ADEQ within 30 days after placement of the tank into operation. An owner or operator of an underground storage tank may be required to comply with other requirements, four of which are discussed below.

TANK PERFORMANCE STANDARDS

A new underground storage tank must comply with federal performance standards governing corrosion protection, leak detection, and spill and overflow protection. An owner and operator must use qualified personnel to install the tank. Existing tanks must be upgraded to meet the performance standards applicable to new tanks. Tanks that fail to meet the standards by designated deadlines must be taken out of service.

FINANCIAL RESPONSIBILITY

An owner or operator of an underground storage tank may be required to demonstrate financial ability to take corrective action in the event of a release. Evidence of financial responsibility can be established by an insurance policy, a guaranty, a surety bond, a letter of credit, or qualification with ADEQ as a self-insurer.

Spill Reporting and Corrective Action Requirements

Owners and operators of underground storage tanks are required to notify ADEQ not later than 24 hours after detection of a release, or suspected release, from a tank. In some instances, particularly if groundwater may be affected by the release, ADEQ may require the owner or operator to implement a corrective action plan.

Tank Closure Requirements

Underground tanks must be closed in a safe and secure manner that prevents release of regulated substances into the environment. A tank that is closed for a period of less than 12 months must continue to comply with federal standards governing corrosion protection, leak detection, spill and overflow protection, and spill reporting requirements. An underground storage tank that is closed for 12 months or longer is subject to special closure requirements, including the requirement to notify ADEQ at least 30 days before closure.

Local Fire Codes

Fire codes established by counties, cities, and towns also regulate the storage and handling of hazardous materials. Requirements under these codes vary greatly, and each applicable code must be reviewed.

Employee Hazard Communication

The Occupational Safety and Health Act (OSHA) imposes a duty on employers to provide employees with a safe and healthful place to work, a workplace free from recognized hazards causing or likely to cause death or serious physical harm. The U.S. Labor Department, which administers OSHA, has issued a specific standard for the use of hazardous chemicals in the workplace known as the "OSHA Hazard Communication Standard."

The OSHA Hazard Communication Standard requires employers to inform employees about any "hazardous chemicals" to which they may be exposed. Hazardous chemicals is defined broadly and includes carcinogens, toxics, irritants, corrosives, sensitizers, agents that damage the skin, lungs or eyes, and chemicals that are combustible, explosive, or flammable. The OSHA Hazard Communication Standard applies to any hazardous chemical known to be present in the workplace to which employees may be exposed under normal working conditions or in a foreseeable emergency. The OSHA Hazard Communication Standard also applies to manufacturers, importers, and distributors of hazardous chemicals. The OSHA Hazard Communication Standard imposes the four requirements discussed below.

LABELING OF HAZARDOUS CHEMICALS

The OSHA Hazard Communication Standard requires chemical manufacturers, importers, or distributors to label, tag, or mark each container of hazardous chemical with the identity of the hazardous chemical and with an appropriate hazard warning. Employers must ensure that all workplace containers of hazardous chemicals are similarly labeled, tagged, or marked. In lieu of affixing labels to individual containers, an employer can provide notice of the presence of hazardous chemicals by posting signs or distributing written materials among employees. All labels and warnings must be legible and in English.

MATERIAL SAFETY DATA SHEETS

Employers must maintain a material safety data sheet (MSDS) for each hazardous chemical in the workplace. The MSDS must identify the specific chemical, the health hazards associated with the chemical, known precautions for safe handling and use of the chemical, and first aid procedures. Employers must make the MSDS available to employees, union representatives, and the Labor Department.

EMPLOYEE INFORMATION AND TRAINING

The OSHA Hazard Communication Standard requires employers to provide employees with information and training on hazardous chemicals in the workplace at the time of their initial employment and whenever a new hazard is introduced into the work area. Employees must be informed of any operations in their work area where hazardous chemicals are present and the location of the MSDS. Employee training must include discussions of available means to detect the release of a hazardous chemical, the physical and health hazards of the chemicals, and the measures that employees can take to protect themselves.

WRITTEN HAZARD COMMUNICATION PROGRAM

Employers must develop, implement, and maintain at the workplace a written hazard communication program. The hazard communication program must describe how the employer will satisfy the requirements relating to labeling, preparation of material safety data sheets, and employee information and training.

EMERGENCY PLANNING AND COMMUNITY RIGHT-TO-KNOW ACT

The Emergency Planning and Community Right-to-Know Act (EPCRA) imposes reporting requirements on businesses that use hazardous chemicals. The reporting requirements are intended to provide the public with important information on hazardous chemicals in their communities, to enhance community awareness of chemical hazards, and to facilitate state and local emergency response plans. The reporting requirements under EPCRA fall into four categories, as discussed below.

EMERGENCY PLANNING REPORTING

An owner or operator of any facility that has present any "extremely hazardous substance" in designated quantities must notify the state and local emergency planning commissions. The presence and location of additional quantities of specified substances must be reported within 60 days of the acquisition, and the notification must include the name of a facility representative who can be contacted in the event of an emergency.

CHEMICAL INVENTORY

Businesses are required to provide an annual inventory of certain chemicals. Any business that prepares a material safety data sheet in compliance with the OSHA Hazard Communication Standard must submit a list of all chemicals for which a material safety data sheet is required that are present at the facility in quantities greater than threshold reporting quantities at any one time during the year, or must submit the actual material safety data sheet. Additionally, businesses must submit an annual chemical inventory report specifying the average daily amount of a chemical on the premises, the maximum amount present on any given day, and the location of the chemicals. A business may be exempted from disclosing the identity of a specific chemical if it can establish that the disclosure would reveal a trade secret.

EMERGENCY NOTIFICATION

The owner or operator of any facility that produces, uses, or stores any hazardous chemical defined under the OSHA Hazard Communication Standard must report the spill or release of any such chemical *outside* the facility. The report must be made to the National Response Center, the state emergency response commission, and the local emergency planning committee. Two notifications are required, an initial notice and a follow-up notice. The initial notice may be by telephone and must include the identity and amount of the chemical released, the duration of the release, and information regarding any health hazard created by the release. The follow-up notice must be in writing, must update the information previously submitted, and must identify the actions taken.

TOXIC CHEMICAL RELEASE REPORTING

EPCRA requires every manufacturing company that has 10 or more full-time employees and that manufactures, imports, processes, or otherwise uses any "toxic chemical" in an amount greater than the designated threshold amount during the calendar year, to submit annual reports of discharge of toxic chemicals into the environment during the preceding year.

SUPERFUND LAWS

IN GENERAL

Federal and state statutes, commonly referred to as "superfund" laws, authorize government actions against responsible parties for reimbursement of cleanup costs and for damages to natural resources caused by the release of hazardous substances into the environment. The federal and state statutes also contain citizen suit provisions which allow private parties in certain situations to bring claims against responsible parties for releases of hazardous substances into the environment. A "responsible party" can include a generator or transporter of the hazardous substance or any present or past owner or operator of a site from which hazardous substances are released.

Liability under the federal superfund law is joint and several. However, recent amendments to the state superfund law have eliminated joint liability. Joint liabilities means that each responsible party may be liable for the entire amount of cleanup costs and damages at a particular site, regardless of the responsible party's actual share of liability. Furthermore, liability is "strict" liability, which means that a responsible party may be held liable without regard to fault. A purchaser of a site contaminated by a prior owner's operations may be liable no matter when or by whom the hazardous substances were disposed.

INNOCENT PURCHASER DEFENSE

An important defense to environmental liability where a site has been contaminated by another party's operations is the "innocent purchaser" defense. A party will not be liable under the federal superfund law if it can be established that after "all appropriate inquiry" a purchaser had no reason to know about the presence of hazardous substances at the site prior to acquisition. Arizona's superfund law has a similar defense available to purchasers of contaminated property who did not cause or contribute to a hazardous substance release. Superfund laws are not explicit about the extent of inquiry required, but minimum inquiry should include site inspection, a full inquiry into any present and past uses of hazardous substances at the site, a "title search" of real estate records to determine prior owners, and a review of regulatory agency records to determine whether enforcement action has occurred or is planned.

Environmental Assessments and Allocation of Liabilities

The acquisition of real property or an existing business should always be preceded by an environmental assessment of the property and/or business. Environmental assessments serve at least two important purposes. First, environmental assessments identify liabilities that may significantly affect the economic viability of an acquisition. Cleanup costs and expenses, and delays in planned operations may make the acquisition economically unattractive. Further, knowledge as to whether operating permits are transferable is important if the business will continue to be operated in the same fashion after acquisition. Second, the prospective purchaser may be able to take advantage of the innocent purchaser defense under the superfund laws, as noted above, if proper due diligence (typically in the form of an environmental assessment) is undertaken.

It is advisable for the parties to a transaction to address the possibility and allocation of environmental liabilities in their agreement through appropriate representations, warranties, and indemnities.

WATER RIGHTS

CHAPTER OUTLINE

SUMMARY

Much of Arizona is arid. As a consequence, Arizona has developed an extensive system of rules for allocating water among competing users. These rules are widely recognized as a fair and effective means of managing Arizona's water resources.

Most who need water in Arizona will have little involvement with Arizona's water laws. Those who locate industrial, commercial, or residential developments within metropolitan areas of Arizona usually will find fully developed water supplies and delivery systems. Hooking up to a water line and paying a usage fee to the municipal water company will be all that is required. But water rights can be an important element in certain types of real estate purchases or industrial ventures, especially in the less metropolitan areas of Arizona. Agricultural, commercial, or industrial developments locating in rural or undeveloped areas may find that the availability of water is a key factor in the successful development of these types of properties.

TYPES OF WATER RIGHTS IN ARIZONA

Water rights in Arizona are classified into three broad categories: (i) rights to use surface water, such as the water found on the surface of the earth in streams, rivers, lakes, ponds, and springs; (ii) rights to use groundwater, which generally is water pumped or withdrawn from wells; and (iii) contractual rights to water.

While each of these categories is generally discussed below, it must be remembered that in Arizona, the nature of a "water right" is defined by the courts and by Arizona's legislature. As our courts or legislature resolve conflicts between competing water users, the nature of a water right is altered. Indeed, as of the date of this publication, there are several appeals of trial court rulings pending before the Arizona Supreme Court , any one of which could result in a significant redefinition of the water rights that are briefly discussed below.

SURFACE WATER RIGHTS

DOCTRINE OF PRIOR APPROPRIATION

In the arid western United States, early miners, irrigators, settlers, and pioneers found that streams, rivers, and lakes were few and far between. These early water users often claimed surface water under an informal process that had previously been used to claim minerals under mining law; a water user would "stake a claim" to surface water by diverting it from its source and applying it to some beneficial use, usually mining, irrigation, or domestic consumption.

This informal process became known as the Doctrine of Prior Appropriation, and it is generally followed in Arizona. Under this doctrine, the first person to divert and beneficially use surface water acquires a "prior right" to the water necessary to continue his beneficial use. Thus, the Doctrine of Prior Appropriation translates into "first in time is first in right."

Under the "first-in-time, first-in-right" concept, an appropriator who previously obtained a water right is entitled to have his or her right protected from interference by subsequent water users. For example, a water user who appropriated water in 1950, is entitled to protection against a person, who in 1991, initiated a water use from the same source.

Rights to surface water uses are appurtenant to the land on which such water rights are used, and thus "follow the land." A property owner with rights to use surface water on a tract of real property can transfer these rights to a successor property owner for use on the same property.

THE ADMINISTRATIVE PROCESS FOR
ACQUIRING A SURFACE WATER RIGHTS

During the final 20 years of the 1800s, most western states adopted a water code of some sort in which the Doctrine of Prior Appropriation was legislatively reduced to an administrative process. The territorial and state legislatures enacted statutes to formalize the Doctrine of Prior Appropriation. Statutes varied widely from state to state, but often the enactments of one state were subsequently adopted by another state. For example, on June 12, 1919, Arizona "plagiarized" a surface water code from Oregon.

Despite the variation from state to state, most statutory schemes based on the Doctrine of Prior Appropriation require a person who desires to appropriate surface water to first file an Application to Appropriate with the applicable state agency. In Arizona, this agency is now the Arizona Department of Water Resources.

After the Application to Appropriate is filed, the Arizona Department of Water Resources issues a Permit to Appropriate under which an applicant is entitled to construct the diversionary facilities necessary to put the surface water to beneficial use. Once the facilities have been constructed and the water has been applied to beneficial use, the Department of Water Resources issues yet a third document recognizing, at least on an administrative level, the validity of the appropriation. In Arizona, this document is referred to as a Certificate of Water Right.

REGISTRATION OF CERTAIN TYPES OF
SURFACE WATER RIGHTS

Arizona's 1919 Surface Water Code did not, however, provide a mandatory, statewide system for registering surface water rights based on uses initiated prior to 1919. Water rights that had been acquired before 1919, were not subject to the Surface Water Code's requirement that a water user first file an application to appropriate surface water. Therefore, no one had a "database" of the water rights that had been perfected or vested prior to June 12, 1919. To deal with specific problems in determining conflicting rights to surface water, Arizona's legislature enacted legislation that required those who claimed these "pre-1919" water rights to register these types of claims with the appropriate state agency.

A similar registration scheme required owners of stockponds to register their water rights claims. A stockpond is a small surface water impoundment that stores 15 acre-feet of water or less for stock watering or wildlife. Generally, stockpond water rights are of limited value to large industrial water users and real estate developers.

GENERAL STREAM ADJUDICATIONS

In Arizona, as in other western states, Indian tribes have asserted significant claims to water. In the mid-1970's, major surface water users initiated lawsuits in the state court system to determine the extent and priority of rights to the waters of two major river systems in Arizona—these suits are known as the *general stream adjudications.* It was hoped that in these adjudications, the Arizona state court would determine the nature and extent of the claims asserted by each of the Indian tribes with lands in Arizona.

Under the current law, it is unclear exactly what claims to water would fall within the scope of a general stream adjudication. In many cases, groundwater may be connected to surface water flow, and therefore, many surface water users in Arizona also have sought to adjudicate rights to groundwater. Many water rights may be affected by the outcome of this litigation. These adjudications have become extremely complex and, as a result, each will continue for many years.

GROUNDWATER RIGHTS

Groundwater means water found under the surface of the earth regardless of the geologic structure in which it is standing or moving. As explained above, Arizona simply does not have enough surface water to meet the demands of all users. As a result, numerous water users in Arizona drilled wells and then pumped groundwater from highly productive aquifers. Municipalities and mining companies usually drilled wells to tap aquifers already pumped by agricultural groundwater users. As a result, groundwater levels declined and pumping costs increased; the increased costs of pumping groundwater led to protracted litigation.

To resolve these disputes, Arizona passed the *1980 Groundwater Management Act*. The 1980 Act governs the use of groundwater in *active management areas* (AMAs), which include most of the metropolitan areas of Phoenix, Prescott, and Tucson, as well as the upper Santa Cruz Valley (near Nogales, Arizona) and Pinal County in central Arizona.

GROUNDWATER RIGHTS IN AMAS

Pursuant to the 1980 Act, the Arizona Department of Water Resources adopted management plans for each AMA that require all groundwater uses in an AMA to gradually implement conservation measures to reach certain management goals. For example, in the Phoenix, Tucson, and Prescott AMAs, groundwater usage is to be managed to achieve *safe-yield* by the year 2025. Safe-yield is a long-term balance between the annual amount of groundwater withdrawn and the annual amount of natural and artificial groundwater recharged or replenished in the same AMA. The management goals for the Pinal and Santa Cruz AMAs are similar to the goal of safe yield, although other management objectives are also recognized.

The right to use groundwater in an AMA is generally determined by the history of groundwater use during the five-year time period prior to January 1, 1980. For example, a property owner who used groundwater for agricultural irrigation on a particular parcel of land during this five-year period acquired an *irrigation grandfathered groundwater right*. The grandfathered irrigation right entitles the owner of the property, or the owner's successors, to continued use of groundwater on that property for agricultural irrigation. The 1980 Act recognizes other types of grandfathered groundwater rights, including several types of rights to use groundwater for non-irrigation purposes, such as industrial uses, electric power generation, golf course watering (which under the 1980 Act is not irrigation), and municipal supply. If a property owner does not have a groundwater right, the owner nevertheless may be entitled to a groundwater use permit. Whether a permit will be issued depends, in part, on whether water is available from an alternative source.

GROUNDWATER RIGHTS OUTSIDE AMAS

Outside of the Active Management Areas, there are areas where property owners are prohibited from using groundwater to irrigate new tracts of land. These areas are designated as *irrigation non-expansion areas* (INAs). There are, however, no restrictions in INAs prohibiting new uses of groundwater for nonagricultural purposes.

The use of groundwater outside of both INAs and AMAs is governed by the *Doctrine of Reasonable Use*. Under this doctrine, a property owner is authorized to withdraw and use groundwater on the owner's property for all "reasonable" purposes, but waste is prohibited. There also are limitations on the transportation of groundwater away from the groundwater basin from which the groundwater is withdrawn.

CONTRACTUAL WATER RIGHTS

Rights to water may be established under contract, as when an owner of property enters into a contract with a municipality or a private water company to obtain water. Often, developers in

Arizona will have to negotiate the terms and conditions of water service with a private water company or a municipality. If the entity that supplies the water is a private water company, then typically, such water service contracts must be approved by the *Arizona Corporation Commission*, an Arizona agency that regulates private companies (but not municipalities) that supply utility service in Arizona.

In addition, various water suppliers have entered into water service contracts to acquire water from the Central Arizona Project, a technologically-advanced aqueduct system that transports water from the Colorado River to water users in central and southern Arizona.

THE CENTRAL ARIZONA PROJECT

The *Central Arizona Project* (CAP) is an aqueduct system consisting of canals and an expanded storage facility (New Waddell Dam) through which Colorado River water is imported from Lake Havasu on the Colorado River to the Phoenix and Tucson metropolitan areas, as well as various irrigation districts and Indian tribes along the aqueduct system. It has a capacity of approximately 1.5 million acre-feet per year[1]. The CAP was constructed by the U.S. Bureau of Reclamation under the authority granted to the Secretary of Interior in the Colorado River Basin Project Act of 1968, which authorized federal funding of this project.

The CAP is now operated by an Arizona agency, the *Central Arizona Water Conservation District*, or CAWCD. The CAWCD is responsible for repaying to the United States a portion of the construction cost of the CAP, as well as operating and maintaining the CAP. Payments to the United States are made with funds acquired by CAWCD from three sources: property taxes levied on taxable real property within Maricopa, Pinal, and Pima Counties; water service charges to all CAP water users, including those municipalities and private water companies that have contracted for CAP water but have not received delivery of such

---

[1] An "acre-foot" is 325,891 gallons, the amount of water necessary to cover a football field to a depth of one foot; it is enough to provide a family of five with water for one year.

water; and the sale of surplus electrical power from several facilities that were constructed to generate electrical power for pumping Colorado River water through the CAP aqueduct system. Water from the CAP is delivered to municipalities, irrigation districts, and other types of non-Indian water users through three-party contracts between the water user, the CAWCD, and the U.S. Bureau of Reclamation.

SPECIAL WATER ISSUES AFFECTING LAND ACQUISITIONS

Because of the importance of water, a prospective purchaser of real property in Arizona should conduct a thorough investigation of all applicable water rights that might either be appurtenant to the land to be acquired or, alternatively, required for future development. This investigation usually is made during a "due diligence" or feasibility review period that is provided for in most purchase agreements for major real estate purchases. If the property is in a metropolitan area, the investigation may involve no more than confirmation of the availability of water and terms of water service from the local municipality or water company. If the property is located outside the area served by a municipality or private water company, or if the property includes existing wells or other water sources, the purchaser must make a more comprehensive analysis of water availability.

REVIEW OF TITLE REPORT AND SURVEY

Most water rights are legally attached, or appurtenant, to specific parcels of real property. The ability to acquire water rights may depend on the geographic location of the real property— often the types of water rights that might be appurtenant to a tract of real property vary from location to location within Arizona. For example, irrigation grandfathered groundwater rights, as discussed above, exist only within the AMAs. Thus, farmland outside of an

AMA or INA lacks such rights. If the real property is served with water from a commonly owned well or irrigated with water received from some surface water source, then sometimes the contractual arrangements under which such water is used will be referenced in a title report.

If the real property to be acquired is of significant acreage, a prospective purchaser may elect to have the property surveyed to determine the existence of wells, ponds, and similar water sources; the survey will aid in the evaluation of what water rights will actually be acquired in connection with the acquisition of the real estate. Close review of title reports and surveys is essential.

WARRANTIES

A seller of property usually makes warranties of title to the purchaser, but warranties relating to water rights are rarely made by the seller because, as noted above, the outcome of the general stream adjudications may affect existing rights to both surface water and groundwater. Sellers are often unwilling or unable to make unqualified warranties regarding the validity of water rights.

POST-ACQUISITION DOCUMENTATION

If real property includes appurtenant water rights, documents should be prepared and filed with the Arizona Department of Water Resources to reflect the transfer of water rights from seller to buyer. In many cases the documentation can be prepared on forms available from the Department.

SPECIAL WATER ISSUES AFFECTING LAND DEVELOPMENT

ASSURED WATER SUPPLY REQUIREMENTS

A purchaser who acquires property within an Active Management Area and who intends to subdivide the property into six or more lots or parcels may be required to demonstrate to the Department of Water Resources that an assured water supply exists for the proposed subdivision. Demonstration of an assured water supply requires a showing that enough water is physically and legally available to meet the demands of the subdivision for a 100-year period. Additionally, projected groundwater use must be consistent with the management plan and the developer must show financial ability to construct the water delivery system. Similar requirements apply to the subdivision of real property located outside of the AMAs, although in such cases the limitations on subdividing real property if adequate supplies of water are not available are somewhat more relaxed.

WATER SERVICE PROVIDERS

A person seeking to subdivide real estate in an area that lacks water service may also have to create a water service provider to build and then operate the water service infrastructure. There are several alternatives for water providers, but two options commonly are considered—a developer might form a private water company or form a public improvement district. Both alternatives involve additional expense and require various governmental approvals, but these alternatives may be the only way to develop a tract of real property estate in areas where no water service provider is available.

FORMATION OF A PRIVATE WATER COMPANY

In some cases a developer may elect to form a private water company. Sometimes several developers will join to form a water company to serve a number of developments. Formation of a water company is a complicated process that may take six months or more to complete. Approval must be obtained from the Arizona Corporation Commission. Additionally, a water company must obtain a franchise from the county or municipality in which it proposes to operate. If the water company conducts business within the boundaries of a municipality, the grant of a franchise requires approval of the municipality's voters. Furthermore, a water company that proposes to operate within an AMA must satisfy conservation requirements imposed by the Department of Water Resources. Approvals are also required from state and local health and environmental departments.

FORMATION OF A PUBLIC IMPROVEMENT DISTRICT

An alternative to the formation of a private water company is the formation of a public improvement district to construct or to acquire an existing water system. Every landowner within such a district pays assessments that are used to pay the costs and expenses of the district. In some cases a district has the capacity to issue bonds, and the proceeds from the bond sale are used to construct water service facilities. There are extensive requirements for the formation of such districts, including obtaining the approval of the board of supervisors of the county in which the district is located, and sometimes obtaining the approval of other districts that operate in the same geographical area.

FEDERAL TAXATION

CHAPTER OUTLINE

SUMMARY

This chapter deals with significant federal tax considerations relevant to foreign persons investing or doing business in the United States. First considered are federal *income* taxes. Two additional income tax classifications are discussed: "resident" and "nonresident." Federal income taxes are then discussed as to corporations, partnerships, and several special situations. Next there is a discussion of federal *estate* tax issues and, as to them, the determination and consequences of resident or non-resident status and the impact of tax treaties. The final part deals briefly with federal *gift* taxes.

INCOME TAXATION OF FOREIGN INDIVIDUALS

Two very different classifications govern the federal income taxation of foreign individuals. One applies to foreign individuals classified as "resident aliens." A second applies to foreign individuals classified as "nonresident aliens."

DETERMINATION OF RESIDENT STATUS

A foreign individual is classified as a resident alien for federal income tax purposes for a particular calendar year if he or she meets any one of three tests: the "green card" test, the "183-day presence" test, or the "cumulative presence" test. A foreign individual is classified as a nonresident alien for federal income tax purposes for a particular calendar year if he or she does not meet any one of the tests. However, certain foreign individuals who fail to meet any of the three tests may elect to be classified as resident aliens if they satisfy the requirements explained below. Also, some tax treaties between the United States and foreign countries address the determination of individual residency for income tax purposes.

GREEN CARD TEST

A foreign individual is classified as a resident alien if he or she enters the United States with an immigrant visa (a "green card"). The length of the individual's presence in the United States if irrelevant under this test.

183-DAY PRESENCE TEST

A foreign individual is classified as a resident alien if he or she is physically present in the United States at least 183 days in a calendar year. Generally, each day during which a foreign individual is present in the United States at any time during the year, must be counted for this purpose, but in some cases days are excluded from the count. For example, days the individual is unable to leave the United States because of a medical condition that arose in the United States.

Certain individuals are exempt from the 183-day presence test, such as an individual representing a foreign government and, under limited circumstances, teachers, students, and employee-trainees.

CUMULATIVE PRESENCE TEST

Under the "cumulative presence" test, a complex mathematical formula is applied to determine whether an individual is classified as a resident alien for income tax purposes. The formula is based on the number of days (other than the same days which are excluded under the 183-day presence test described above) during which a foreign individual is present in the United States during the most recent *three-year period*.

A foreign individual will be classified as a resident alien under the cumulative presence test in any calendar year if present in the United States for at least 31 days and if the person's presence during that year and the two preceding years equals a "weighted" aggregate of at least 183 days. The weighting discounts presence in the first preceding year by two thirds and in the second preceding year by five-sixths, as illustrated by the following example, which assumes the foreign citizen to have been in the United States for 126 days in each of 1995, 1996, and 1997.

Current year - 1997	126
First preceding year - 1996 (126 x 1/3)	+ 42
Second preceding year - 1995 (126 x 1/6)	+ 21
Total number of days	189

Notwithstanding the general rule, a foreign individual will *not* be classified as a resident alien, even if he or she otherwise satisfies the cumulative presence test, if the individual can prove the existence of a "tax home" in a foreign country and a "closer connection" to the foreign country than with the United States. Factors taken into consideration include the locations of the individual's family and business, location of bank accounts, and the individual's social, political, cultural, and religious affiliations. An individual who otherwise satisfies the cumulative presence test must file a statement justifying the claim to the "closer connection" exception. The statement must be filed with the Internal Revenue Service (the IRS), the principal enforcement agency of the U.S. tax laws.

Certain individuals are also exempt from the cumulative presence test, such as representatives of foreign governments and certain teachers, student, and employee-trainees.

ELECTION TO BE TAXED AS A RESIDENT ALIEN

An individual who arrives in the United States too late in the year to satisfy either the 183-day presence test or the cumulative presence test may nonetheless elect to be treated as a resident alien for such year if three requirements are satisfied: the individual is present in the United States for at least 31 consecutive days during the election year; the individual is present in the United States 75 percent of the days between the first day of the 31 day period and the last day of the election year; and the individual is classified as a resident alien for the year following the year of the election under either the 183-day presence test or the cumulative presence test. The election is made by attaching a special statement to the individual's tax return of the election year.

IMPACT OF TAX TREATIES

Because of the conflicting laws of many countries, an individual may qualify as a resident of more than one country. The United States has entered into treaties with a number of countries that resolve the issue of residence under "tiebreaker" rules. An individual deemed to be a resident of a foreign country under tiebreaker rules is classified as a U.S. nonresident alien for all tax issues addressed by the treaty.

DUAL STATUS YEARS

Special rules govern the first year and the last year in which a foreign individual is classified as a resident alien. A foreign individual may be taxed as a nonresident alien for a portion of a calendar year and taxed as a resident alien for the remainder of that year, a year sometimes referred to as a "dual status" year.

INITIAL YEAR AS RESIDENT ALIEN

A foreign individual who is classified as a resident alien is regarded as a resident alien only for the portion of the calendar year which begins on his "residency starting date." The residency starting date is the day the individual receives a green card or, for an individual who meets either the 183-day presence test or the cumulative presence test, the individual's first day of presence in the United States.

FINAL YEAR AS RESIDENT ALIEN

A foreign individual who is classified as a resident alien is deemed to terminate his or her residence in the United States on the last day present in the United States, provided that the individual has a closer connection to a foreign country than to the United States following departure from the United States and is not a resident alien at any time during the following calendar year.

TAXATION OF RESIDENT ALIENS

IN GENERAL

A foreign individual who is classified as a resident alien for federal income tax purposes is taxed in the same manner as a U.S. citizen. Accordingly, the individual's income earned worldwide is taxed at graduated rates from 15 to 39.6 percent. The United States, unlike certain other countries, does not permit a capital gains tax adjustment in the tax basis of a capital asset to fair market value upon arrival; all appreciation in the value of capital assets, including the appreciation accumulated prior to arrival in the United States, is potentially subject to tax.

In many instances, classification as a resident alien will result in greater U.S. taxes than if the individual were classified as a nonresident alien. However, there are circumstances in which a resident alien pays lower taxes than a nonresident alien. For example, a resident alien may claim various deductions that may not be claimed by a nonresident and may claim a credit for certain taxes paid to foreign countries.

Various techniques may be available to reduce taxes in situations in which resident alien status is likely. It will generally be advantageous for a foreign individual to collect payments prior to becoming a resident alien if the foreign individual's home country either does not impose a tax on such payments or imposes taxes at a lower rate. Also, it may be advantageous for a foreign individual to dispose of capital assets or other property prior to becoming a resident alien if the individual's home country does not impose a tax on such assets.

SPECIAL RULES

Special rules apply in determining the income of a resident alien. For example, ownership in certain corporations may result in the recognition of "deemed" dividend income, even though a dividend is not actually paid to the shareholder. Ownership of stock in a "controlled foreign corporation" can result in deemed dividend income. A controlled foreign corporation is a corporation formed outside the United States of which more than 50 percent, by vote or value, is owned by U.S. shareholders. For this purpose a "U.S. shareholder" is a U.S. citizen, resident alien, or domestic corporation, partnership, trust, or estate, that owns, directly or indirectly, at least 10 percent of the voting stock of the foreign corporation.

The ownership by a resident alien of stock in "foreign personal holding companies," "U.S. personal holding companies," and "passive foreign investment companies" can also result in deemed dividend treatment. Restructuring of stock ownership may minimize or eliminate deemed dividend treatment.

TAXATION OF NONRESIDENT ALIENS

IN GENERAL

Two sets of rules apply to the taxation of nonresident aliens. *Investment income* earned by nonresident aliens is taxed in accordance with one. *Trade or business income* is taxed in accordance with another.

INVESTMENT INCOME

IN GENERAL

Investment income (sometimes referred to as "fixed or determinable annual or periodic income") earned from *U.S. sources* by a nonresident alien is generally taxed in the United States at a 30 percent tax rate. The tax, collected by withholding at the source, is a tax on *gross* investment income. The amount of investment income subject to federal income taxation is computed without any deductions. Investment income is income not associated with a U.S. trade or business and includes interest, dividends, rents, and royalties. Investment income earned from foreign sources by a nonresident alien is not subject to U.S. taxation.

SOURCE RULES

As noted, a nonresident alien is generally taxed at a 30 percent rate on investment income earned from U.S. sources. The following rules apply in determining whether investment income is "U.S. source" income.

■ Interest

Interest paid by a U.S. corporation is generally treated as U.S. source income, unless 80 percent or more of the corporation's gross income for the three-year period preceding the payment of interest is derived from foreign sources. However, if the recipient of the interest owns 10 percent or more of the stock of the payor-corporation, the interest paid is apportioned between U.S. and foreign sources, unless 100 percent of the payor-corporation's gross income is derived from foreign sources. In contrast, interest paid by a foreign corporation is generally treated as U.S. source income only if the foreign corporation conducts a trade or business in the United States.

■ Dividends

Dividends paid by a U.S. corporation are generally treated as U.S. source investment income. Dividends paid by a foreign corporation are generally treated as U.S. source income only if 25 percent or more of the corporation's gross income for the three-year period preceding the payment is associated with the operation of a U.S. trade or business.

■ Rents and Royalties

Rents are U.S. source investment income if the property producing the rents is located in the United States. Royalties from the licensing of intangible property, such as patents, copyrights, secret processes, goodwill, and similar properties are treated as U.S. source income if the intangible property is used in the United States.

Special Rules

A number of special rules apply to the treatment of investment income earned by a nonresident alien. Several of the most important are:

■ Exempt Interest

Not all interest earned from U.S. sources is subject to taxation. Interest paid on deposits with U.S. banks, insurance companies, and savings and loan associations is not taxed to a nonresident alien. Certain "portfolio" interest, including interest paid on bonds issued in the Eurobond market, is not taxed to a nonresident alien, unless the recipient owns 10 percent or more of the issuer. Interest on state and municipal obligations is totally exempt from U.S. taxation.

■ Impact of Tax Treaties

The United States has entered into tax treaties with certain countries that reduce the rate of taxation on investment income earned by residents of the treaty county. Many treaties reduce the rate of taxation on interest to zero and reduce the rate of taxation on dividends to 5 to 15 percent.

DOING BUSINESS IN ARIZONA

■ Rental Income

United States source rental income not associated with a trade or business is treated as investment income subject to the 30 percent tax rate. The nonresident alien may elect to treat rental income as income associated with a trade or business. The election permits a nonresident alien to claim rental expenses as deductions and results in the taxation of the net income (rather than gross income) from rentals at graduated tax rates. The election, which remains in force for subsequent taxable years unless permission to revoke is granted by the IRS, applies to all rental income from real property.

■ Capital Gains

Most capital gain income earned by a nonresident alien is exempt from U.S. taxation. An exception applies with respect to capital gain attributable to an interest in "U.S. real property." Capital gain associated with a U.S. real property interest is treated as income associated with a U.S. trade or business, as described in further detail below.

TRADE OR BUSINESS INCOME

IN GENERAL

In contrast to the 30 percent rate of taxation on gross investment income, income of a nonresident alien that is "effectively connected" with a U.S. trade or business is taxed on a *net* basis. Thus, certain expenses associated with the trade or business can be claimed as deductions. The rates of taxation on net trade or business income vary between 15 and 39.6 percent, the same rates that apply to U.S. citizens and resident aliens. Although most effectively connected income is derived from U.S. sources, a non-resident alien may be taxed on certain foreign source income effectively connected with a U.S. trade or business.

There are no specific guidelines for determining whether a nonresident is considered to be engaged in a U.S. trade or business. The most important factor is the "continuity and regularity" of activities carried on in the United States. The number of transactions and the nature and kind of undertakings carried on are important criteria. Isolated sales or "net leases" by a foreign person (leases that do not compel the foreign person to provide any services in connection with the leased property) to only one tenant are not considered to constitute trades or businesses. Trading in securities or commodities, through brokers or for one's own account, does not constitute a trade or business. The purchase and sale of goods, and the regular solicitation and advertising of sales in the United States, are both regarded as involving a trade or business.

Even if a foreign person is not directly engaged in a U.S. trade or business, the person may be deemed to be engaged in a trade or business as a result of the activities of others. For example, activities engaged in by a partnership (foreign or domestic) in which the foreign person is a partner are attributed to the foreign partner. Similarly, activities engaged in by an agent on behalf of a foreign person may be attributed to the foreign person.

SPECIAL RULES

Several special rules apply with respect to the taxation of income "effectively connected" with a U.S. trade or business:

■ Compensation for Personal Services

Compensation for the performance of personal services in the United States is treated as income effectively connected with a U.S. trade or business. A limited exception applies in the case of a nonresident alien who is present in the United States for up to 90 days during a taxable year and who here earns less than $3,000 for such services. Income that qualifies for this exception is exempt from U.S. income taxation. Additionally, certain tax treaties exempt from U.S. income taxation all or a portion of the compensation earned in the United States by a nonresident alien covered by the treaty who is in the United States for less than 183 days in a calendar year.

■ United States Real Property Interests

Gain or loss associated with the disposition of a "U.S. real property interest" is treated as income effectively connected with a U.S. trade or business and is subject to special tax withholding requirements, whether or not the ownership and operation of the real property actually constitute a trade or business.

A U.S. real property interest for this purpose includes direct and indirect ownership of real property in the United States. Stock in a U.S. corporation generally constitutes a U.S. real property interest if, at any time during the five-year period preceding the nonresident alien's disposition of the stock, the corporation held U.S. real property worth 50 percent or more of the fair market value of the corporation's total assets. Publicly traded stock of a U.S. corporation does not constitute a U.S. real property interest connected with a U.S. trade or business, unless a foreign individual directly or indirectly owns more than five percent of the corporation's stock.

■ Impact of Tax Treaties

Most tax treaties exempt from U.S. taxation income earned by a nonresident alien from a business effectively connected with the United States if the nonresident alien does not have a "permanent establishment" in the United States, such as an office, branch, factory, or similar facility. A permanent establishment generally does not include a facility for the storage, display, or delivery of merchandise, nor maintenance of a fixed place of business solely to purchase goods or to conduct activities of a preparatory nature.

Income Taxation of Corporations

Two different tax categories govern federal income taxation of corporations. One applies to U.S. or "domestic" corporations. A second applies to "foreign" corporations.

Determination of Status

The "place of incorporation" determines the status of corporations for federal income tax purposes. A U.S. corporation is a corporation created or organized in the United States. A foreign corporation is any corporation not a U.S. corporation.

Taxation of United States Corporations

In General

United States corporations are taxed much like U.S. citizens or resident aliens. A U.S. corporation is taxed on its income earned worldwide. However, the tax rates that apply to U.S. corporations differ from the rates that apply to U.S. citizens or resident aliens. Generally, a U.S. corporation is taxed on its income at rates between 15 and 35 percent.

In addition to the income tax at the corporate level, shareholders of a corporation are subject to tax on dividends distributed, or deemed to be distributed, from the corporation. Corporate profits thus are generally subject to double taxation, once when earned by the corporation and a second time when distributed or deemed distributed to shareholders.

S Corporations

Certain U.S. corporations may avoid the imposition of corporate taxes by making a special election under Subchapter S of the federal income tax code. In lieu of taxes payable by the S corporation, only the *shareholders* of the corporation pay taxes on income earned by the corporation. A corporation can make this election only if, among other requirements, its shareholders are limited to estates, certain trusts, and individuals other than nonresident aliens and the number of permissible shareholders does not exceed 75. Accordingly, corporations owned in whole or in part by nonresident aliens, partnerships, unqualified trusts, or other corporations cannot avoid corporate liability for taxes.

Taxation of Foreign Corporations

In General

Foreign corporations are taxed in a manner similar to taxation of nonresident aliens. Gross investment income earned by a foreign corporation is subject to withholding at the source and, except as may be provided by treaty, is taxed at a rate of 30 percent. Net income effectively connected with a U.S. trade or business is not subject to withholding and, except as may be provided by treaty, is taxed at the same tax rates that apply to U.S. corporations.

Branch Profits Tax

In addition to the tax on net income effectively connected with a U.S. trade or business, a foreign corporation may be liable for the "branch profits tax." The branch profits tax subjects a foreign corporation which directly engages in a U.S. trade or business to taxes roughly equivalent to those that would be payable if the U.S. trade or business were incorporated as a U.S. subsidiary of the foreign corporation.

When a foreign corporation is engaged in a U.S. trade or business through a U.S. subsidiary, income generated by the U.S. subsidiary is taxed twice. First, the subsidiary is subject to the regular U.S. corporate tax. Second, dividends from the subsidiary to the foreign parent corporation are generally taxed at the flat rate of 30 percent on the U.S. source investment income. Without the branch profits tax, a foreign corporation would be subject to the regular U.S. corporate tax on net income effectively connected with a trade or business, but because the earnings of the foreign corporation when repatriated abroad would merely be transferred and would not be paid out as dividends, there would be no second tax.

To eliminate the distinction, the branch profits tax imposes a tax on the amount deemed to be repatriated abroad by the U.S. branch. The amount is roughly the difference between the profits earned by the branch and the amount of branch profits reinvested in branch operations. Unless reduced by treaty, the tax is imposed at a rate of 30 percent. A similar tax is imposed on interest received by a foreign corporation from a U.S. branch.

INCOME TAXATION OF PARTNERSHIPS

IN GENERAL

A partnership, as such, is not liable for the payment of taxes unless it elects to be treated as a corporation. Assuming such election is made, income earned by the partnership is taxed directly to the partners. United States standards govern characterization of any entity for income tax purposes, notwithstanding the characterization of the entity under foreign law.

WITHHOLDING TAX LIABILITY ON BEHALF OF FOREIGN PERSONS

Although a partnership generally is not liable for the payment of taxes, a special rule applies to any partnership, whether organized in the United States or abroad, that is engaged in a U.S. trade or business and has one or more "foreign partners," a term which includes nonresident alien individuals and foreign corporations. In such a situation, the partnership is generally required to pay to the IRS a withholding tax on the portion of partnership income attributable to the U.S. trade or business allocable to any foreign partner. When the foreign partner files an income tax return, the amount paid by the partnership on behalf of the foreign partner is treated as a refundable credit against the tax due by the foreign partner. There are several methods by which a partnership can recoup from a foreign partner the withholding taxes payable by the partnership on behalf of the partner.

SPECIAL INCOME TAX CONSIDERATIONS

TRANSFER PRICING

Transactions between foreign taxpayers and "related parties" under "common control" are closely scrutinized by the IRS. The principal purpose of such scrutiny is to insure that the corporations deal with each other at arm's length and do not unreasonably inflate or reduce the costs of goods and services between the two in an effort to shift income artificially from one entity to the other for tax advantage. The IRS has extensive authority to reallocate income and deductions among related parties if it determines that arm's length dealing has not occurred.

Special Disclosure and Recordkeeping Requirements

The federal tax code imposes disclosure and recordkeeping requirements on corporations used by foreign persons for investment or business in the United States. The disclosure and recordkeeping requirements apply to any "reporting corporation" which is either a foreign corporation that is engaged in business in the United States or a U.S. corporation that has at least one "foreign person" who directly or indirectly owns at least 25 percent of the vote or value of the corporation's stock. A "foreign person" includes a nonresident alien or foreign corporation.

A reporting corporation must file an annual return that discloses the name, business, principal business location, and country of incorporation or residence of any related party who engaged in one or more transactions with the corporation during the year. "Related party" is defined very broadly.

A foreign reporting corporation must maintain all records necessary to determine the corporation's correct U.S. tax liability. A domestic reporting corporation must maintain all records necessary to establish the correct tax treatment of any "related party" transactions. Recordkeeping requirements are relaxed for smaller corporations.

The disclosure and recordkeeping requirements for reporting corporations are complex and subject corporations to sanctions for noncompliance.

Tax Treaty Abuses

The benefits of tax treaties entered into by the United States are available to nationals of the treaty country and to corporations and other entities organized under the laws of the treaty country. Opportunities often exist for investors to arrange investments and business operations to exploit the availability of treaty benefits, and concern has been rising of perceived abuses. Efforts to restrict "treaty shopping" will likely increase. There is expected to be more vigilance by the IRS, and new tax laws, new tax treaties, and new limitations under existing treaties when renegotiated, are anticipated.

STATE AND LOCAL TAXATION

CHAPTER OUTLINE

SUMMARY

The State of Arizona and various local governments also impose taxes in connection with investments and business operations in Arizona. This chapter outlines several of the most significant state and local taxes in Arizona. The first portion deals with taxes levied only by the state, such as state individual and corporate income taxes and estate taxes. The next deals with taxes that may be levied by the state, by counties, and by municipalities, such as the transactional privilege (sales) tax and taxes on real and personal property.

INCOME TAXATION OF INDIVIDUALS

Two different classifications govern state income taxation of individuals. One applies to "Arizona residents," the other to "Arizona nonresidents."

DETERMINATION OF RESIDENT STATUS

An individual is classified as an Arizona resident for state income tax purposes if in the state for other than a temporary or transitory purpose or if domiciled in Arizona. An individual is considered to be domiciled in Arizona if present in the state with the intent to remain in the state permanently. An individual who spends more than nine months of a year in the state is presumed to be an Arizona resident for that year, but evidence that the individual is in the state for a temporary or transitory purpose can overcome the presumption. An individual is classified as an Arizona nonresident if he or she is not classified as an Arizona resident under either of the above two tests.

TAXATION OF ARIZONA RESIDENTS

An individual classified as an Arizona resident for state income tax purposes is taxed by the state on the individual's income worldwide. The income tax rate ranges from 3.0 to 5.6 percent of taxable income.

TAXATION OF ARIZONA NONRESIDENTS

An individual classified as an Arizona nonresident for state income tax purposes is taxed by the state only on income earned from sources within the state. The tax on an Arizona nonresident is at the same rate as on an Arizona resident.

SIMILARITIES TO FEDERAL TAXATION

The income tax in Arizona is imposed on "Arizona taxable income." For residents, an individual's Arizona taxable income is the individual's federal adjusted gross income, modified by certain additions and subtractions. Two of these modifications relate to interest income. First, interest received on obligations issued by any state or municipality, although excluded from federal taxable income, is included in Arizona taxable income tax unless paid by the state of Arizona or by an Arizona municipality. Second, interest received on U.S. government obligations, such as savings bonds and treasury bills, although included in federal taxable income, is not subject to tax by Arizona or any other state.

INCOME TAXATION OF CORPORATIONS

IN GENERAL

Arizona taxes 9.0 percent of the taxable income of corporations, or $50.00, whichever is greater. Except for corporations that derive income attributable to business activities in more than one state, a corporation's Arizona taxable income is determined by reference to the corporation's federal taxable income, with certain adjustments. Several of the most significant adjustments are:

- Net operating losses, which for federal tax purposes can be carried back three years and carried forward for 15 years, for state tax purposes cannot be carried back at all and can be carried forward for only five years.

- The 70 percent and 100 percent dividends-received deductions permitted for federal tax purposes are not allowed under state law. However, a deduction is available for dividends received from a corporation "the principal business of which is attributable to Arizona," and also for dividends received from a corporation, 50 percent or more of whose stock is owned by the recipient. Dividends received from a "foreign corporation," one organized outside the United States, are also excluded.

- Deductions for taxes based on income paid to states other than Arizona, permitted for federal tax purposes, are not deductible from taxable income under Arizona's income tax.

- Interest received on obligations of any state other than Arizona, or of any municipality outside of Arizona, which are excluded from federal taxable income, must be included in state taxable income.

- Interest received on obligations of the United States, included in income for federal tax purposes, are excluded from state income taxes.

MULTI-STATE ACTIVITIES

If a corporation has income attributable to activities in more than one state and more than one state imposes a corporate income or similar tax, the corporation's aggregate income must be "apportioned" among the states. Only the amount properly apportioned to Arizona is subject to the Arizona corporate income tax.

For purposes of apportioning "business income," Arizona uses the three-part formula method of the Uniform Division of Income for Tax Purposes Act. Over 40 states use a similar formula to apportion the business incomes of corporations. Under this method, business income is generally apportioned among the states on the basis of three factors: the relative value of the corporation's real and personal property in Arizona as compared to the value of the corporations property nationwide; the relative amount of compensation paid by the corporation in Arizona as compared to the corporation's payroll nationwide; and the relative amount of sales made in Arizona as compared to the corporation's sales nationwide. Under Arizona law, this last factor has the most significant impact, being given twice the weight of each of the other factors.

"Nonbusiness income," income received by the corporation outside the regular course of its trade or business, is allocated under different rules. Dividends and interest received by a corporation are allocated to the state from which the corporation is directed or managed. Income from real property rentals is allocated to the state where the real property is located. Patent and copyright royalties are generally allocated to the state where the patent or copyright is used.

MULTI-STATE CORPORATIONS INVOLVING RELATED CORPORATIONS

Multi-state corporations that are part of an affiliated group of corporations may be required to aggregate their income in a combined return for apportionment to Arizona if those corporations are operationally integrated and united by a direct or indirect stock ownership or control of 50 percent or more, i.e., are unitary. Alternatively, if the related corporations do not constitute a unitary group for the reason that they are not operationally integrated, the corporations may nevertheless elect or be required to aggregate their income in a consolidated return for apportionment to Arizona. In order to file a consolidated state income tax return, multi-state corporations must:

- file a consolidated income tax return at the federal level and

- be united by direct or indirect stock ownership of 80 percent or more.

ESTATE TAXATION OF INDIVIDUALS

The death of a foreign individual may have estate tax implications under Arizona law. Different tests govern, depending on whether the individual is an "Arizona resident" or an "Arizona nonresident."

DETERMINATION OF RESIDENT STATUS

The location of the individual's "domicile" is determinative of the individual's status for state estate tax purposes. An individual is classified as an Arizona resident for Arizona estate tax purposes if domiciled in Arizona at the time of death; otherwise the decedent is classified as an Arizona nonresident. An individual is considered to be domiciled in Arizona if present in the state with the intent to remain permanently.

ESTATE TAXATION OF ARIZONA RESIDENTS

A state tax is imposed on the estate of an Arizona resident equal to the maximum credit for state death taxes allowed for federal estate tax purposes. The specific amount is prescribed by a table issued by the federal taxing authorities.

ESTATE TAXATION OF ARIZONA NONRESIDENTS

A state tax is imposed on the estate of an Arizona nonresident equal to a portion of the maximum credit for state death taxes allowed for federal estate tax purposes. The credit is the value of the estate property taxable in Arizona in proportion to the value of all of the estate property taxable under federal law. Property of an estate taxable in Arizona includes real property located in the state and tangible personal property that has an "actual situs" in the state.

Transaction Privilege (Sales) Taxes

The state of Arizona, most municipalities, certain counties, and various Indian tribes, impose a "transaction privilege" tax, sometimes called a "sales" tax. The tax is imposed on the privilege of engaging in certain specific business activities, including retail sales, mining, personal property leasing, real property leasing, contracting, and "owner/builder sales." The tax is imposed on the person who engages in the taxable business activity. The person who engages in the business is permitted to charge the customer an amount equal to the tax and so pass through the tax to the customer.

Any person wishing to engage in a business covered by one of the statutory taxable classifications must first obtain a license from the state and the particular municipality in which the business is to be operated. In most instances a monthly tax return is required and is submitted to the particular taxing jurisdiction with payment of the tax owed.

The tax base is the gross income or gross proceeds from the business activity. The rate of tax imposed by the state is five percent for most categories of taxable activities. Municipal tax rates vary, but generally range from one to three percent. Additionally, Maricopa County, which includes the city of Phoenix, imposes a tax of three-quarters of one percent. Various tax exemptions and deductions, specific to the business activity being taxed, may be utilized to reduce or eliminate some of the tax liability.

Real Property Taxes

All levels of government, including state, county, and local jurisdictions, have the authority to impose taxes on real property. The counties are primarily responsible for property tax assessment and collection.

The tax is determined by the use of the property and its value. Real property is classified into one of several use categories, including commercial and industrial, owner-occupied residential, rental residential, and agricultural. The use or class of the property determines the percentage of the property's value which is subject to tax. Each parcel is assigned a primary "limited" value and a higher secondary "full cash" value. The taxes assessed against the taxable portion of the property's limited value are used for the general maintenance and operation of counties, cities, towns, school districts, community college districts, and the state. Taxes assessed against the taxable portion of the property's full cash value are used for specific purposes, such as the funding of bonds, budget overrides, and special assessment districts. Increases in a property's limited value are governed from year to year by the Arizona Constitution and by statute. There is no limit on the amount that a property's full cash value can increase from year to year and the property's full cash value is intended to reflect the property's fair market value. Beginning in 1997, if a property owner in either Maricopa or Pima County protests a property valuation and the appropriate county assessor's office is unable to resolve the dispute, the property owner can appeal to The State Board of Equalization, a new independent agency intended to streamline the administrative appeals process in Arizona.

Personal Property Taxes

Personal property used for a commercial purpose is also subject to taxation in Arizona. Although there are exceptions, most commercially owned personal property is subject to tax. The owner or person in control of personal property subject to tax is required to file with the local county assessor a list of all taxable personal property, with values if requested by the assessor. If no return is filed, the county assessor can estimate the property and its value. After receiving the property list, the county assessor assigns a depreciated market value to each item of personal property. An accelerated administrative appeal process is available for challenging the valuation or classification assigned by the particular county. Additionally, various tax exemptions are available which may reduce or eliminate some of the property tax liability. Exemptions must be applied for annually.